AUTHENTIC REGIONAL CUISINE

Real AMERICAN Food

Restaurants, Markets, and Shops Plus Favorite Hometown Recipes

★ BURT WOLF ★
AND ANDREW F. SMITH

RIZZOLI
NEW YORK

First published in the United States of America in 2006
by Rizzoli International Publications, Inc.
300 Park Avenue South
New York, NY 10010
www.rizzoliusa.com

2006 2007 2008 2009 / 10 9 8 7 6 5 4 3 2 1

Distributed in the U.S. trade by Random House, New York
Printed in the United States of America

ISBN-10: 0-8478-2792-5 / ISBN-13: 978-0-8478-2792-3

Library of Congress Control Number: 2006923437

Recipe, page 49: Reprinted with permission from The Second Avenue Deli Cookbook, by Sharon Lebewohl and Rena Bulkin (Villard Books, a division of Random House, Inc., October 1999). Recipe, page 72: Reprinted with permission from City Tavern Cookbook, by Walter Staib (Running Press, © 1999).

Photo Credits:
(Numbers in *italics* refer to full-color photo insert pages.) © City of Chicago: 21 (Chris McGuire), 208–09 (Mark Segal). © Kristen Ciappa: *5* top left. © Corbis: 10–11, *10* top right (Bob Krist); 19, 25 (Rick Friedman); 23 (Greg Probst); 32–33 (John Hicks); 84 (Lynda Richardson); 126, *11* center left (Richard Cummins); 137, 189 (Robert Holmes); 152, *16* top left (Sandy Felsenthal); 158 (Lindsay Hebberd); 164–65, *13* bottom (Robert Landau); *1* top left (Kelly-Mooney Photography); *4* top right (James Leynse); *8* top right (Richard Bickel), center right (Tony Arruza); *10* top left (Bob Sacha); *11* top right, *14* bottom right (Phil Schermeister); *12* top right (David Butow); *13* top right (Frank Trapper). © Bob Krist: 56–57; *4* bottom left & right; *5* top right & bottom left. © Peter Medilek: Jacket (back) left top & bottom, 35, 42, 171, 175, 186–87, *2* bottom left & right, *9* top right & left, *12* center left, *13* top left, *14* top right, *15* top right & left. © 2003 RightMinds. Courtesy Richmond Metropolitan Convention and Visitors Bureau: 78–79, *7* top right. © San Antonio Convention and Visitors Bureau: 142–43 (Nancy Belcher), *10* bottom right (Doug Wilson). All other photos are copyrighted by Burt Wolf.

Contents

Richmond 78

BARBECUED PULLED-PORK SANDWICHES
DEVIL'S MESS
CORNBREAD-STUFFED PORK CHOPS WITH PEACH COMPOTE
ROAST PORK WITH BLACK PEPPER, GARLIC, AND PAPRIKA
SOFT-SHELL CRAB SANDWICH
SWEET POTATO-STREUSEL PIE
SPOONBREAD
PEANUT BUTTER COOKIES

Miami 100

CRISPY CRAB CAKES WITH MANGO SALSA
BLACK BEAN SOUP
SAUTÉED FLOUNDER WITH SHRIMP
CLAM CAKES WITH BLACK BEAN SALAD WITH LIME TARTAR SAUCE
TROPICAL FRUIT WITH MINT DRIZZLE
KEY LIME PIE
FLAN

New Orleans 120

CHICKEN AND SAUSAGE GUMBO
SHRIMP BISQUE
MINI CRAB CAKES WITH RÉMOULADE SAUCE
SHRIMP CREOLE
BRENNAN'S BANANAS FOSTER
CREOLE PRALINE CANDIES
PEANUT BUTTER PIE
CHOCOLATE BREAD PUDDING

San Antonio 142

HUEVOS RANCHEROS
MEXICAN-STYLE CHICKEN APPETIZERS
TORTILLAS
ALAMO BURGERS

PECAN-BREADED CHICKEN
BBQ-RUBBED SWEET POTATOES
CHILE CON CARNE
PECAN PIE

Los Angeles

GUACAMOLE
CAESAR SALAD WITH GARLIC CROUTONS
MEXICAN-STYLE CHICKEN IN A BAG
TILAPIA WITH LEMON SAUCE
PIZZA WITH SMOKED SALMON AND CAVIAR
LEMON SOUFFLÉS WITH CHOCOLATE ICE CREAM

San Francisco

IRISH COFFEE FROM THE BUENA VISTA CAFÉ
BEEF WITH BROCCOLI
MANDARIN CHICKEN SALAD
MINESTRONE SOUP
CHICKEN WITH CITRUS SAUCE AND RAISINS
COLD NOODLES WITH ASPARAGUS AND GINGER
MONTEREY JACK CORN FRITTERS
RICOTTA CHEESECAKE

Chicago

FRENCH ONION SOUP
HORSERADISH-CRUSTED FILET MIGNON
CHICKEN WITH MUSTARD CREAM SAUCE
STEAK WITH GARLIC BUTTER
PARMESAN-CRUSTED CREAMED SPINACH
LEMON BARS
CHOCOLATE DEEP-DISH PIZZA
SWEDISH CARDAMOM CAKE
CHICAGO-STYLE CHOCOLATE CHEESECAKE

Introduction

EVERY CITY IN THE WORLD has a local flavor, a flavor that comes from the signature dishes of the town, from a group of preferred ingredients, or from a type of restaurant that originally developed in the area. The flavor might also come from the appreciation of a particular piece of cooking equipment or a technique. There are dozens of influences, but the local flavor is always the result of the interaction of the region's geography, history, economics, and the ethnic groups that settled in the neighborhood.

The story of real American food is the story of home cooks and fancy restaurateurs, family farmers and agribusiness giants, street vendors and supermarket magnates, artisanal cheese makers and massive food conglomerates, burger barons and vegetarians, wine makers and brewery magnates, and an extraordinary collection of ethnic and religious groups. They have each made a unique contribution.

This book is not intended as a comprehensive review of American food; neither is it a detailed examination of the culinary life of the cities we have selected. This book takes a look at the local flavors of ten cities in the United States that, to a great extent, represent the signature foods of their region and have made a significant contribution to our national cuisine.

The focus of eating in America has changed a great deal in recent years. Once much of the great dining in this country was provided expressly for travelers. Hotel dining rooms and railroad dining cars were symbols of the best this country had to offer or had imported from Europe.

Today more and more meals are eaten away from home. More and more effort and imagination is being spent on creating distinctive restaurants. From Philadelphia to Los Angeles, explosions of restaurant activity are being inspired and supported by generations with money to spend, with the sophistication to demand accurate reproductions of foreign cuisines and the creation of new ones.

As we were writing the chapter on New Orleans, Hurricane Katrina hit and destroyed much of the city. We were concerned about the future of one of America's most important culinary centers, but we decided that New Orleans was too important to exclude and went ahead with the chapter. As we write this introduction, we are delighted to see that the city is coming back to life. As is true with any of the restaurant and shop listings in this book, it is a good idea to call ahead to make sure they are still in place and to check on their hours of operation.

We hope this book will help you understand why people in America eat what we do and why you owe yourself a taste.

BOSTON

Massachusetts

I N 1630, a fleet of eleven ships carrying 750 Pilgrims set sail from England. The Pilgrims called their new home in America New England, which gives you a pretty clear idea of what they hoped would be their daily lifestyle. Many of the new arrivals were Puritans, members of a religious sect that valued a pure and simple existence, an approach to life that was reflected in their attitude toward cooking.

Their Sabbath began at sundown on Saturday and ended at sundown on Sunday—a twenty-four-hour period in which cooking was forbidden. They would prepare a baked dish on Saturday that could be easily reheated for Saturday night or Sunday.

As part of their structured lives, some families developed the habit of serving the same meal on the same day each week. Monday was boiled dinner day, Friday was fish chowder day, and Saturday was baked beans and Boston brown bread day. The first Tuesday evening after the first Monday in October was reserved for sex.

LEARNING FROM THE NATIVE AMERICANS

The English colonists brought European seeds with them. Most of the imports did not grow well in the New World, but, luckily, American Indians introduced colonists to a wide variety of other New World plants. Without their help, the first colonists to New England would not have survived, nor would they have learned so quickly about crops like corn, which, unlike other plants, did not need smooth and properly tilled earth. Corn became the colonists' most important food, as it could be grown in small areas that were still covered with stumps from trees that had just been cut. Colonists consumed corn in many ways. They boiled ears of corn, or roasted them in hot ashes, as the Indians did, and then flavored them with salt and butter. Corn was also ground into cornmeal, which was cooked in dishes such as samp, which was coarsely ground corn boiled with vegetables and meat, and mush, or hasty pudding, which was frequently served with milk and flavored with whatever was available, such as milk, cider, or syrup. Various versions of corn-bread, also called pone or johnnycakes, were made from cornmeal and served at most meals.

The second most important New World food that American Indians introduced to the English colonists was beans. Numerous types of beans had been domesticated in North America prior to the arrival of the Europeans. The kidney bean was disseminated widely throughout the continent in pre-Columbian times. Native Americans typically planted beans with corn. The bean runners climbed the corn stocks. Many Native Americans boiled beans with corn, and one Indian name for this combination, succotash,

REVENGE OF THE COB

Ideally, fresh corn should be cooked within an hour of its being picked. The objective is to get it into boiling water before it realizes it has been harvested and has a chance to pay you back by loosing its sweetness. Since few of us have the opportunity to boil fresh corn at the edge of a field, some cooks have come up with a method that can recover some of the lost flavor. Bring equal amounts of water and milk to a boil. Use sufficient quantities to cover the amount of corn you are about to cook. Add 1 tablespoon butter and 1 teaspoon sugar for each quart of liquid. Cook the corn in the boiling liquid for 8 minutes.

survives today. Native Americans also slow-cooked beans by combining them with water in earthen pots and burying them in fire pits. Colonists adopted this method, adding new ingredients to suit their tastes. Later colonists in Boston added molasses and meat to the baked beans, which eventually evolved into "Boston baked beans." Beans became so important to the culinary life of Boston that the city is still affectionately called "Beantown."

American Indians also taught the colonists about squash, especially the pumpkin. Pumpkins were solid enough to be stored through the winter, while squash was more frag-

---

★ **WHAT TO TASTE AND WHERE TO TASTE IT** ★

Thanksgiving Dinner

PLIMOTH PLANTATION
137 Warren Avenue ★ Plymouth ★ (508) 746-1622

Since 1863, Thanksgiving has been a national holiday, and most Americans celebrate it with the traditional meal of roast turkey, stuffing, cranberries, and candied sweet potatoes. But the place to enjoy a real traditional Thanksgiving dinner is at Plimoth Plantation, a re-creation of how Plimoth looked in 1627. The annual dinner served in November includes ciderkin (a kind of weak hard cider), hasty pudding, sauced turkey, stewed pumpkins, and a cheesecake made with spice and dried fruit.

ile and was usually consumed in the late fall or early winter. Native Americans dried slices of pumpkins and squash, which could be kept for years. Colonists roasted, boiled, stewed, and mashed both pumpkins and squash. Winter squash was mixed with cornmeal and baked into bread and cakes. Later, pumpkins and squash were used to make puddings, tarts, and pancakes, and they were eaten as accompaniments to meat. But it is the pumpkin pie, served particularly at Thanksgiving, that became an American culinary icon.

Native Americans introduced colonists to a wide variety of other New World plants. Cranberries, which resembled English barberries, were an instant success, particularly in New England, where the berries were baked into tarts or mashed into a sauce for poultry and game. Groundnuts (*Apios americana*—not peanuts) and Jerusalem artichokes were boiled and served as vegetables. Sunflower seeds were consumed as a snack, and later were used to make oil. Nuts, such as American chestnuts, filberts, hickory nuts, and black walnuts, were gathered and served after meals, and some colonists added them occasionally to bread. Colonists, especially in frontier areas, also gathered wild foods such as acorns, elderberries, grapes, leeks, onions, plums, pokeweed, and strawberries. Blackberries, blueberries, and huckleberries were sun-dried Indian-style and substituted for currants and raisins.

Just as important, American Indians introduced colonists to the processing of maple sap. All along the Atlantic coast and as far west as Minnesota, Native Americans sliced the barks of maple trees and drained their sap, which was boiled down and added to porridges and meat and fish stews. They also mixed it with cold water to produce a beverage that they drank during the summer heat—early Kool-Aid.

American Indians also taught colonists how to hunt bears, deer, and wild birds, including turkeys, cranes, and swans, which were easily caught. Unfortunately, the Indians taught the colonists too well. These animals were hunted to such an extent that they almost disappeared. It wasn't until the twentieth century that wild turkeys were reintroduced into New England.

With the help of Native Americans, early colonists learned to fish and harvest seafood in the New World. Bostonians feasted on fish and seafood taken from rivers and coastal waters. The favorite fish included freshwater bass, catfish, saltwater flounder, and migrating salmon, shad, herring, perch, pike, shad, sturgeon, and trout.

Fresh fish had to be promptly prepared and consumed; more frequently, it was salted and dried or smoked for future use. By 1665, over a thousand vessels were regularly engaged in fishing off the coast of Massachusetts.

In the early days, there were more than two hundred different species of fish in the waters near Boston. The deep Atlantic offered the colonists flounder, mackerel, halibut, salmon, haddock, cod, and young cod called scrod. (The finest scrod comes from New England and consists of cod that weighs between one and two pounds. My preferred method of preparation consists of splitting the fish in half then frying or broiling it.) Cod became a major export for the colony, and some of the earliest colonial fortunes were made in the dried cod business. Some historians believe that by the early 1700s food supplies were so plentiful that cooks took a less creative approach to cooking.

Shellfish was also plentiful. American lobsters were large and abundant. Lobsters were not considered a delicacy, but were mainly used to stave off hunger when other foods were unavailable. Indentured servants put clauses in their contracts limiting lobster to two meals each week. Lobster was also used as bait for cod and fertilizer for beans. Likewise, oysters were so common in coastal areas that they were considered food for the poor, though they were enjoyed by all. Oysters were eaten raw, boiled, baked, and broiled. They were also pickled, and the shells were saved and burned to make lime, which was used in construction and later as a fertilizer. Next in importance were crabs and clams. New England became famous for its quahog clam chowder. The New England clambake was standard-op in the area long before the first colonists arrived. Algonquin tribes would pile wet seaweed over hot stone, followed by corn and shellfish. Steam coming up from the seawater did the cooking.

★ WHAT TO TASTE AND WHERE TO TASTE IT ★

Clams

CLAM BOX
246 High Street ★ Ipswich ★ (978) 356-9707

Clams have been a New England tradition since prehistoric times. The best way to eat clams is right on the beach, with a professional cook preparing them. If you can't do this, the best place to taste them is at the Clam Box in Ipswich, about thirty miles north of Boston. It was built in 1938 by Dick Greenleaf, and the building really is shaped like a box. We recommend it not for its unique structure, but for the clams that are prepared by true masters of the art. Bring cash, as they don't take credit cards.

THE CHOWDER WARS

Whether chowders were introduced to New England by French, Nova Scotian, or British fishermen is undocumented, but in America chowders were important dishes by the beginning of the eighteenth century. The first known American recipe for chowder was published in Boston in 1751. Chowders are quite distinct from broths and soups. Chowders, originally stews, were composed of fish, seafood, and vegetables in various proportions. The object was to prepare a thick, highly seasoned compound without reducing the ingredients to the consistency of a puree. Chowder recipes were identified as coming from a variety of different geographical locations. The debate as to whether clam chowder should contain tomatoes was exaggerated by Representative Cleveland Sleeper, who introduced a bill in the Maine legislature in 1939 to "make it an illegal as well as a culinary offense to introduce tomatoes to clam chowder." Those were the good old days, when legislators tended to deal with subjects that were in keeping with their individual level of intelligence. Within a few years of the outbreak of the Clam Chowder Wars, Chef Louis P. DeGouy, author of *The Soup Book*, concluded that it was one of those subjects, like politics and religion, that could never be discussed lightly. In his book, he offered ninety-eight chowder recipes, all of which originated in various communities in and around Boston.

THE OLD NEW WORLD

When English colonists settled in America, they craved the same foods they had eaten in the old country. But they soon found that they had to adapt their cooking in order to make it work in the New World. An example of this "fusion" cuisine was hasty pudding—a generic term for porridge made by stirring a starch into boiling liquid. It was commonly served in Boston during colonial times. Based on a traditional British recipe, its main ingredient depended on where one lived: In England, hasty pudding was made of wheat, while in Scotland oats were used. In Boston, hasty pudding, also called Indian pudding (or simply "mush"), was made from corn flour and, if the cook's budget ran to such luxuries, might include eggs, raisins, butter, spices, sugar, and molasses. Following English custom, hasty pudding was frequently served as a filling first course, meant to check the appetite for the meat course, but as puddings increasingly became sweet, they were reserved for the end of the meal. Hasty pudding largely disappeared from America's table during the nineteenth century as commercial corn-based cereals, such as cornflakes, replaced traditional American breakfast foods. The dish is memorialized in the name of Harvard's famed dramatic club—the Hasty

Lobster, Chowder, and Other Seafood

JASPER WHITE'S SUMMER SHACK
149 Alewife Brook Parkway ★ Cambridge ★ (617) 520-9500

In Cambridge, just across the Charles River from downtown Boston, you will find Jasper White's Summer Shack, which despite its name is open all year round. Jasper is considered to be the dean of American fish cookery. His restaurant is huge, filled with wooden picnic tables, banquettes from the 1960s, and dangling strings of lights. In the center of the room is a fifteen-hundred-gallon lobster-cooking apparatus that is so unusual it was given a patent by the federal government. Live lobsters are held in a giant tank. At the proper moment, they are lifted into two enormous steam kettles, where they are cooked. Each basket can hold about a hundred lobsters, which is good, because Jasper has a couple of nights each week when he runs through more than a thousand. In addition to lobster, Jasper is well known for his fried clams, old-fashioned cod cakes with beans, and homemade pies.

LEGAL SEA FOODS
26 Park Plaza ★ Boston ★ (617) 426-4444

Launched in Cambridge in 1968, Legal Sea Foods owns and operates more than thirty restaurants on the East Coast, from Massachusetts to Florida. But it's not your typical chain restaurant. Legal has had a strong dedication to using only the freshest ingredients. Its straightforward approach to cooking fish and shellfish works well and has made the chain a magnet for both locals and out-of-towners. Highlights are first-rate clam chowder and baked clams.

GREAT BAY
550 Commonwealth Avenue ★ Boston ★ (617) 532-5300

Located in the Hotel Commonwealth, near Boston University, Great Bay attracts a trendy younger crowd, and not-so-trendy visiting parents; however, all agree on the high-quality local and far-flung seafood lovingly prepared by Maine-raised and California-trained chef Jeremy Sewell. New England chowder gets an Asian twist, but don't panic—it's not in the preparation, but rather in the presentation: The creamy chowder is poured from an elegant Japanese teapot. There's also an exceptional raw bar.

LOCKE-OBER
3 Winter Place ★ Boston ★ (617) 542-1340

Excellent for a special occasion or a romantic evening, Locke-Ober serves classic New England dishes tastefully updated in a guardedly modernized landmark building. Smart and polite service.

American

EAST COAST GRILL

1269 Cambridge Street ★ Cambridge ★ (617) 868-4278

The East Coast Grill is owned and operated by Chris Schlesinger, who has a national reputation as a grilling expert. His advice has been concentrated into a series of books including *The Thrill of the Grill, License to Grill,* and *Let the Flames Begin.* If it is on the menu, try the "Jerk Duck Leg from Hell." The duck is spicy but quite edible. The yellow sauce on the side is satanic.

Pudding Club—and the homey dessert is still occasionally served in Boston restaurants.

Another strong craving the early colonists shared was wheat bread. Unfortunately, the early wheat varieties imported from Britain never flourished in New England (with a couple of geographic exceptions, such as in the Connecticut River Valley), and wheat remained a marginal crop throughout the colonial period. So Bostonians improvised. Rye grew well in New England; accordingly, it was mixed with cornmeal (also called Indian meal) to make sturdy bread known as "rye 'n' Injun."

The price of flour remained high in the Northeast until the Erie Canal was completed in 1827; the new waterway made it easy and inexpensive to transport wheat grown

Boston Cream Pie

OMNI PARKER HOUSE

60 School Street ★ Boston ★ (617) 227-8600

In 1856, a French chef named Sanzian, who worked at the Parker House Hotel in Boston, served several versions of cream "pies," which were actually cake layers, split and filled with custard and topped with a pourable icing. It gradually became know as Boston cream pie. In 1996, it was proclaimed the official Massachusetts State Dessert. While you can get Boston cream pie throughout the United States, the best place to eat it is at its point of origin. The Omni Parker House Hotel in Boston is also the home of the Parker House roll, made by folding a butter-brushed round of dough in half; which produces a pleasing abundance of crusty surfaces. The Parker House is also the point of origin for Boston scrod. They also serve a traditional Boston chowder and fish cakes.

in central New York and the Midwest to the eastern seaboard. This wheat was processed with a new type of mill, which removed the germ as well as the hull from the wheat kernels and produced very white flour.

Cheap white flour, however, was not universally appreciated. In fact, it sparked America's first culinary revolt, led by a minister named Sylvester Graham. Graham believed that only whole-grain flour should be used for making bread, and, thanks to his campaign, whole-wheat flour became known as Graham flour. This term has largely faded from the American lexicon, although it lives on in the modern-day Graham cracker. Graham flour was also mixed with rye flour and cornmeal to make "Boston brown bread," a moist loaf that's steamed, not baked, and traditionally served with Boston baked beans.

Unlike many other early European imports, English apples fared well in New England. Within two decades of the arrival of the Pilgrims, apple orchards were common throughout eastern Massachusetts. Apples were eaten raw, baked, or stewed, dried for wintertime use in pies, and pressed to make cider, which was drunk fresh or fermented.

The primary apple product in colonial times was hard cider, usually with an alcohol content of about 5 percent. The otherwise abstemious John Adams downed a large tankard of hard cider every morning, and it was even served to children. Until the early nineteenth century, hard apple cider was America's most common alcoholic beverage. Apples were so important to New Englanders that many carried seeds with them when they moved west. John Chapman, a Massachusetts native who made it his

THE BOSTON DUNK

Boston has been responsible for many firsts. It is the site of Harvard University, the first university in America, and of the first public garden. The city built the first public library. It is the home of the world's oldest annual foot race, the Boston Marathon. In a somewhat less significant category, but still of importance to many people, including me, it is the home of the first Dunkin' Donuts shop. The donut is the most popular pastry in the United States and, as opposed to bagels, which are consumed primarily in restaurants, donuts are eaten primarily in automobiles.

mission to plant apple trees in western Pennsylvania and in Ohio, was nicknamed "Johnny Appleseed."

Until the twentieth century, cattle, sheep, and hogs were generally butchered (that is, cut into portions for preserving or cooking) on the farm or by butchers in nearby towns. Butchering resulted in prime cuts like steaks, roasts, and chops, and also yielded organs and scraps. The scraps were used to make pot pies, which were signature foods in New England. When the hand-cranked home meat grinder became popular in the late nineteenth century, these scraps would be ground together, to be shaped and cooked in various ways. To give the impression of a "roast," the chopped meat could be formed into a good-sized block—a meat loaf. Meat loaf could be made of beef alone, or some combination of beef, veal, and pork. Beaten eggs were incorporated to bind the mixture together with extenders such as oatmeal, bread crumbs, or rice, which produced an economical family dish. Meat loaf became a regular feature on diner menus, and this filling, savory staple became a real American food during the Depression, when thrift was the order of the day. In the 1950s, when virtually every cookbook and food magazine included recipes for it, meat loaf became emblematic of the American home and family. Today, it has had a resurgence as an old-fashioned comfort food.

HEARTS AND WAFERS

In 1847, Oliver R. Chase founded Chase and Company in Boston. The company thrived because Chase invented several candy machines. One of his earliest products was Conversation Hearts, which the company renamed "Sweethearts" in 1902, when they became associated with Valentine's Day. Chase and Company merged with other Boston candy manufacturers in 1901 to form the New England Confectionary Company (NECCO). At the time, it was the largest candy manufacturer in America. Released in 1912, the company's most famous product was NECCO wafers, which are hard disks of various flavors and colors. Today, NECCO is one of the few small candy companies left in America—the largest companies, Hershey and Mars, control 70 percent of the shelf space in grocery stores. NECCO sells a number of confections, including Sweethearts, NECCO Wafers, Mary Janes, and the Clark Bar, which it acquired in 1999. NECCO is the oldest continuously operating candy company in America.

Corn Bread with Chives

MAKES 8 SERVINGS

If you check a dictionary you will find that the English word corn refers to a country's most important grain. If a country makes its daily bread with wheat, then wheat is described as the corn of that country. Oats are the corn of Ireland. Rye is the corn of Sweden. When the first English speakers arrived in America, they saw that maize was the basic food of the natives and so they called it Indian corn. Native Americans showed the New England settlers how to cultivate the rocky soil and maximize the short growing season in order to produce corn.

Oil or nonstick vegetable oil spray, for the pan
1 cup coarsely ground cornmeal
1 cup all-purpose flour
2½ tablespoons baking powder
1 teaspoon salt
¼ teaspoon baking soda
⅛ teaspoon cayenne pepper
1 tablespoon sugar
2 tablespoons chopped fresh chives
¼ cup vegetable oil
1 cup buttermilk
2 egg whites, lightly beaten

1. Preheat the oven to 400 degrees F. Lightly grease an 8-inch-square baking dish.

2. In a medium bowl, combine the dry ingredients. Stir in the chives.

3. Add the oil to the dry ingredients. With your fingers, blend until the oil is evenly mixed through.

4. In a small bowl, combine the buttermilk and egg whites. Pour this mixture into the other ingredients. Stir quickly to blend.

5. Spread the batter evenly in the prepared baking dish. Bake for 20 minutes, until the top is golden and a toothpick inserted in the center comes out clean. Cool on a rack before serving.

Wok-Seared Salmon with Soy-Lime Vinaigrette

SERVES 6

Salmon ranks among the most popular of finfishes in the world. Wild salmon is caught in the coastal waters of both the east and west coast; and much salmon is now farm raised.

FOR THE SALMON

2 tablespoons chopped garlic

2 tablespoons chopped ginger

2 tablespoons sesame oil

6 (7-ounce) salmon fillets with skin

Salt and freshly ground black pepper

3 tablespoons canola oil

FOR THE SALAD

3 tablespoons fresh lime juice

½ cup soy sauce

1 teaspoon chopped garlic

1 teaspoon chopped ginger

1 teaspoon chopped shallots

½ cup canola oil

1 teaspoon freshly ground black pepper

1 (4-ounce) package alfalfa sprouts

6 ounces pea shoots

6 ounces sunflower sprouts

6 ounces mung bean sprouts

1 small red bell pepper, julienned

1 small green bell pepper, julienned

1 small yellow bell pepper, julienned

1 small red onion, thinly sliced

1 bunch cilantro, leaves removed

18 radicchio or bibb lettuce leaves

1. TO MARINATE THE SALMON: In a glass or porcelain baking dish, combine the garlic, ginger, and sesame oil. Place the fillets, skin side up, into the marinade, cover with plastic wrap, and refrigerate for 4 hours or overnight.

2. TO PREPARE THE SALAD: In a medium bowl, whisk together the lime juice, soy sauce, garlic, ginger, and shallots. Slowly whisk in the oil, stir in the pepper, and set aside. In a large salad bowl, gently toss together the alfalfa sprouts, pea shoots, sunflower sprouts, mung bean sprouts, bell peppers, red onion, and cilantro. Set aside in the refrigerator, undressed.

3. TO COOK THE SALMON: Season the fish with salt and pepper. Heat a wok over medium high heat. Add the oil and then lay the filets, skin side up, into the hot oil. Cook the fish 2 or 3 filets at a time, searing, 3 to 4 minutes per side depending on the thickness of the fillets. Remove the fish to a warm spot while you cook the remaining fillets.

4. TO PRESENT THE DISH: Reserve 4 tablespoons of the vinaigrette for the fish. Drizzle the Soy-Lime Vinaigrette over the salad and toss it to coat. Arrange 3 radicchio or bibb cups around the perimeter of each large dinner plate and fill each cup with a small mound of dressed salad and a small mound in the center of the plate. Place the salmon on top of the salad in the center of the plate and drizzle with the reserved vinaigrette.

Clam Chowder

MAKES 6 SERVINGS

Early European explorers returned from the Grand Banks of the coast of New England with reports of a sea with fish so plentiful they could be caught by swimming in the waters of the area.

Today you can find respectable versions of classic chowder all over, but for the real thing in an old Boston institution, go to the Locke-Ober restaurant (shown opposite).

6 slices bacon, finely chopped
1 cup of finely chopped onions
½ teaspoon paprika
3 cups cold water
3 cups peeled, diced potatoes
½ teaspoon dried thyme
3 (6½-ounce) cans chopped clams
1 cup half-and-half
Salt and freshly ground black pepper
⅓ cup minced parsley or fresh chives for garnish, optional

1. In a medium saucepan over medium heat, heat the bacon, covered, for a minute or until some of the fat has rendered. Uncover the saucepan and continue to sauté, stirring constantly for 2 minutes or until a thin film of fat coats the bottom surface of the pan.

2. Add the onions and paprika, cover and cook, over low heat for 5 to 6 minutes, stirring on occasion. Add the water, potatoes, and thyme and bring the liquid to a boil.

3. Reduce the heat and simmer the soup, covered, for about 20 minutes or until the potatoes are tender but not falling apart.

4. Add the clams with their juices and the half and half. Bring the soup just to a simmer and season with salt and pepper to taste. Serve immediately, each portion garnished with parsley or chives.

Dutch-Oven Brown Bread

MAKES 3 OR 4 BREADS

Boston brown bread is traditionally served with Boston baked beans because both could be prepared ahead of time—which was essential for the early colonists, who were not permitted to cook on the Sabbath. These meals provided good nutrition during the New England winters.

To make the characteristic loaf shape, you'll need three empty 20-ounce food cans or four 16-ounce cans. Remove the labels and make sure that the open tops are free of jagged, dangerous edges. Leave the bottoms intact. Clean the cans and lightly oil the insides.

2 cups buttermilk
¾ cup molasses
1 cup raisins
¼ cup chopped walnuts
1 cup whole-wheat flour
1 cup rye flour
1 cup yellow cornmeal
¾ teaspoon baking soda
½ teaspoon salt

1. In a bowl, mix together the buttermilk and molasses. In a second bowl, mix together the raisins, walnuts, whole-wheat and rye flours, cornmeal, baking soda, and salt.

2. Stir the dry ingredients into the wet ingredients. Add only one-quarter of the dry ingredients at a time, and make sure that they are fully incorporated before adding more. (This technique helps avoid lumps in the batter and is valuable for all baking recipes when the dry and wet ingredients are brought together.)

3. Divide the batter among the food cans. Cover the tops of the cans lightly with aluminum foil, and put them into a Dutch

ABOUT MOLASSES

Molasses was a profitable export from the West Indies to colonial New England, and an important sweetener in the days when white sugar was heavy and expensive to transport. Famous early American dishes like Boston baked beans and Indian pudding are made with molasses. Molasses is the thick, black, syrupy residue left from the process of refining white sugar. There are three grades of molasses: First boil, the finest, is used as a table syrup. Second boil is darker and less sweet. Blackstrap molasses is very black, and a tablespoon of it contains one-third of the adult minimum daily requirement for iron.

In baking, molasses is usually used with baking soda. It adds sweetness to gingerbread and cookies. It also acts as a natural preservative and keeps cakes moist for long periods of time.

oven or stockpot, or any other pot that is deep enough to hold them. Pour boiling water into the Dutch oven until it comes about 2 inches up the side of the cans. Cover the Dutch oven, place it over low heat, and keep the water at a simmer for 3 hours. Check periodically. As the water level in the Dutch oven begins to drop, add more boiling water.

4. To remove the breads from the cans, cut out the bottom of the can and push out the bread through the other open end. Allow them to cool on a rack.

Triple-Berry Muffins
MAKES 12 MUFFINS

Blueberries and cranberries grow throughout New England.

Nonstick vegetable oil spray (optional)
3 large eggs
¼ cup packed brown sugar, plus 2 tablespoons for topping
½ cup vegetable oil
½ cup whole milk
2 tablespoons oat bran
1 teaspoon baking powder
1 teaspoon baking soda
½ teaspoon salt
1 cup whole-wheat flour
1 cup unbleached all-purpose flour
¾ cup raspberries, cranberries, or blueberries or ¼ cup each type of berry

1. Preheat the oven to 375 degrees F. Line a 12-cup muffin tin with paper liners or spray them with nonstick vegetable oil spray.

2. In a large mixing bowl, with a whisk, blend the eggs with the brown sugar and whisk until frothy. Add the oil and milk and beat until blended. Blend in the bran.

3. In a separate mixing bowl, with a whisk or fork, combine the baking powder, baking soda, and salt with the whole-wheat and all-purpose flours.

4. Gradually incorporate the dry ingredients into the egg mixture and beat with a wooden spoon until the batter is smooth. Fold in the berries and let the batter set for 5 minutes.

5. Fill the muffin cups three-quarters full and sprinkle about ¼ teaspoon brown sugar over each muffin. Bake for 22 to 25 minutes, until a toothpick inserted in the center of the muffin comes out dry. Cool on a rack.

Codfish Cakes

MAKES 6 SERVINGS

Cape Cod was named for the cod found swimming in the waters of the area.

2 pounds all-purpose or Yukon Gold potatoes, peeled and quartered
Salt and freshly ground black pepper
1 pound boneless fresh cod
½ cup finely diced salt pork or bacon (4 slices)
¾ cup finely chopped onion
½ cup finely chopped celery
½ teaspoon dried sage
¼ cup all-purpose flour, for dredging
2 tablespoons vegetable oil
1½ cups tomato sauce
6 sprigs dill
6 lemon wedges

1. Boil the potatoes in lightly salted water for about 20 minutes, until tender. Drain and immediately mash them with a potato masher or fork. (Don't do this in a food processor or they will turn gluey.) Place the mashed potatoes in a mixing bowl, season with salt and pepper to taste, and set aside.

2. Simmer the fish in lightly salted water for about 5 minutes, until just cooked through. Drain the fish and transfer to a paper towel–lined plate. Allow the fish to dry while you prepare the seasonings.

3. Heat a medium saucepan and add the salt pork. Cook for 5 minutes or until the fat has rendered and the pork is golden. Add the onion and celery, cover, and cook over low heat for a few minutes, until the vegetables are tender. Mix in the sage, and add the mixture to the potatoes. With your fingers, flake the fish into the mixture and combine; adjust the seasoning.

4. Shape the mixture into 12 cakes about 2½ inches in diameter and ½-inch thick. Dip the fish cakes in the flour and shake off any excess. In a large skillet, heat the vegetable oil over medium heat. Add the fish cakes and cook for 5 minutes on each side or until golden brown. In a separate saucepan, heat the tomato sauce. Serve 2 fish cakes per person, drizzled with tomato sauce. Garnish each portion with a sprig of dill and a lemon wedge.

Rum Cake

MAKES 8 SERVINGS

Christopher Columbus first planted sugarcane in the West Indies, and African slaves were brought in to grow the sugarcane and produce molasses. The molasses was shipped to New England (most likely through Boston Harbor), and the rum was made. Rum was the staple drink of the American colonies until the British enacted the Molasses Act and the Sugar Act, unpopular taxes that led to the American Revolution.

During the eighteenth century, the rum produced in New England was considered to be the world's finest.

4 tablespoons (½ stick) unsalted butter, at room temperature, plus more for the pan
1½ cups cake flour, plus more for the pan
2 teaspoons baking powder
½ teaspoon salt
⅔ cup granulated sugar
4 eggs
4 to 6 tablespoons dark rum or orange juice or 3 tablespoons rum extract
1 (8-ounce) can crushed pineapple, drained
Confectioners' sugar, for dusting

1. Preheat the oven to 350 degrees F. Lightly butter and flour a 6-cup Bundt pan.

2. In a bowl, combine 1½ cups flour, the baking powder, and salt. Set aside.

3. In another bowl, beat together 4 tablespoons butter and the sugar. Add the eggs, one at a time, beating after each addition until blended. Stir in the rum and pineapple.

4. Add half of the dry ingredients to the wet ingredients, beating until blended, and then beat in the remaining dry ingredients. Pour the batter into the prepared Bundt pan.

5. Bake for 30 to 35 minutes, or until a wooden toothpick inserted in the cake comes out clean. Cool the cake in the pan on a rack for 10 minutes, then remove it from the pan and cool completely.

6. Dust with confectioners' sugar before serving.

Old-Fashioned Strawberry Shortcakes

MAKES 8 SERVINGS

Strawberries grow wild on many continents. The American Indians were already eating strawberries when the colonists arrived. They mixed crushed berries with cornmeal and baked it into strawberry bread. Strawberries were so abundant in New England that an early colonist said that you couldn't put your foot down without stepping on one. During the 1850s, strawberry fever swept New England, leading a contemporary observer to say, "Doubtless the Almighty could make a better berry—but doubtless He never did."

FOR THE SHORTCAKES

12 tablespoons (1½ sticks) chilled, unsalted butter, cut into bits,
    plus more for the baking sheet
4 cups all-purpose flour, plus more for kneading
¼ cup plus 2 tablespoons sugar
1 tablespoon plus 2 teaspoons baking powder
1 teaspoon salt
1½ cups heavy cream
2 tablespoons (¼ stick) unsalted butter, melted and cooled

FOR THE TOPPING

2 pints fresh ripe strawberries, washed and stemmed
2 tablespoons sugar, or to taste
Heavy cream, sweetened and whipped

★ WHAT TO TASTE AND WHERE TO TASTE IT ★

Real Yankee Food

DURGIN-PARK
340 Faneuil Hall Market Place ★ Boston ★ (617) 227-2038

In the beginning, American food was English. Unique regional foods emerged in America as a result of a culinary drift that took place over hundreds of years and the introduction of new ingredients that were not common in English cookery. The best place to sample real Yankee food, however, is at Durgin-Park, which was launched about 130 years ago by John Durgin and Eldridge Park. It has been, and continues to be, famous for its Indian puddings, Boston baked beans, clam chowder, home-style apple pandowdy, johnnycakes, pot pies, and old-fashioned strawberry shortcake.

1. Preheat the oven to 425 degrees F. Lightly butter a large baking sheet.

2. TO MAKE THE SHORTCAKES: In a large bowl, mix together the dry ingredients. Add the cold butter pieces, and with a pastry blender or fingertips, rub the butter into the dry ingredients until the mixture resembles coarse meal.

3. Add the cream and mix thoroughly until a soft dough forms.

4. Gather the dough into a compact disk and place on a lightly floured board or work surface. Gently knead the dough for about 1 minute, folding it end to end and pressing down and pushing forward several times with the heel of your hand.

5. Roll out the dough into a ½-inch-thick round. With a 3-inch cookie cutter, cut out 8 rounds. With a 2½-inch cookie cutter, cut the remaining dough into 8 rounds. (If there isn't enough dough, gather the scraps, knead briefly, and roll out again.) Arrange the 3-inch rounds on the prepared baking sheet. Brush each with melted butter and top with a ½-inch round.

6. Bake shortcakes in the center of the oven for 15 minutes, until firm to the touch and golden brown. Remove to a rack to cool.

7. TO MAKE THE TOPPING: Coarsely chop half the strawberries, reserving the most attractive ones for the top.

8. Pull the tops away from the bottoms of the shortcakes. Spread a layer of chopped strawberries on the bottom halves, sprinkle with sugar, and gently replace tops. Garnish with whipped cream and whole strawberries.

> Strawberries were always the first fruit of spring in temperate zones. The strawberry season used to last from one to three months, but with new breeds and methods, it now runs from February through November in California. Production is greatest in May.
>
> When buying strawberries, look for clean, bright berries with uniform red color. Their green stem caps should be attached. Don't wash or remove the stems until right before you eat them. Strawberries should be used the day of purchase.

Two elements are responsible for the gastronomy of New York City, money and immigration, and they have been dependent on each other since the city was first settled.

The great cities along the Atlantic coast of North America were originally colonized by people who wanted to build communities based on their religious beliefs: Puritans in Boston, Quakers in Philadelphia, Anabaptists in Rhode Island. The exception was New York City. New York City was founded in 1620 as a trading post by the Dutch West India Company. It was a profit center for a corporation, and the directors of the company had one objective, to make as much money as they could as quickly as possible; all other issues were secondary.

During the 1640s, Peter Stuyvesant was the governor of the colony. He ruled with an iron fist and a wooden leg and was New York's first official bigot. He petitioned the company to let him keep out free blacks and Jews. The company's response was firm and direct: All races and religions were to be allowed into New York City so long as they enhanced the colony's economic standing, and for the past four hundred years that has been the city's general policy.

In 1625, there were five hundred people living on the island of Manhattan, and they spoke eighteen different languages. Today the residents of Manhattan speak more than a hundred different languages—and some even speak English.

By the middle of the nineteenth century, thousands of immigrants were arriving each day and they were allowed in for the simple reason that the city needed cheap labor for its new factories and construction projects. The largest groups came from Germany, eastern Europe, Ireland, and Italy. They were common people who made an uncommon

American

UNION SQUARE CAFÉ
21 East 16th Street ★ New York City ★ (212) 243-4020

Union Square Café enjoys an international reputation but remains a characteristically local New York restaurant—it's elegant but rustic, sophisticated but casual, spacious and inviting, and the staff is attentive but not stuffy. And then there's the food! Chef Michael Romano prepares consistently delicious and innovative American dishes that are often inspired by the best Italian home cooking. If they're on the menu, try the lobster shepherd's pie or the roast suckling pig. And don't miss the calamari. I like to eat at the long mahogany bar close to their excellent wine collection, which is arranged not by country of origin but by aroma.

NATHAN'S FAMOUS
1310 Surf Avenue ★ Brooklyn ★ (718) 946-2202

Sausages have been around for centuries, but the first person known to have placed one in a bun was Charles Feltman, a pie vendor in New York's Coney Island. Finding an eager audience for the new combination, he traded his pie cart for a sausage cart and his business took off. Nathan Handwerker, a Polish immigrant who worked for Feltman, decided to open his own hot dog stand in 1916, ensuring success by selling a more flavorful dog at a much lower price. When the subway opened in the 1920s, crowds of New Yorkers flooded Coney Island during the sweltering summers, and Nathan's became the place to eat. But after World War II, Coney Island's popularity declined; Feltman's closed in 1954. The following year, Nathan's began to extend its operation, opening outlets in other cities. It expanded rapidly during the 1980s when investors encouraged the growth of larger restaurants. You can still buy a Nathan's hot dog in Coney Island, and that's still the best possible place to eat one.

PARK SLOPE CHIP SHOP
383 5th Avenue ★ Brooklyn ★ (718) 832-7701

The Twinkie may have been invented in a Chicago bakery, but it took Christopher Sell, who operates a British-style fish and chip shop in Brooklyn, to come up with deep-fried Twinkies. (The deep-fried Mars Bar, a staple of Scottish "chippies," was the likely inspiration.) Served with vanilla ice cream, the deep-fried Twinkie is just what you need to offset the healthful omega-3 fatty acids you've gotten from your order of fish.

decision. They wanted to be free, free of the poverty, free of the persecution, and free of the despair that had dominated their lives in the countries in which they had been living. They changed their lives, but they also changed the United States.

The author Patrick Gallo quotes an immigrant shortly after his arrival in New York: "I have learned three things. First, the streets are not paved with gold. Second, most of the streets are not paved at all. Third, I am expected to pave them." In addition to becoming America's labor force, the immigrants also became a force for creativity, cultural development, and gastronomic change.

In 1909, my twenty-one-year-old grandmother arrived on New York's Ellis Island holding her one-year-old daughter, my mother, in her arms. As it was for most immigrants, Ellis was the site of her first meal in America. She had beef stew, boiled potatoes, rye bread, stewed fruit, and tea. In comparison to what she had been eating on the voyage, Ellis was a gastronomic paradise. The one disturbing note came on the ferry from Ellis to Manhattan. A social worker gave her something she had never seen before and indicated that she should eat it and feed some to her child. The first bite sent her into tears and she feared that she and her infant daughter would starve in America. It was a banana, but no one told her it had to be peeled.

Massive immigration to the city is still going on. U.S. census figures indicate that during the 1990s more than 1 million immigrants settled in New York City. Today, over 40 percent of the city's residents are foreign born. One result of the enormous immigrant population is the extraordinary diversity of cuisine that is available in the city. Every nation represented in the United Nations has at least one restaurant in New York serving its traditional dishes.

Immigration is responsible for the diversity of cuisine in New York City. Money, however, is responsible for its quality. The first big money came floating into town when the Erie Canal opened in 1825. The canal was 135 miles long and it connected New York City with the Great Lakes. Suddenly, products that had once taken months to get to New York were arriving in weeks. Shipping charges dropped, from a dollar to a dime. New York City was connected to the heartland of America, and the products that were being made or grown there were now shipped through the port of New York.

The Erie Canal made New York City the mercantile center of the New World. The stocks issued to fund the canal and the money needed to deal with the city's rapid growth made it the financial center of the country.

New money is usually the result of creativity. It can be as simple an idea as selling things cheaper, a concept that has made over $20 billion dollars for Sam Walton, or as complex as Microsoft, which made Bill Gates the wealthiest man in the world. These days, people of great wealth and creativity live throughout the United States, but during the second half of the 1800s and the first half of the 1900s most of America's wealthiest families lived in New York City. And whenever you have a town packed with creative people and their recently acquired money, you have a town interested in food, and that was clearly the case in New York. Immigrant cooking skills and American money made New York City one of the great restaurant towns of the world.

In the beginning, most of the cultural and gastronomic influences in the city came from England. In 1700, 90 percent of the people in the colonies were English. As a result, we speak English, our laws are based on English common law, and much of our cooking is based on English recipes: Roast beef, pies with top crusts, tea, steamed puddings, oatmeal, marmalade, and most of the dishes associated with a traditional Christmas celebration came here from England. We often say that something is as American as apple pie, what we should really be saying is that it's as *English* as apple pie.

HOW THE ITALIANS CONQUERED AMERICA

As immigrant groups arrived, they wanted to assimilate and be like everybody who was already here, so they accepted the English tradition. There was, however, one group who thought that the food in the United States was appalling. They flatly refused to give up their old-country ways and ended up changing American gastronomy to meet their traditions. The key decade was the 1880s, and the immigrants were Italian.

During the mid-1800s, American researchers developed a set of theories about the relationship of food and health and began teaching their theories as if they were scientific fact. They thought that fruits and vegetables had so high a water content that they were nutritionally useless, and green vegetables were the worst of all. They thought that eating different foods at the same time put too much stress on your digestive system. Consuming a plate of meat loaf, mashed potatoes, and string beans at one meal was a self-inflicted wound. Many of the researchers worked for the federal government, and their credentials intimidated most immigrants. The Italians, however, being more sophisticated in the ways of government, rejected the researchers and held on to their traditional approach to eating and drinking. The Italians are directly responsible for America's acceptance of vegetables, pasta, pizza, olive oil, wine, ice cream, and espresso.

The word *pizza* means "pie," and in one form or another it has been part of the diet of people in the Near East and around the Mediterranean for thousands of years. It is descended from an ancient Roman breakfast that was made up of a flat piece of baked dough with an assortment of toppings. It had a raised edge so you could eat it easily by hand and not lose any of the topping. It could have come to America with a number of immigrant groups. But it came with the Italians. In 1905, Gennaro Lombardi, from Naples, opened the first New World pizzeria, in New York City.

On January 16, 1919, the United States passed the Eighteenth Amendment to the Constitution, which prohibited the manufacture, sale, and distribution of alcoholic beverages. For ten years, distilled spirits, wine, and beer were illegal. Before Prohibition, popular restaurants served food that was basically English with a few French recipes adapted for the American consumer. When Prohibition arrived, it was impossible for people to go to these restaurants and have a glass of wine or beer with their meal.

Italian

SAN DOMENICO
240 Central Park South ★ New York City ★ (212) 265-5959
Sophisticated food based on the cuisine of northern Italy. The *New York Times* described the work of Chef Odette Fada as the best Italian cooking in the city. Tony May and his daughter Marissa treat every guest as if he or she were their most important client. The three-course prix fixe lunch is one of New York's gastronomic bargains.

BABBO
110 Waverly Place ★ New York City ★ (212) 777-0303
Mario Batali's Babbo celebrates Italian food to the fullest. Superb ingredients are used to reinterpret classic Italian dishes, and the results are wonderful. On the adventurous side, check out the lamb's tongue or fennel-dusted sweetbreads. Or, if you prefer something more middle-of-the-road, try goat cheese tortellini or the spicy lamb sausage called Mint Love Letters. In either event, the flavors are explosive but very well balanced. And where else can you have a five-course pasta tasting menu that includes two desserts?

GRIMALDI'S PIZZERIA
19 Old Fulton Street ★ Brooklyn ★ (718) 858-4300
Located under the Brooklyn Bridge on the Brooklyn side of the river, this small pizzeria serves the most delicious coal oven–baked pizza pies in the city—my favorite on all counts. The pies come out of the oven perfectly crisp, oozing a light and pleasingly charred aroma. Most topping ingredients are made on the premises, including fresh mozzarella and a savory tomato sauce. My favorite toppings are bits of fresh sausage with strips of roasted red peppers. They don't deliver or take reservations, so be prepared to wait outside, especially on busy weekends. Cash only.

There was, however, a way around this disheartening situation. If you went to an Italian neighborhood on the Lower East Side of Manhattan and ate in a dining room that was part of an Italian rooming house, wine and beer came with the meal. For decades, the owners of the rooming houses in New York City's Little Italy had been making their own wine, beer, and brandy to serve to the people who lived in the house. The local authorities, who usually lived in the neighborhood and were often related to the owners of the rooming houses, tended to overlook the practice. The general "uptown" public soon realized that they could go downtown for a good, inexpensive meal that came with the alcoholic beverage of their choice. Suddenly, Italian restaurants became extremely popular. Even today they are America's most common choice.

Deli-Style

JUNIOR'S
386 Flatbush Avenue Extension ★ Brooklyn ★ (718) 852-5257

New York–style cheesecake relies for its dense richness on cream cheese, which became available toward the end of the nineteenth century. The classic is made of cream cheese sweetened with sugar, enriched with eggs and cream, flavored with vanilla, and baked in a crumb, cookie-dough, or sponge-cake crust. It is sometimes dressed up with fruit toppings—cherry, blueberry, strawberry, pineapple—and new variations are constantly appearing—chocolate swirl, mocha, and pumpkin, for example. The "World's Most Fabulous Cheesecake" is served at Junior's in Brooklyn, founded by Harry Rosen in 1950. The dense cheesecake continues to be made in the restaurant's original location, and you can sample a slice on site or take a whole cake home.

BARNEY GREENGRASS
541 Amsterdam Avenue ★ New York City ★ (212) 724-4707

This Upper West Side restaurant has been rated New York's finest kosher deli. Opened in 1908, it specializes in everything that you would expect—cheese blintzes, chopped chicken livers, bagels and cream cheese, borscht, and Nova Scotia salmon scrambled with eggs—all of which are worth it. But Barney Greengrass is the "Sturgeon King," so don't miss the sturgeon, which should be eaten on rye with raw onion, of course.

KOSSAR'S BIALYS
367 Grand Street ★ New York City ★ (212) 473-4810

Not a place to settle in for a cozy meal, this bakery is all business—and a delicious business it is. Bialys are chewy, flat rolls with sunken centers, something like a bagel without a hole. Often slightly charred on the edges, lightly dusted with flour (you'll end up lightly dusted yourself if you stay at Kossar's for more than a few minutes), bialys are best eaten warm from the oven, plain or with cream cheese.

YONAH SHIMMEL'S
137 East Houston Street ★ New York City ★ (212) 477-2858

A knish is like a baked dumpling. A potato knish has filling of well-seasoned mashed potato wrapped in thin, flaky pastry. Kasha, meat, and liver knishes are the other classics, and nowadays there are innovative fillings to suit all tastes. Yonah Shimmel's, on the Lower East Side, is nearing its one-hundredth anniversary of preparing knishes. There's nothing like a sturdy, steaming-hot knish on a cold winter day, and if you have one for lunch you won't be hungry 'til dinnertime.

LET'S GET PICKLED

During the 1880s, eastern Europe was in constant turmoil, crops were failing, there was agonizing poverty throughout the population, and religious persecution was rampant. Millions of Russians, Poles, Hungarians, Austrians, and Romanians headed for New York City.

When they arrived, they began baking rich, whole-grain breads, which they preferred to the overly processed white breads that were eaten by most Americans. They chose water as their favorite drink, infused it with bubbles, and introduced New York to seltzer. They called it the worker's Champagne. They were masters at smoking fish and meat and gave New York its great delicatessens with their pastrami and corned beef. They also popularized the drinking of tea, which had lost much of its standing since the Boston Tea Party. They introduced whipped cream, sweet pancakes, yogurt, cookies in dozens of shapes, and the idea of drinking coffee throughout the day, not just at breakfast.

The Germans have been coming to America since our earliest colonial days. So many arrived during the early 1700s that Ben Franklin suggested limiting German immigration—he feared that the colonies would end up with German as the most common language.

Gastronomically, the Germans introduced Hamburg steaks, frankfurters, potato salad, jelly donuts, numerous cakes and cookies, and good beer as well as pretzels, sauerbraten, and sauerkraut. During the mid-nineteenth century, German beer gardens, restaurants, and saloons sprang up in New York and became social centers for German immigrants as well as native-born Americans, who ate, drank, talked, and played cards and other games in the establishments. Lüchow's, on Fourteenth Street, was built in 1840 and it was one of New York's most popular restaurants until the late twentieth century.

Delicatessen is a German word meaning "to eat delicacies"; in Germany it referred to a retail store selling specialty food items. Nineteenth-century German delicatessens sold pickled, roasted, and smoked hams, sausages, fowl, smoked and pickled fish, and game. They also offered prepared salads made from chicken, herring, or potatoes, as well as sauerkraut and pickles of all descriptions. Frequently, a wild boar's head, the quintessential symbol of a feast, was placed in the window of the shop to symbolize the abundance within.

German immigrants introduced the delicatessen to the United States. The first delicatessen in America opened on Grand Street in New York City in around 1868. At that time, Manhattan's Lower East Side had a substantial German immigrant population, but the exotic groceries attracted shoppers of all ethnicities. During the late nineteenth century, delicatessens filled the gap between butcher shops (which mainly sold uncooked meats) and grocery stores (which mainly sold generic and packaged goods). Delicatessens soon opened in other cities.

The first American delicatessens sold cooked, ready-to-eat meats, poultry, and fish, as well as specialty products like cheeses, teas, mushrooms, caviar, olive oil, pickled foods, and imported canned goods. Later, delicatessens sold tuna and chicken salads, coleslaw, and potato salad. Originally, the prepared foods were taken away for home consumption, but as delicatessens thrived and expanded, some made space for customers to sit down and eat in the store, particularly at lunchtime.

By the time of World War I, German-owned delis had been largely replaced by Jewish-owned delis. Kosher delis served only meat and pareve (neutral—neither dairy nor meat) dishes. The standard menu came to include chicken soup, corned beef, gefilte fish, lox, knishes, pastrami, chopped liver, tongue, and garlic pickles. Establishments that did not adhere to kosher laws expanded their menus in the 1920s to include bagels, bialys, cream cheese, and cheesecake. Delis also popularized Jewish-style breads, notably rye and pumpernickel. Famous kosher or Jewish-style delicatessens in New York City include Katz's, the Carnegie Deli, and the Second Avenue Deli. During the mid-twentieth century, some delicatessens became full-fledged restaurants and remained delicatessens in name only.

Delicatessens were the birthplace of a number of prepared foods that reached national markets. In New York, a German immigrant, Richard Hellmann, opened a delicatessen in 1905. He began selling commercial mayonnaise in 1912 under his own name and later expanded his product line. Hellmann's is still one of the most popular brands of bottled mayonnaise in the United States.

Other entrepreneurs created businesses catering to delicatessens. Frank Brunckhorst, for instance, began supplying provisions to other New York delicatessens in 1905. Brunckhorst opened a manufacturing plant in Brooklyn in 1933 and sold his products under the brand name "Boar's Head." Today, Boar's Head Provision Company is one of the largest suppliers of prepared meats to delicatessens and supermarket deli counters.

During the mid-twentieth century, mainstream America adopted many traditional "deli" specialties. Supermarkets

Steak

PETER LUGER
178 Broadway ★ Brooklyn ★ (718) 387-7400

There is considerable difference of opinion as to the best spot for a New York steak. However, I have been a devoted fan of Peter Luger's for over fifty years, and my judgment is shared by many of the top food authorities in the city. It opened in 1887 and has the feeling of an old German beer hall. The waiters like to play at being crusty but can also be very charming. The standard meal is sliced tomatoes and onions with the restaurant's special steak sauce for dipping, sliced Porterhouse steak, home-fried potatoes, creamed spinach, a mug of beer, and cheesecake for dessert.
Note: You'll need a reservation, and they only take cash.

POST HOUSE
28 East 63rd Street ★ New York City ★ (212) 935-2888

Post House is a refined and elegant version of the classic New York institution that is the steak house. Leather banquettes and armchairs, gilt-framed paintings, and carefully chosen china give the room a look of a private gentlemen's club, but the atmosphere is more family friendly than stuffy. No matter what you order—a grand porterhouse, a Cajun rib steak, or a buttery filet mignon—it will arrive at the table in a ceremonial way. Proprietor Alan Stillman's enthusiasm for wine manifests itself in a carefully chosen wine list.

DELMONICO'S
55 Beaver Street ★ New York City ★ (212) 509-1144

In 1826, John Delmonico pronounced New York a culinary wasteland and promptly decided to right that situation by opening an eating establishment. A few years later, he and his brother Peter started Delmonico's restaurant, which is credited for the invention of the dish Lobster à la Newberg. Situated in the Wall Street district, it provides a great window into the past but also a way to savor a beefy lunch or dinner among the city's financial power brokers.

OLD HOMESTEAD
56 Ninth Avenue ★ New York City ★ (212) 242-9040

This historic restaurant opened in 1868 and catered to the butchers who worked in the neighboring meat market. So from the start it had to serve good stuff; you can't pass off a low-quality piece of meat on a butcher. Plus, its location ensured that its cooks could acquire the freshest and choicest picks of meat. Today the meatpacking district has gone haute and is filled with more upscale bars than butchers. But you can still dine on porterhouse or prime rib under the tin ceilings and stained-glass lamps of Old Homestead.

THE SEOUL OF NEW YORK

Historically, New York greengrocers were of Italian or Greek descent. This began to change in 1975, when Kyung T. Sohn, a college graduate, bought out a small greengrocery store owned by an Italian-American. Although he knew nothing about produce, he worked hard and expanded his operation. Sohn was one of the first Korean-Americans to open a greengrocer in New York. He was extremely successful and others followed his example, opening greengrocery stores throughout the city. These stores not only sold produce but also began to supply spicy Korean foods, such as kimchi, to New York's estimated 100,000 Koreans. Today, 85 percent of New York produce stores are Korean owned.

incorporated delis into their operations, and foods such as pastrami, corned beef, and lox have become popular across the country.

The word *delicatessen* remains current in American cities, but today the term is used quite loosely. As new immigrants—Italians, Greeks, Puerto Ricans, West Indians, Asians, Russians, and Mexicans—moved into American cities, many found that deli ownership was one way to enter American economic life. Some of these delis serve traditional delicatessen foods, but most have incorporated culinary elements from the own-

---

★ WHAT TO TASTE AND WHERE TO TASTE IT ★

French

BALTHAZAR
80 Spring Street ★ New York City ★ (212) 965-1414

This SoHo French brasserie has good food and an atmosphere that feels like Paris. The main attraction, however, is the "scene"—fashion models, famous actors, hot investment bankers, and those who enjoy looking at fashion models, famous actors, and hot investment bankers. The dishes we filmed for a public broadcasting special on New York are probably still on the menu—*brandade de morue* (a puree of codfish and potatoes), steak with pepper sauce and French fries, and apple tarts.

CAFÉ BOULUD
20 East 76th Street ★ New York City ★ (212) 772-2600

Café Boulud is a small, casually elegant café where the atmosphere is warm and welcoming and the food is always dependably good. There are four different menus: Classic, offering Chef Daniel Boulud's French-country signature dishes, like roasted duck breast or chocolate soufflé; Seasonal, with a focus on remarkably fresh fish, meats, fruits, and vegetables of the season; Vegetarian; and an International menu featuring inventive international specialties. It's a chic Upper East Side spot for laid-back dining either at lunch or dinner.

Power Lunch

THE FOUR SEASONS
99 East 52nd Street ★ New York City ★ (212) 754-9494

Designed by Philip Johnson, the restaurant is an architectural landmark. The food is outstanding and straightforward in its preparation and presentation. Powerful people need to know what's on their plate. The service is excellent and the wine list superb. The Grill Room at lunch is where the elite meet to eat. Last time I was there I saw former secretary of state Henry Kissinger, opera star Beverly Sills, Barnes & Noble president Steve Riggio, and public relations guru Bob Dilenschneider—and that was without turning around to see who was seated behind me.

"21" CLUB
21 West 52nd Street ★ New York City ★ (212) 582-7200

The "21" Club started out during Prohibition as a speakeasy, and by the time the dry years came to an end it was a favorite eatery for the rich and powerful. It's smack in the middle of New York's television district, with ABC, NBC, and CBS headquarters within easy walking distance. Chef Erik Blauberg has done a fine job of updating the restaurant's traditional favorites while adding new life to the menu. The walls and ceiling of the bar area are covered with models that relate to the companies run by the restaurant's regular clientele. It's famous for the "21" Hamburger and the Sunset Salad (chopped cabbage, lettuce, ham, and chicken) with Lorenzo Dressing.

ers' homelands. For instance, some Korean-American deli owners offer kimchi, which can be described as Korean sauerkraut.

Other "delis" are small grocery stores, which might or might not sell prepared food. Today, there are more delicatessens than ever, and several chains now franchise "New York" delis throughout America, although many are related to traditional delicatessens in name only.

LUNCH-HOUR POWER

The combination of top-quality restaurants in New York City and the desire to do business throughout the day led to the introduction of the "power lunch." There are a half-dozen restaurants in the city that have become the chosen watering holes for the city's power brokers. I use the term watering hole because for centuries a town's water well was where people came to meet each other. In fact, it often acted as a singles bar for young people in search of a suitable lover. The Grill Room in the Four Seasons Restaurant and the bar room in the "21" Club are the new wells.

Sunset Salad with Lorenzo Dressing

MAKES 4 SERVINGS

A quintessential landmark New York restaurant, the "21" Club was once a speakeasy. Built into a four-story townhouse, its hidden Prohibition wine cellar is presently used as a private dining room. The restaurant is famous for a solid American menu including their "21" Burger and the Sunset Salad with Lorenzo Dressing.

FOR THE SALAD

½ medium head green cabbage
½ medium head iceberg lettuce
5 thin slices cooked beef tongue or ham
2 whole chicken breasts, poached and cooled, skin and bones removed,
  or 1 pound skinless cooked turkey

FOR THE LORENZO DRESSING

1 cup chili sauce
½ cup finely chopped watercress
½ cup French dressing

1. Cut all of the salad ingredients into thin, match-size strips. Combine them in a large bowl.

2. TO MAKE THE DRESSING: Combine the chili sauce and the watercress. Add the French dressing and blend thoroughly.

3. Just before serving, toss the salad with the Lorenzo dressing.

Watercress is a peppery-tasting green leafy plant that grows along streams and creeks. It is a member of the nasturtium family, whose edible leaves and petals offer a similar peppery flavor. Watercress has been used as a food for over 3,000 years. It is a good source of vitamins C and A.

Watercress is very perishable. Look for bright green bunches with leaves and stems as undamaged as possible. Wash and store in a plastic bag in the refrigerator for only 1 or 2 days.

Manhattan Clam Chowder

MAKES 6 SERVINGS

Tomato-based clam chowders were in fact developed in New England. By the 1930s, this tomato version had come to be called Manhattan clam chowder.

4 tablespoons (½ stick) unsalted butter
1 cup diced potatoes
½ cup diced celery
½ cup chopped onions
¼ cup all-purpose flour
6 cups homemade clam broth or bottled clam juice
2 tablespoons tomato paste
1 cup drained canned chopped tomatoes
2 cups chopped cooked fresh or drained canned clams
  (If using canned clams, reserve the juice and include in step 2.)
1 teaspoon dried thyme
Salt and freshly ground black pepper
Crackers

1. In a large pot, melt the butter over moderate heat. Add the potatoes, celery, and onion and sauté for 2 minutes. Stir in the flour. Cook for 1 minute, stirring, until thoroughly mixed.

2. Add the clam broth, tomato paste, and tomatoes. Mix well. Simmer for 1 hour, stirring occasionally. Add more clam broth or water if the chowder looks too thick.

3. Add the clams and thyme and simmer for 3 minutes. Season with salt and pepper to taste.

4. Serve the chowder with large plain white crackers.

ABOUT CRACKERS

Nineteenth- and early-twentieth-century American grocery stores displayed barrels full of crackers for sale; for the customers these functioned as a center for small talk. That is the origin of the expression "heard around the cracker barrel." What the English call biscuits, Americans call crackers. Crackers get their name from the cracking sound they make when they are broken. In their most primitive form, crackers are simply wheat or rye flour mixed with water, rolled thin, and baked until crisp. All sorts of flavorings, butter, salt, sugar, and spices have been added over the years to create dozens of different crackers.

New Potato Salad

MAKES 6 SERVINGS

Delicatessen is a word of German origin meaning "delicacies." New York is famous for it delicatessens that offer pastrami, corn beef, coleslaw, and potato salad. This recipe is has been adapted from one of New York's finest delicatessens.

3 pounds new potatoes, scrubbed
2 tablespoons salt
1 tablespoon caraway seeds
1 clove garlic, peeled
Salt and freshly ground black pepper
1 cup sour cream or plain yogurt, or a combination of the two,
    or Low-Fat Dressing (recipe follows)
¼ cup minced fresh dill
Lettuce leaves, tomato wedges, and a sprig of dill, for garnish

1. In a large saucepan combine the potatoes, caraway seeds, garlic, and 2 tablespoons salt. Add water to cover and cook over moderately high heat for 20 minutes or until the potatoes are tender. Drain and cool. Discard the garlic and caraway seeds.

2. Quarter the potatoes and place in a mixing bowl. Add salt and pepper to taste and stir in the sour cream or yogurt and dill.

3. Line a serving bowl with lettuce leaves, add the potato salad, and garnish with tomato wedges and a sprig of dill.

One of the best ways to reduce the calorie content of your salad dressings is to use buttermilk made with skim or low-fat milk, low-fat or nonfat plain yogurt, nonfat sour cream, or reduced-fat mayonnaise.

LOW-FAT DRESSING

MAKES 1 ¼ CUPS

1 tablespoon fresh lemon juice
⅓ cup buttermilk (made from skim or low-fat milk)
1 cup low-fat or nonfat cottage cheese or nonfat sour cream

Combine the ingredients in a blender for 5 seconds.

BOSTON CLOCKWISE FROM TOP LEFT: Clambake on the beach ★ Fresh fish for sale ★
Blueberries and strawberries ★ Berry Muffins

BOSTON ABOVE LEFT: Strawberry Shortcake ★ ABOVE RIGHT: Lobster dinner

NEW YORK BELOW LEFT: Nathan's Famous Hot Dogs ★ BELOW RIGHT: Ice cream

NEW YORK ABOVE: Hot pretzel with mustard ★ BELOW LEFT: Deli-smoked Fish ★
BELOW RIGHT: Chinatown window

NEW YORK ABOVE LEFT: Classic New York diner ★ ABOVE RIGHT: Street vendor

PHILADELPHIA BELOW LEFT: Buddakan restaurant ★ BELOW RIGHT: Ricali's Seafood

PHILADELPHIA CLOCKWISE FROM ABOVE: Reading Terminal Market ★ Rocco's Famous Italian Hoagies ★ Scoop de Ville ★ Jim's Steaks ★ Lemon meringue pies

RICHMOND CLOCKWISE FROM TOP
LEFT: Home-canned vegetables ★
Janice's Sweet Shop ★ Picnic on the dock
★ Frogmore stew ★ Produce stand

RICHMOND CLOCKWISE FROM ABOVE:
17th Street farmer's market ★
String beans ★ Freshly shucked oysters

MIAMI BELOW: Stone crab farmers ★
LEFT: Joe's Stone Crabs Restaurant

MIAMI CLOCKWISE FROM ABOVE: Key
Lime Pie ★ Crab cakes ★ Cuban sandwiches
★ Haitian band at Tap Tap restaurant ★
Oranges and grapefruit for sale at gas station

The Best Chicken Soup

MAKES 8 SERVINGS

The Second Avenue Deli was an East Village landmark, serving traditional Jewish delicacies for fifty years. This recipe is from *The Second Avenue Deli Cookbook: Recipes and Memories from Abe Lebewohl's Legendary Kitchen.*

1 pound chicken parts
2 ribs celery, including leafy tops, cut into 3-inch pieces
1 whole chicken, thoroughly rinsed
Salt to rub inside chicken, plus 2 teaspoons salt
1 large whole onion, unpeeled (find one with a firm, golden-brown peel)
1 large whole carrot, peeled
1 medium whole parsnip, peeled
¼ teaspoon pepper
1 bunch of dill, cleaned and tied with a string

1. Pour 12 cups of cold water into a large stockpot, and throw in the chicken parts and celery. Bring to a boil. While the water is heating, rub the inside of the whole chicken with salt.

2. Add the chicken to the pot, cover, reduce heat, and simmer for 30 minutes. Test chicken with a fork to see if it's tender and fully cooked; then remove it from the pot, and set aside on a large platter. Leave the chicken parts in the pot.

3. Add onion, carrot, parsnip, 2 teaspoons salt, and pepper. Let soup simmer for 1 hour and 15 minutes.

4. When whole chicken cools, remove skin and bones and cut the meat into bite-sized pieces. You can add it to the soup, just before serving, or save it for chicken salad.

5. Strain the soup, and discard everything solid except for the carrot.

6. Drop in the dill for a minute before serving and remove. Add salt and pepper to taste. Slice the carrot and toss it into the soup. Also add the chicken pieces if desired.

The Deli's recipe calls for both a whole chicken plus 1 pound of chicken parts. You can, however, use just 1 large chicken and cut off both wings, the neck, and a leg to use as parts. You may want to skim the foam off the surface as the soup simmers. For serving, you can add cooked noodles, rice, kasha, or matzo balls.

New York Firehouse Chile

MAKES 8 SERVINGS

Firefighters everywhere love to cook, eat, and talk about food. Their mainstays are one-pot meals that are hearty and down-to-earth. This is a classic recipe from **New York's Bravest.**

5 tablespoons vegetable oil
2 pounds ground beef round
1 pound hot Italian sausages, skinned and crumbled
4 cups beef stock
1 pinch saffron threads
2 cups coarsely chopped shallots
2 tablespoons minced garlic
1 (7-ounce) can green chiles, drained, chopped to a rough puree
1 teaspoon crushed dried oregano
1 teaspoon ground cumin
½ teaspoon cayenne pepper
2 tablespoons chili powder
1 teaspoon salt
Freshly ground black pepper
1 (6-ounce) can tomato paste
2 (15- to 16-ounce) cans red kidney beans, drained

1. In a large heavy skillet, heat 2 tablespoons of the oil over medium-high heat. Add the ground meat and sausage and sauté until browned.

2. Drain the fat off and transfer the meat to a 4-quart pot. Add the beef stock to the skillet, and bring to a boil. Remove from the heat. Crumble the saffron into the stock. Set aside.

3. In another large skillet, heat the remaining 3 tablespoons oil over medium-high heat. Add the shallots and garlic and sauté for 5 minutes, until lightly browned. Remove from the heat.

4. Stir in the chilis and seasonings, and black pepper to taste. Stir in the tomato paste and mix thoroughly.

5. Pour the contents of both skillets into the pot of meat and mix well. Place over medium-high heat and bring to a boil. Reduce the heat to low and simmer, half-covered, for 1½ hours.

6. Add the beans and cook for 10 minutes more before serving.

Saffron comes from the stigma of the crocus, and 75,000 must be hand picked to get a pound. That explains why it is one of the most expensive food products on the planet—about $2,000 a pound. Fortunately, the flavor is very powerful and only a pinch is needed for a whole pot of food. Saffron is sold in long, thin threads, and crushing them in a little hot liquid will bring out all of the flavor.

Egg Cream
MAKES 1 SERVING

Egg creams contain neither eggs nor cream. Originally they were produced almost exclusively in the soda fountains of New York. It is believed that the egg cream was invented in 1890 by Louis Auster, a Jewish candy store owner in Brooklyn, New York.

A cousin (on my mother's side) owned a candy store in New York next to Yankee Stadium. The following is his recipe, modified for home use.

½ cup milk, chilled
⅓ cup Fox's U-Bet Chocolate Syrup
¾ cup seltzer, chilled

1. Pour the milk into a 12-ounce glass. Add the syrup and ¼ cup of the seltzer.

2. Briskly stir the milk, syrup, and seltzer together until all ingredients are fully incorporated. Add the remaining ½ cup seltzer while trying to avoid disturbing the foam that has formed.

Homemade Pasta

MAKES ABOUT 1 1/2 POUNDS

In New York, Italian immigrants have made some of the most lasting contributions to the city's cuisine. In the early days of Little Italy, small shops opened to sell homemade fresh pasta just like in the old country. Today fresh pasta is sold in outlets all over the city.

3 cups all-purpose flour
4 large eggs, at room temperature
Cornmeal
1 tablespoon salt

1. Mound the flour on a clean work surface and make a well about 6 inches wide in the center. Crack the eggs into the well. With a fork, break the eggs and gradually combine them with the flour. Do not let the eggs run out of the walls of the flour. When the eggs have mixed with the flour to make a loose paste, use the palms of your hands to bring the walls of flour and the eggs together to form a soft dough. The amount of flour the eggs will absorb will vary from batch to batch.

2. When you have a pliable dough, clean your hands and the work surface of any excess flour and egg. Knead the dough until it is smooth and elastic, about 5 to 7 minutes. Set the dough aside, covered with a towel or wrapped in plastic, and let it rest for at least 20 minutes or up to 2 hours. (Do not refrigerate the dough or it will get too wet.)

3. Set up a pasta machine. Cut off a quarter of the dough (keep the rest covered while you work) and flatten it into a square that will fit through the widest setting of the machine. Feed the dough through the machine and then fold the flattened dough like a business letter. Pass the folded dough through the machine again and repeat this process until the dough is satiny smooth. Close the machine's rollers down a notch and feed the dough through the machine again. Repeat this process at each setting down to the thinnest. Lay the pasta sheet out to dry on a towel. Repeat this procedure with the rest of the dough. Before cutting, let the dough dry until it is leathery but still pliable, about 1 hour.

4. Cut the dough into foot-long pieces and pass the sheets through the small tonnarelli or wide fettuccini cutters. Lay the pasta out on a tray to dry and dust it with cornmeal to prevent the pasta from sticking together.

5. When ready to serve, bring 4 quarts of water to a boil, and add the salt. Add the pasta and cook at a rapid boil for 1 to 2 minutes, depending on the size and how long it has been drying. Drain and serve with the sauce of your choice.

OXTAIL TOMATO SAUCE

MAKES ABOUT 5 CUPS

3 tablespoons olive oil

1½ pounds oxtails (or beef short ribs or beef shin), trimmed of excess fat

2 teaspoons kosher salt

½ teaspoon freshly ground black pepper

1 medium onion, diced

1 carrot, sliced

1 tablespoon minced garlic

½ teaspoon crushed red pepper flakes

1½ cups dry red wine

4 cups tomato puree

½ teaspoon freshly grated nutmeg

½ teaspoon fresh sage (4 medium leaves) or ½ teaspoon dried sage, crushed

½ pound spicy Italian sausage

1. Heat the oil in a large saucepan. Season the oxtails with some of the salt and pepper and brown them on all sides over medium-high heat. Remove the oxtails from the pan and sauté the onion, carrot, garlic, and pepper flakes until translucent, 4 to 5 minutes. Return the oxtails to the pan, add the red wine, tomato puree, nutmeg, and sage and bring to a simmer.

2. Press the sausage out of its casing and break the meat apart. Fry the sausage meat in a small skillet for 5 minutes. Drain the excess fat and add the cooked sausage meat to the simmering sauce.

3. Season the sauce to taste with the remaining salt and pepper and cook, covered, over low heat for 45 minutes. Remove the oxtails from the sauce before serving.

New York Hazelnut Cheesecake

MAKES 10 TO 12 SERVINGS

There are hundreds of different cheesecake recipes that claim to represent the authentic New York style. However, New York cheesecake is always made with cream cheese.

Commercial cream cheese in the familiar eight-ounce blocks was first made by the Lawrence dairy in upstate New York at the turn of the century. The name Philadelphia cream cheese came from another upstate New York dairyman who made such good cream cheese that he named it after the gracious city of Philadelphia. It should be noted that at that time Philadelphia was famous for the high quality of its dairy products. When the New York farmer called his cheese Philadelphia, it was a clear case of false advertising.

3 (8-ounce) packages cream cheese (1½ pounds), at room temperature
1 cup sugar
3 eggs
1 cup finely chopped hazelnuts
1 teaspoon vanilla extract
1 cup heavy cream
2 tablespoons rum
Butter for the pan
Plain bread crumbs

1. Preheat the oven to 375 degrees F.

2. In the bowl of an electric mixer beat the cream cheese until fluffy. Add the sugar, eggs, hazelnuts, vanilla, heavy cream, and rum; beat until well combined.

3. Butter a 10-inch springform pan and coat the sides and bottom with bread crumbs.

4. Pour the batter into the prepared pan. Set the springform pan in a larger pan and add hot water to the outer pan to reach halfway up the side of the springform. Bake for 1 hour. Turn the oven off and leave the cheesecake inside for 1 hour, without opening the oven door. The cool air may cause the cheesecake to crack.

5. Remove the cake from the oven and allow it to cool completely.

Baked Apples

MAKES 6 SERVINGS

In the early twentieth century, apple was used to describe the numerous race courses in and around New York City. The prizes for the races were substantial and they were also referred to as apples. By the early 1920s, New York City came to be known as the Big Apple. It's believed that jazz musicians were responsible for this moniker because in show business there was an old saying: "There are many apples on the tree, but only one Big Apple." New York City, being the best place to perform, was referred to as the Big Apple. Apples also happen to be one of the major crops of New York State.

¾ cup packed light brown sugar
1 teaspoon ground cinnamon
¼ teaspoon grated nutmeg
⅓ cup raisins
⅓ cup cinnamon red hot candies
6 baking apples (ideally a mix of several varieties), cored but not peeled
½ cup maple syrup

1. Preheat the oven to 350 degrees F. Lightly butter a loaf pan or square baking pan large enough to hold all the apples.

2. In a bowl mix together the sugar, cinnamon, nutmeg, raisins, and red hot candies. Spoon this mixture into the centers of the apples.

3. Place the apples in the prepared pan. Pour the maple syrup over the apples. Bake for 30 to 40 minutes, until tender. (Baking time can vary slightly with the variety and size of the apples.

PHILADELPHIA

Pennsylvania

DURING THE 1670S, Englishmen who followed the Quaker faith were persecuted by King Charles II, who found their beliefs unacceptable. He threw ten thousand Quakers into prison, including his fellow aristocrat William Penn, whose father (Sir William Penn) was an admiral in the British navy.

The king owed Admiral Penn sixteen thousand pounds, and the debt was due. King Charles, however, was a little short of cash, so he offered the Penns a win-win deal: He would free the admiral's son and his Quaker brethren, and grant them a huge tract of land in North America—a tract that was actually larger than all of England. William Penn would take his Quakers to a new home in the New World, and the king's debt would be cancelled.

The Penns agreed, William went off to found the colony of Pennsylvania (which he named after his father, not himself), and the king was delighted. The Quakers were out of his hair. Penn would be conducting his experiment in religious freedom and representative government in a heathen wilderness three thousand miles away, and since the king had stolen the land from the Native Americans in the first place, it was a painless resolution of his debt.

There was only one problem: The ideas that came to Pennsylvania with the Quakers were the very ideas that laid the groundwork for the Declaration of Independence and the American Revolution. But that wouldn't happen for another hundred years.

Philadelphia was the capital of Penn's colony and America's first truly diverse society. The ability of Philadelphians to tolerate radical ideas made the city so attractive that on the eve of the American Revolution, it was the largest city in the English-speaking world after

London, and the wealthiest city in the Americas. It was the logical place to plan the revolution and became the first seat of our new national government.

Because of its Quaker founders, Philadelphia became known as the City of Brotherly Love, and one of the things the Quaker brothers loved most was good food. The city became

famous for its bakeries and pastry shops, its ice-cream makers and restaurateurs. And it still is. It's the place where a visitor can trace and taste many of the major influences on the history of American eating and drinking.

The plantations that grew up around Philadelphia were based on the English manor system. A central element was the bake and brew house, where yeast was used to produce both beer and bread. Wheat was the major cash crop of the colony; it supplied the funds that the colony needed to trade with England, and provided the raw material for some extraordinary bakers.

The city became a haven for bakers. Mennonites from Germany and the Amish from Switzerland were attracted to Philadelphia because of its promise of religious freedom, but they were also master bakers and skilled in the use of spices. (Philadelphia was a great trading port, and among the cargoes unloaded were spices from the West Indies and fresh produce from the Caribbean—coconuts, bananas, pineapples, and limes.) Because they spoke German (Deutsch), when they settled in the

Old Philadelphia

READING TERMINAL MARKET

Twelfth and Arch Streets ★ 51 North 12th Street ★ Philadelphia ★ (215) 922-2317

The Reading Terminal Market is a cornucopia of multiethnic eateries and mini-markets attached to the Convention Center. This is a gastronomical, geographical, and cultural experience all in one square block.

CITY TAVERN

138 South Second Street ★ Philadelphia ★ (215) 413-1443

For history in a meal, this is a delightful place to dine. Try the pepper pot soup and the colonial turkey pot pie. For those who can't make it to Philadelphia and want to taste the foods of the American Revolution, you can do so through Walter Staib's wonderful cookbooks, *City Tavern Cookbook* and *City Tavern Baking and Dessert Cookbook: 200 Years of Classic Recipes from America's First Gourmet Restaurant.*

BOOKBINDER'S OLD ORIGINAL

125 Walnut Street ★ Philadelphia ★ (215) 925-7027

Since 1865, Bookbinder's has served seafood, crab cakes, and old-fashioned snapper soup. Bookbinder's is an early-nineteenth-century restaurant that many consider an important destination in Philadelphia.

area these groups became known as Pennsylvania Dutch. To this day, they are known for their wonderful farmstead meals, including hearty dishes like chicken pot pie (topped with squares of noodle dough) and schnitz und knepp (ham cooked with dried apples and served with dumplings). They were also experts at the production of homemade pickles, relishes, and sauces to accompany every meal.

Their traditional sweets included cinnamon buns, donuts, crullers, funnel cake (made by siphoning batter through a funnel into hot fat), and shoofly pie, with its filling of molasses and streusel-like crumbs.

WAS AMERICA BORN IN A TAVERN?

During colonial times, taverns occupied an important place in American life. They weren't just places to drink and have a bite to eat. In the days before social clubs and debating societies, taverns were gathering places where colonists could express and defend their notions of the politics of the day. The drinks helped keep the discourse flowing, and the food sustained the drinkers as they debated until the early hours of the morning.

The City Tavern played a special role in Philadelphia—and in our nation's history. In fact, it could be said that the United States had its beginnings in this tavern. Built in 1773, the City Tavern opened just in time to serve as the meeting place of the First Continental Congress. When Congress moved to Carpenter's Hall, the tavern served as a hotel for America's most important leaders—and, of course, George Washington slept there. The City Tavern burned down in 1834, but was faithfully reconstructed in preparation for the national bicentennial in 1976. In 1994, Chef Walter Staib took over the City Tavern and started to faithfully re-create American dishes from the late eighteenth and early nineteenth centuries. In this tavern you can truly take a bite out of history.

The American Revolution introduced a new government, and Philadelphia was its first capital. The new government brought hundreds of well-heeled politicians to town, and Philadelphia became a gathering place for lovers of fine food. Within a few years, the situation had gotten even better. As the American Revolution ended, the French Revolution began, and at the same time an uprising took place in Haiti. By the mid-1790s, hundreds of Frenchmen had come to Philadelphia seeking refuge. Among them were professional chefs, pastry cooks, confectioners, wine experts, and epicures. Philadelphia became the gastronomic center of the young nation.

★ **WHAT TO TASTE AND WHERE TO TASTE IT** ★

Mediterranean

DIMITRI'S
795 South Third Street ★ Philadelphia ★ (215) 625-0556
This restaurant is known for its Mediterranean seafood dishes that have a decidedly Greek influence. BYO and sit at the counter and watch the chefs at work. No reservations are taken, so be prepared to line up outside with all the regulars.

FAIR FOOD

When America's one-hundredth birthday arrived in 1876, Philadelphia was the center of the nation's festivities. The city hosted a Centennial Exposition, where both Americans and foreigners were fascinated by the many new foods and beverages that were on display and for sale. In the Horticultural Hall, a forty-acre exhibition of exotic tropical fruits included a banana tree heavy with fruit. While bananas had been imported into the United States since the 1840s, they were still a novelty to most visitors. During the exposition, guards were posted near the banana tree to prevent visitors from helping themselves to samples. Outside the hall, bananas in foil wrappers were sold for ten cents apiece. It wouldn't be long before the banana was America's favorite fruit.

Commercial canning had gotten under way in America in the 1820s, but it wasn't until the start of the Civil War that government contracts spurred widespread development of canneries. Many canning companies were represented at the exposition, and most received awards for their products. The Joseph Campbell Preserve Company, located right across the Delaware River from Philadelphia in Camden, New Jersey, was among the medal winners. Later renamed the Campbell's Soup Company, the firm featured its exposition gold medals on every can label until they won a medal at an international exposition in 1900—and that medal remains on their cans today.

TWISTED AND THRIFTY

Pretzels, which probably originated in Germany, were sold by German immigrants in Philadelphia during colonial times. A big, soft pretzel, served with a ribbon of yellow mustard and eaten warm as you stroll the streets of the city, is a Philadelphia classic. But Philadelphia also has a history in the hard-pretzel business. In 1861, the first commercial pretzel company was launched in Lancaster County, Pennsylvania. The first automatic pretzel-twisting machine was developed by the Reading Pretzel Machinery Company in 1933, and pretzel manufacturing remained concentrated in Pennsylvania until it emerged as a national snack in the 1960s.

Another Philadelphia specialty is scrapple. Introduced to America by Pennsylvania Dutch farmers and based on culinary traditions from northern Germany, scrapple is a thrifty farmer's way of using up every bit of the pig: Bits of pork trimmed off at butchering time are cooked in broth and thickened with cornmeal and buckwheat. The mixture is formed into a loaf and then sliced and fried. Served with eggs for breakfast, scrapple is a uniquely American sausage. Unlike other Philadelphia foods, however, scrapple has yet to capture the culinary imagination of the rest of the country.

FIZZY WATER

Another taste sensation at the Philadelphia Exposition was soda (as in soda water, soda pop, and soda fountain). While the technique of carbonating water with bicarbonate of soda had been known for centuries, it had not yet been applied to commercial products—but that would change after the Centennial Exposition.

Temperance supporters had managed to ban the sale of hard liquor at the exposition, so James W. Tufts and Charles Lippincott plunked down the astronomical sum of fifty thousand dollars for the privilege of selling soda water on the exposition grounds. Tufts and Lippincott constructed a three-story edifice with a thirty-foot soda fountain as its featured attraction. They also set up counters around the grounds to provide thirsty fairgoers with soda, syrup, and ices. The summer of 1876 was a hot one, and the refreshment counters were heavily patronized.

Although Tufts and Lippincott somehow managed to lose money at the exposition, soda still proved a profitable investment. In the succeeding years, they made a fortune selling soda fountains and dispensers to drugstores around the country. Drugstore soda fountains soon became social gathering places in towns throughout America. Carbonated soft drinks are today a multibillion-dollar business that spans the globe, and it can truly be said that they got their start in Philadelphia.

★ WHAT TO TASTE AND WHERE TO TASTE IT ★

Japanese

POD

Inn at Penn ★ 3636 Sansom Street ★ Philadelphia ★ (215) 387-1803

POD, located on the Penn campus, is considered one of the most stylish Japanese restaurants in Philadelphia, with its choose-your-own-color lighting in special podlike booths. Its sushi bar is excellent, but POD also serves dishes from other Asian and Pacific nations.

MORIMOTO

723 Chestnut Street ★ Philadelphia ★ (215) 413-9070

Morimoto is owned by Philadelphia restaurateur Stephen Starr, but the real star is Chef Masaharu Morimoto, of the Japanese television program *Iron Chef*. Morimoto prepares traditional Japanese food with unique twists. Try Chef Morimoto's line of sake or the omakase meals, in which the chef selects what looks best each day.

Philly Cheese Steak

JIM'S STEAKS

400 South Street ★ Philadelphia ★ (215) 928-1911

Although Jim's Steaks did not invent the Philly cheese steak, they did perfect it.
This restaurant has a colorful dinerlike atmosphere, but be prepared to wait in line.
And be warned: Know what you want before you get to the counter.

CHEESY PHILLY

Sandwiches may have been invented in England by the Fourth Earl of Sandwich, who was determined to eat and play cards at the same time, but it was in America that the sandwich was popularized and perfected: From hamburgers, hot dogs, and BLTs to peanut-butter-and-jelly and grilled cheese, Americans have mastered the art of the sandwich. Philadelphia can lay claim to a few of its own classics.

One such Philadelphia tradition was the Philly cheese steak, which supposedly originated at Pat's King of Steaks. In 1930, Pat Olivieri was a hot-dog vendor. Tired of eating hot dogs, Pat brought his own lunch composed of thin slices of round steak and cheese on a thin roll. If you are determined to experience the taste of Philadelphia, subject yourself to a famous Philly cheese steak: thin slices of chuck-eye steak cooked on a grill, topped with Cheese Whiz, smothered in grilled onions, and served on a roll—with a side of Roll-Aids.

DO THE HOKEY-POKEY

The Philly cheese steak is not the only sandwich to originate in Philadelphia. One of Philadelphia's most interesting gastronomic innovations appeared in 1879, when Gilbert and Sullivan were giving the first Philadelphia performance of their new operetta *H.M.S. Pinafore.* To help celebrate the event, the bakers of the city introduced a bread in the shape of a boat, which they called a Pinafore. Street vendors known as hokey-pokey men had been selling a variety of foods, including ice cream, since the exposition of 1876. When the Gilbert and Sullivan operetta was presented, they began serving their "anti-pasta"—sliced meats, salami, cheese, fish, and vegetables—on that boat-shaped bread. People called the sandwich a "hoagie," using a contracted form of *hokey-pokey.* These days, a hoagie is made from luncheon meats, lettuce, tomato, onions, cheese, and mayonnaise and presented on long Italian bread. A former mayor of Philadelphia, Edward G. Rendell, declared hoagies to be the official sandwich of Philadelphia.

MARKETING THE TERMINAL

During the 1890s, the Reading Railroad tried to have a group of market stalls demolished so it could build a new terminal. The farmers who had been using the stalls to sell their products banded together and forced the railroad to build the station above the market. For many years, the market and the railroad worked as a team. Someone in the suburbs would place an order, the market would pack it up, put it on the right train, the conductor would drop it off at the right station, and the station master would hold the basket until the customer came for it. As the nation developed a national railroad system, food manufacturers in Philadelphia learned how to distribute their products throughout the country.

The Reading Market has supplied the cooks of Philadelphia with excellent products for more than a hundred years. But it is also a good market for tourists. In addition to all of the foods that are meant to be used by local residents, the market has foods that are meant to be eaten on the spot or taken back to a hotel. If you visit Philadelphia, stop into the market and try a soft pretzel with a drizzle of mustard from Fisher's Soft Pretzels, or a hoagie or a cheese steak, signature foods in the history of Philadelphia gastronomy. Beiler's Bakery offers a hearty Pennsylvania Dutch breakfast or lunch. If you want seafood, Pearl's Oyster Bar is the place to go for broiled or fried seafood platters and homemade snapper soup. For dessert, stop at the Bassett's Ice Cream counter. Founded in 1861, it is the nation's oldest ice-cream brand. Bassett's also serves a terrific milkshake.

★ WHAT TO TASTE AND WHERE TO TASTE IT ★

Asian

SUSANNA FOO'S
1512 Walnut Street ★ Philadelphia ★ (215) 545-2666
Susanna Foo is one of the masters of Asian cooking in America. She's written outstanding cookbooks: *Susanna Foo Chinese Cuisine* and her latest, *Susanna Foo Fresh Inspiration*. The food in her restaurant reflects her sophistication, attention to detail, and her ability to blend Asian and French influences. One of her signature dishes is chicken with mango, asparagus, and ginger.

AUTOMATED FOOD

The idea that food could be dispensed from machines originated in Europe in the late nineteenth century. One of the most celebrated American applications of this principle was the Automat, first opened in 1902 by Philadelphians Joseph Horn and Frank Hardart. Portions of food were prepared, plated, and displayed in compartments with little glass doors, so customers could see what was available. Put a nickel or two in the adjacent slot, turn a knob, and the door popped open. Heated or refrigerated compartments kept food hot or cold. Beverages were dispensed from taps in the shape of a lion's head. Glittering palaces of glass and chrome, they offered simple, satisfying food—and a bit of amusement—for the urban workforce.

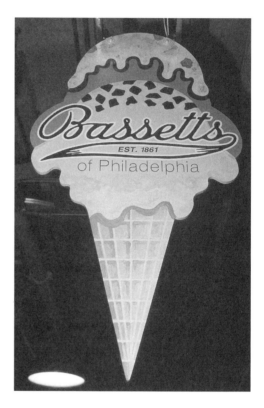

In 1848, Eber Seaman patented a machine that produced ice cream on a large scale. It turned a luxury food into something that could be distributed to a mass market and made Philadelphia-style ice cream famous throughout the country. Philadelphia is also home to a wide selection of water ices that were introduced by immigrants from southern Italy. Philadelphia was also well known for its cheesecake. A shop called the Cheesecake House was in operation during the 1730s.

★ WHAT TO TASTE AND WHERE TO TASTE IT ★

Pan Asian

BUDDAKAN
325 Chestnut Street ★ Philadelphia ★ (215) 574-9440
Buddakan offers a creative and delicious Asian fusion menu in a beautiful atmosphere. Modeled after the Buddha Bar in Paris, you are served in the shadow of a ten-foot golden Buddha.

Pretzel-Crusted Pork Chops

MAKES 4 SERVINGS

This unusual pork recipe produces delicious results with a Philadelphian accent.

2 cups heavy cream
½ cup Dijon-style mustard
½ cup honey mustard
1 teaspoon grated orange zest
8 tablespoons (1 stick) unsalted butter
4 (1-inch-thick) boneless pork chops
Salt and freshly ground black pepper
1 cup all-purpose flour
2 eggs, beaten
2 cups crushed hard pretzels

1. In a small saucepan, gently simmer the heavy cream over low heat until it has reduced to ½ cup; this will take about 1 hour. In a medium bowl, whisk together the mustards, orange zest, and the reduced cream. Set aside.

2. Preheat the oven to 350 degrees F. In a small skillet, melt the butter over medium-low heat until it begins to foam. Skim off the foam and carefully pour the clarified butter into a large ovenproof skillet, leaving behind the milk solids in the bottom of the pan. Season the pork chops with the salt and pepper on both sides. Lightly dredge the pork in the flour, shaking off the excess, then dip into the beaten egg, and coat in the crushed pretzels, gently pressing in the coating.

HISTORY OF THE HARD PRETZEL

The hard pretzel had its beginnings in Pennsylvania. The story tells of a baker's assistant who fell asleep while baking soft pretzels. When he woke the oven had died down and he thought the pretzels had not baked long enough so he fired up the furnace again baking them twice as long. To his delight he discovered they were crisp, crunchy, and delicious. He was especially pleased to learn that the hard pretzels retained their freshness much longer than soft ones.

3. Heat the butter over medium-high and add the chops. Cook for 1 minute per side and place into the oven until the pork is just cooked through, about 5 minutes. Allow to cool for 5 minutes. Pour the sauce on top and serve.

Pan-Seared Chicken with Creamy Onion Sauce and Chive Mashed Potatoes

MAKES 6 SERVINGS

Botanically, onions are members of the same family as lilies and daffodils. They were first grown for food in the Middle East. The Spaniards brought them to the Americas and now billions of pounds are grown in the United States each year.

Thomas Jefferson's loved the potatoes that he ate in France while he served as American ambassador in the 1780s. When he became president a few years later, he instructed the White House chef to prepare potatoes for his frequent guests.

FOR THE ONION SAUCE

2 tablespoons (¼ stick) unsalted butter
1 large yellow onion, diced
2 tablespoons all-purpose flour
1½ cups chicken stock
½ cup half-and-half
1 teaspoon chopped fresh sage
Salt and freshly ground pepper

FOR THE CHIVE MASHED POTATOES

8 russet potatoes, peeled but left whole
Salt
1 cup whole milk, warmed
4 tablespoons (½ stick) unsalted butter, at room temperature
2 tablespoons chopped fresh chives
Freshly ground black pepper

FOR THE CHICKEN

6 whole skin-on, bone-in chicken legs with thigh attached
6 skin-on, bone-in chicken-breast halves
Salt and freshly ground black pepper
2 tablespoons (¼ stick) unsalted butter
4 tablespoons vegetable oil

1. Preheat oven to 450 degrees F.

2. TO MAKE THE ONION SAUCE: In a medium saucepan, melt the butter over medium heat. Add the onion and cook for 20 minutes, stirring occasionally, until the onion is golden brown. If the onion browns too fast, reduce the heat to medium-low. Add the flour and stir constantly for 5 minutes. Gradually whisk in the chicken stock and simmer for 5 minutes. Add the half-and-half and simmer 5 minutes more. Stir in the sage and season with the salt and pepper. Cover and set aside.

3. TO MAKE THE MASHED POTATOES: In a large pot, cover the potatoes by 2 inches with cold water and season with salt. Cook the potatoes over medium-high heat for 30 minutes or until the potatoes are tender when pierced with a fork. Drain the potatoes and return them to the pot. Add the milk and butter and mash with a potato masher until smooth. (Alternatively, you can warm the milk and butter in the pot and pass the potatoes through a ricer. Whisk until smooth.) Stir in the chives and season with salt and pepper. Keep warm while you make the chicken.

4. TO MAKE THE CHICKEN: Season the chicken pieces with salt and pepper. In a large skillet, heat the butter and vegetable oil over medium-high heat. Sear the chicken in batches until golden brown, 3 to 4 minutes per side. As they are browned, transfer the pieces to a baking pan. Bake for 30 to 35 minutes, a few minutes less for the breasts, until the juices run clear when deeply pierced with a fork.

5. When ready to serve, gently reheat the onion sauce over low heat. Place a generous mound of the mashed potatoes in the center of each plate and ladle the onion sauce over the potatoes. Place one whole leg and one breast on top of the potatoes.

> Buy onions as you need them and store them in a cool, dry place. Look for onions that are hard and firm, with no soft spots or green sprouting tips; the flatter the base the better the taste.

Steak Au Poivre

MAKES 4 SERVINGS

Most edible fungi are called mushrooms. There are close to 2,000 varieties. Most of the mushrooms we buy as white button mushrooms are grown in underground caves in Pennsylvania and near St. Louis. In the last few years a number of companies in the United States have started cultivating wild mushrooms including shiitake, chanterelle, boletus, and oyster mushrooms.

FOR THE SAUCE

½ *pound beef scraps, chopped (Ask your butcher for these, or use any inexpensive,*
  fatty cut of beef, or use ground chuck.)
1 tablespoon olive oil
3 shallots, chopped
3 cloves garlic, chopped
6 button mushrooms, sliced
3 sprigs thyme
2 cups red Burgundy wine
2 cups veal demi-glace
3 tablespoons chilled salted butter, cut into cubes
Salt and freshly ground black pepper

FOR THE STEAKS

Four 10-ounce center-cut New York strip steaks, about 1½ inches thick,
  at room temperature
½ cup coarsely cracked black pepper
Salt
1 tablespoon salted butter

1. TO MAKE THE SAUCE: In a large heavy-bottomed skillet, brown the beef scraps in the oil over medium-high heat. Add the shallots, garlic, mushrooms, and thyme and sauté until the mushrooms are soft. Deglaze the pan with the red wine and boil to reduce the wine by half, about 5 minutes. Add the demi-glace and reduce by half again, 12 to 15 minutes. Using a rubber spatula or the back of a spoon, press the sauce through a fine mesh strainer into a small saucepan. Discard the solids. Finish the sauce by whisking in the butter, and season with the salt and pepper to taste. Keep the sauce warm over low heat while you cook the steaks.

2. TO PREPARE THE STEAKS: Preheat the oven to 450 degrees F. Coat one side of each steak with the cracked black pepper and season with salt. Press the pepper into the meat so that it adheres to the surface.

3. In a large heavy-bottomed, ovenproof skillet melt the butter over medium-high heat. Add the steaks, cracked pepper side down, and sear until the meat is a rich burnished brown on the first side, 2 to 4 minutes. Turn the steaks over and place the skillet in the oven. Cook for 5 minutes for rare to medium-rare, or until you reach the point of doneness you desire. Allow the steaks to rest for 5 minutes before serving. Serve steaks with the sauce.

Mushrooms are of little nutritional value, providing only a few minerals and B vitamins. The word *mushroom* stems from the Teutonic word for moss, *mousse*. After the Norman invasion, the English began calling them mushrooms. In France they are called *champignons*, after the French word for field, *champs*. The Italians simply call them *funghi*.

★ **WHAT TO TASTE AND WHERE TO TASTE IT** ★

French

LE BEC-FIN
1523 Walnut Street ★ Philadelphia ★ (215) 567-1000

Le Bec-Fin is Philadelphia's most famous—and best—classic French restaurant. The owner, Georges Perrier, was born in Lyon, France, but after forty years in Philadelphia he is a local celebrity. The restaurant faithfully re-creates the space of a Parisian salon. Le Bec-Fin's food creates a balance between rich and light. Perrier has also launched other eating establishments, including Café Lyonnaise, a wonderful small French bistro located within Le Bec-Fin, and Brasserie Perrier [1619 Walnut Street; (215) 568-3000], which is less formal than Le Bec-Fin.

Pepper Pot Soup

MAKES 10 SERVINGS

City Tavern is a Philadelphia landmark, serving classic recipes from America's first gourmet restaurant. Walter Staib, chef-proprietor of the City Tavern, explains: "This recipe is the grandfather to the traditional Philadelphia Pepper Pot Soup—and to my taste, the superior recipe of the two. By far the most popular soup on the City Tavern Menu, our pepper pot soup is made from an authentic West Indian recipe that is more than 250 years old. Back then, English ships traveled through the islands transporting slaves as well as exotic foodstuffs, so that West Indian cookery found its way into the very fabric of Philadelphia life. I learned this recipe from Miss Betty, a great Jamaican lady of undetermined age, who prepared it on the banks of the Rio Grand River in Port Antonio."

The allspice must be freshly ground or the flavor will be compromised. The only substitution you can make in this recipe and still achieve the intended flavor is to use collard greens instead of callaloo, the leafy top of the taro root. You can find both the taro root and callaloo at most Asian and West Indian markets.

To salt-cure pork and beef shoulder, choose meat that appears well-marbled. Then rub with coarse (kosher) salt, cover and refrigerate for at least three days. Wash the salt off the meat before cooking as directed.

3/4 pound salt-cured pork, diced
3/4 pound salt-cured beef, diced
2 tablespoons vegetable oil
1 medium white onion, chopped
4 cloves garlic, chopped
1/4 Scotch bonnet pepper, seeded and chopped
1 bunch scallions, chopped (about 1 cup)
1 pound taro root, peeled and diced
4 quarts (1 gallon) chicken stock
2 bay leaves
1 teaspoon chopped fresh thyme
1 tablespoon freshly ground allspice
1 tablespoon freshly ground black pepper
1 pound callaloo or collard greens, rinsed and chopped
Salt and freshly ground black pepper

1. In a large stockpot, sauté the pork and beef in the oil over high heat for 10 minutes, until brown.

2. Add the onion, garlic, and Scotch bonnet pepper; sauté for 3 to 5 minutes, until the onion is translucent.

3. Add the scallions and sauté for 3 minutes.

4. Add the taro root and sauté for 3 to 5 minutes more, until translucent.

5. Add the chicken stock, bay leaves, thyme, allspice, and ground pepper. Bring to a boil over high heat. Reduce the heat to medium and cook about 30 minutes, until the meat and taro root are tender.

6. Stir in the callaloo or collard greens. Reduce the heat and simmer about 5 minutes, until wilted.

THE FIERY POT

As spices and exotic foods came up from the Caribbean, so did settlers. Many members of Philadelphia's first African-American community came from the Caribbean, and they brought their West Indian recipes with them. It was Philadelphia's African-American cooks who, in the late 1700s and early 1800s, helped create the city's catering trade. They introduced the first catering contracts and changed the way people entertained.

One Caribbean dish that found a permanent home in Philadelphia was pepper pot, a chunky soup or stew that could include mutton, pickled pork, vegetables, and lobster or crab; its defining ingredient was hot cayenne chile powder. Philadelphians took to this spicy stew, and to this day its invention is generally credited to their city.

7. Season with salt and pepper to taste, remove and discard the bay leaves, and serve.

The heat factor of peppers is measured by Scoville heat units. A jalapeño has 80,000 Scoville heat units while habaneros from Jamaica or the Yucatán and Scotch bonnet peppers have been found to have 550,000 heat units.

★ WHAT TO TASTE AND WHERE TO TASTE IT ★

Cuban/Caribbean

ALMA DE CUBA
1623 Walnut Street ★ Philadelphia ★ 215-988-1799

Alma de Cuba offers Nuevo Latino dishes—new interpretations of traditional Cuban dishes. The mojitos are incredible. The décor is dark, so bring your night-vision goggles.

Roasted Pepper and Corn Soup

MAKES 4 SERVINGS

Corn was introduced to the colonists by Native Americans, who held corn as a sacred food and used it as the foundation of their diet. Fresh corn or maize was dried so that it could be stored and used later in soups, stews, chowders, and other recipes. Corn could also be ground and used in place of flour.

2 small red bell peppers
3 tablespoons unsalted butter
1 small white onion, peeled and diced
1 clove garlic, minced
2 cups fresh or frozen corn kernels
5 tablespoons all purpose-flour
4 cups chicken stock
1½ cups half-and-half
2 teaspoons chopped fresh marjoram, thyme, or sage
Salt and freshly ground black pepper

1. **TO ROAST THE PEPPERS:** Preheat the broiler or a grill. Place the peppers on a baking sheet or metal pie pan. Broil or grill them about 4 inches from the heat source. Rotate every 3 minutes until all sides of the peppers are black and blistered. Remove the peppers and place them in a bowl to cool. When cool enough to handle, remove the stems. Cut the peppers into quarters and remove the skin, ribs, and seeds, and chop them coarsely. Set aside.

2. In a heavy-bottomed medium saucepan, melt the butter over moderate heat. Sauté the onion and garlic, stirring often, for 5 minutes or until the onion is soft and golden. Add the corn and reserved peppers. Cook for 10 minutes.

3. Stir in the flour and cook, stirring, for 3 minutes. Add the chicken stock in thirds, stirring well after each addition. Bring the soup to a boil.

4. Reduce the heat to a simmer and cook 10 minutes. Add the half-and-half and cook for 10 minutes more.

5. In a food processor or blender, puree the soup until smooth.

6. Return the soup to the pan and stir in the marjoram, thyme or sage. Season with salt and pepper to taste.

Most bell peppers begin green and become red, sweeter, and more nutritious as they ripen. Bell peppers are very high in vitamins A and C.

For stuffing, large "fancy-style" bell peppers are best, but for cooking and salads the "choice" grade is fine. Peppers should be firm and dark. Peppers that have been picked too early are pale, soft, and thin-skinned; overripe ones are dull. Avoid shriveled or wilted peppers. Take a good look at the stem side of the pepper—that's where decay usually starts.

★ WHAT TO TASTE AND WHERE TO TASTE IT ★

Nouvelle Mexican

LOLITA
106 South 13th Street ★ Philadelphia ★ (215) 546-7100
Bring your own tequila and they provide mixers. The food is great nouvelle Mexican, where the traditions of Mexico connect with fresh local ingredients and others imported from around the world.

Skillet Fruit Pie with Cream-Cheese Crust

Sweet pie was an English tradition brought to America by immigrants, but Americans expanded the art of pie making. Skillet Fruit Pie is an example of this.

1½ pounds Granny Smith or other tart cooking apples
12 tablespoons (1½ sticks) unsalted butter, at room temperature
6 tablespoons sugar
¼ teaspoon ground cinnamon
4 ounces cream cheese, at room temperature
1 cup all-purpose flour, plus more for rolling
1½ cups frozen raspberries
3 tablespoons heavy cream
Vanilla ice cream and Caramel Sauce (recipe follows), for serving

1. TO MAKE THE FILLING: Peel, quarter, core, and cut the apples into ½-inch-thick pieces. In a 10-inch cast-iron skillet or large skillet, melt 4 tablespoons butter over medium-low heat. Add the apples, arranging them in a single layer. Sprinkle 4 tablespoons sugar over the apples and cook for 10 to 20 minutes, until the apples are soft. Be sure to turn them to cook all the sides evenly. Sprinkle the cooked apples with the cinnamon. Remove the pan from the heat and allow the apples to cool to room temperature.

2. Preheat the oven to 375 degrees F.

3. TO MAKE THE PIE DOUGH: In the bowl of a stand mixer fitted with the paddle attachment, cream the remaining 8 tablespoons butter and the cream cheese together until smooth. Add the flour and 1 tablespoon sugar. Continue to beat for 2 minutes or until the dough becomes smooth. On a lightly floured surface, roll the dough out to a 10-inch circle.

4. Add the frozen raspberries to the apple mixture. Carefully lay the dough on top of the fruit and tuck the edges into the skillet. Brush the top of the pastry with heavy cream and sprinkle with the remaining 1 tablespoon sugar.

5. Bake the pie for 40 minutes, until the pastry is golden brown. Remove the finished pie from the oven and cool on a rack. Serve warm, topped with vanilla ice cream and Caramel Sauce.

Cream cheese is a soft, fresh, cow's milk cheese with a smooth, creamy texture made by mixing cow's milk of a very high cream content with rennet until the milk coagulates. (Rennet is a digestive enzyme taken from the stomachs of cows or sheep. It causes milk to coagulate and form curds.) The mixture is then drained and pressed into blocks or placed in containers. The method of making cream cheese has changed little in hundreds of years. Modern techniques simply speed up the process and add ingredients to make the cheese firmer and prolong shelf life.

PHILADELPHIA CREAM CHEESE?

Pennsylvania dairy products developed a national reputation for quality. So highly valued were Philadelphia dairy foods that some products that were never made in Philadelphia carried the Philadelphia name so people would think well of them. Cream cheese, for instance, was first commercially produced in Chester, New York. In 1880, A. L. Reynolds, a New York cheese distributor, began distributing cream cheese wrapped in tin-foil wrappers. He called it Philadelphia Brand because he thought the name Philadelphia stood for top-quality food products.

CARAMEL SAUCE

⅓ cup brown sugar
⅓ cup heavy cream
4 tablespoons (½ stick) unsalted butter

Combine all of the sauce ingredients in a small saucepan. Stir over low heat until the sugar dissolves. Bring to a boil, reduce heat, and simmer, stirring, for 3 minutes.

THE PART OF VIRGINIA that extends from Virginia Beach, on the Atlantic Ocean, to Richmond, the state capital, contains some of the most important historical sites in the United States. Jamestown, the first successful English colony in the New World, was established here, and not far from Jamestown is Yorktown, where Lord Cornwallis surrendered to George Washington, effectively ending the American War for Independence. Less than one hundred years later, this area saw some of the most savage fighting of the Civil War. This is also the birthplace of real American food.

Virginia Beach, at the mouth of the Chesapeake Bay, is the largest estuary in North America. Although more than two hundred miles long and up to thirty-five miles wide, the bay is extremely shallow. The first European to sail into the bay was Vicente Gonzalez, a Spanish explorer, in 1561; for the next ten years, the Spanish tried unsuccessfully to settle

★ WHAT TO TASTE AND WHERE TO TASTE IT ★

Colonial

COLONIAL WILLIAMSBURG
Williamsburg ★ (757) 229-1000

From 1699 to 1780, Williamsburg was the political, cultural, and educational center of what was then the largest and most populous of the English colonies. When the capital was relocated to Richmond, the city of Williamsburg began to decay. In 1926, restoration of Williamsburg began. John D. Rockefeller, Jr., funded the preservation of more than eighty of the original structures and the reconstruction of many buildings. Today, Colonial Williamsburg presents a re-creation of eighteenth-century American life, and visitors can enjoy meals like those eaten by the colonists who frequented the King's Arms and Josiah Chowning's tavern. In these and other establishments, you'll find dishes like cornbread-stuffed quail, wild-boar sausage, bubble and squeak (crisply fried puffs of whipped potatoes and cabbage), and syllabub, a colonial dessert made by whipping cream with sweet wine.

the area. On April 26, 1607, English colonists anchored at the mouth of the Chesapeake Bay, then traveled up a river and founded a small colony. They named the river and their settlement in honor of King James I of England.

At the time of the English colonists' arrival, the Powhatan Indians were the major native group in the area. *Chesapeake* is derived from their word chesepiooc, meaning "Great Shellfish Bay." Indeed, Chesapeake Bay teemed with fish, shellfish, and migratory birds, and game was abundant on its shores.

One of the English settlers, Captain John Smith (later made famous for his relationship with Pocahontas), was the first European to explore the Chesapeake Bay. What he found astounded him. He wrote home that he had seen so many sea bass in the Chesapeake that he thought he could walk across their backs without getting wet. If he wanted fish, he wrote, he had only to put a pot in the water, and the fish would jump in.

John Smith no doubt exaggerated, but the waters of the bay and its tributary rivers were filled with fish and shellfish, and the forest with game—especially deer and wild turkeys. Fruit, nuts, and berries were there for the taking. Despite this abundance, many colonists almost starved, for they disdained to eat any food with which they were not already familiar and they lacked the skills needed to hunt fish or grow plants. The population of Jamestown barely survived.

TALKING TURKEY

Lacking a supply of domestic livestock, Virginia's early settlers lived on game, notably wild turkey. The colonists were quite familiar with the turkey before they arrived in the Americas. It had been domesticated in Mexico in prehistoric times. In 1519, it had been "discovered" by Spanish conquistadores, who exported it to Spain, where turkeys were immediately adopted by the upper classes. The turkey is relatively easy to raise and so prolific that they were readily accessible throughout western Europe by the 1570s.

The good news about wild turkeys was that they were numerous and much larger than the domesticated turkeys the settlers had known in Europe. Colonists shot and snared wild turkeys that weighed between forty and sixty pounds—they were so fat, in fact, that they couldn't fly. The hunting was so intensive that wild turkeys began to disappear from the woods surrounding European settlements. Yet they were still common along the frontier, where they provided food while settlers cleared fields and planted crops.

As wild turkeys disappeared from settled areas of America, domesticated turkeys arrived from Europe. While the turkey did not become America's national symbol, as Benjamin Franklin would have liked, it did become an unofficial national icon with the establishment of Thanksgiving and the formalization of the traditional holiday meal. Also, due to extremely successful conservation programs, wild turkeys are now numerous in most states and hunting them has become an important sport.

Virginians also hunted game in addition to wild turkeys. Deer were always important, as were bears and smaller game. One of the most unusual Virginian dishes is Brunswick stew, which emerged in the mid-nineteenth century. It was commonly made with leftovers: The cook would throw in whatever was available, such as squirrel, chicken, or other meats, along with bacon, green corn, tomatoes, lima beans, potatoes, and other vegetables. Named for Brunswick County, Virginia, which is in the southern part of the state along the border with North Carolina, Brunswick stew remains a regional southern specialty with many recipes claiming to be "authentic."

TOBACCO TURKEYS?

Early European settlers in Virginia and Maryland were interested in growing and curing tobacco, which was America's preeminent colonial export—perhaps the first modern agribusiness. A major challenge in growing this crop was the control of tobacco hornworms, which infested the tobacco fields from June to August. Before the invention of pesticides, planters were helpless to fight hornworms except by sending hordes of slaves through the fields to hand-pick the worms off the leaves. Even then, planters could expect to lose half their crop to these voracious insects. The turkey came to the rescue. Turkeys found the large, meaty tobacco worm irresistible, and by the mid-eighteenth century it was common practice to herd flocks of turkeys into tobacco fields to eat the worms. One turkey could eat worms from an estimated 1,000 plants, but if properly managed, fifty turkeys could handle an estimated 100,000 plants.

Elsewhere in the country, turkeys performed the same function: eating insects that plagued crops. When the crops were harvested, the turkeys were fat and ready to be slaughtered for the holidays—Thanksgiving, Christmas, and New Year's Day. Although commercially raised turkeys are no longer fattened on insects, Virginia remains a major turkey-producing state.

A CORNY BEGINNING

One of the familiar foods the early settlers craved was wheat, a dietary staple. But when they tried to grow wheat in Virginia, it did not mature. The Powhatans grew a grain called maize, which they introduced to the English. It was only after the colonists adopted maize that their settlements began to thrive, and in many ways corn has remained at the center of the American diet ever since. In colonial times, green corn was eaten off the cob, and ground dried corn was used to make grits, mush, and porridge. Because cornmeal does not have the gluten that wheat flour does, European-style yeast breads could not be made from it. But cornmeal was used on its own for what are now classic American baked goods like spoonbread, hoecakes, and corn pone. Early settlers also fed excess corn to their hogs and cattle, which gave the meat a delicious, distinctive flavor. Since colonial times, corn has continued to play a significant role in American cooking—from our summer sweet-corn feasts to our morning muffins and cornflakes to our buckets of movie popcorn to the corn oil and corn syrup that go into many of our processed foods and beverages. We also consume corn indirectly when we sit down to a meal of corn-fed beef, pork, or poultry.

IN AND OUT OF THE SHELL

For more than four hundred years, residents of the Chesapeake Bay area have enjoyed a great variety of seafood—oysters, sturgeon, lobster, crabs, and shrimp. Although early colonists fished in the Chesapeake for sustenance, commercial fishing did not begin until a century after the first European settlement. The watermen of Virginia harvest more than eighty different species that are shipped fresh to cities throughout the world.

One of the oldest harvests is for clams. Hundreds of years ago, the local native tribes used clam shells as money. They found the purple streak on the inside of the shell particularly attractive, and thought them valuable enough for use as currency. Virginia watermen also continue to bring in scallops, as well as oysters, which were a mainstay of the early colonial diet and are still one of Virginia's most prized seafoods. And of course there are blue crabs, especially relished in the season when they're served as soft-shells and at any time in the form of crab cakes.

BEAUTIFUL SWIMMERS

Blue crabs are common to the east coasts of both North and South America, but it is in the Chesapeake that they thrive in greatest abundance. The blue crab is an unusual marine organism in that it mates and spawns at different times. During mating, the male crab transfers his sperm into special saclike receptacles in the female crab. These receptacles store the male's sperm, to be used for egg fertilization at a later time. After mating in the upper reaches of the Chesapeake, the female crab, called the "sook," forages for weeks in beds of eelgrass at the northern end of the bay. When ready, she migrates to the high-salinity spawning grounds near the mouth of the bay to release her eggs. Today, crabbing remains an important industry for the Chesapeake, although crab catches have declined in recent years.

Seafood

LUCKY STAR
1608 Pleasure House Road ★ Virginia Beach ★ (757) 363-8410

Lucky Star is an upscale restaurant with a relaxed atmosphere, considered one of the best in the Hampton Roads area. The menu includes regional foods (like low-country stew), Asian-inspired dishes, and Chesapeake Bay seafood.

CHICK'S OYSTER BAR
2143 Vista Circle ★ Virginia Beach ★ (754) 481-5757

Chick's opened in 1987 as a down-home neighborhood eatery. But the freshly shucked oysters, local fish, and simple, straightforward cooking have given the place a wide and devoted following. You can sit at the counter inside, or out in the open dock room. We ate through the menu, and our collective favorites were crab soup Annapolis, the blackened crab-cake sandwich with homemade coleslaw, and chocolate volcano pie.

LYNNHAVEN FISH HOUSE
2350 Starfish Road ★ Virginia Beach ★ (754) 481-0003

The Lynnhaven Fish House opened in 1979 on the same beach where the first colonists stopped to rest before moving up the Chesapeake to establish their settlement at Jamestown. If the restaurant had been there at the time, Captain John Smith would certainly have treated Pocahontas to lunch—most likely at one of the window tables. You can't go wrong with a whole steamed lobster, hush puppies, crab Louis, and coconut cream pie.

THE WAR THAT CHANGED EVERYTHING

After the Revolutionary War, Virginia's capital was moved from Williamsburg to Richmond. In 1861, Richmond became the capital of the Confederacy, and many significant Civil War battles were fought near the city before it fell to Union forces in 1865. General Ulysses S. Grant, commander of the Union forces, who accepted the surrender of Confederate general Robert E. Lee, said that the Civil War changed everything in America, and our national foodways can be included in that statement. Prior to the war, most people ate food that was locally grown or raised, from their own farms and gardens; small surpluses were traded locally. After the Civil War, with commercial canning under way and rail transportation a reality, American food was on its way to being nationalized and industrialized. When northern soldiers occupied the South, Yankee farm boys were exposed to southern food. When they returned home, they missed the fried chicken, peanuts, and gumbo, and began incorporating them into their diet.

THE HAND THAT STIRRED THE POT

African slaves were brought to Virginia beginning in 1619. They performed the manual labor on tobacco plantations, and planted, cultivated, and harvested the foods eaten on the plantations. Slaves also cooked their masters' meals, adapting their traditional recipes and cooking techniques to the new ingredients they encountered in Virginia. Slaves were sometimes permitted to have their own gardens, where they planted the vegetables they knew best, thereby introducing new foods to the American South. Many slaves also raised chickens, and became experts at preparing chicken recipes.

Interestingly, some of the foods that the slaves introduced to their new home were originally brought to Africa from the Americas. These include guinea fowl, chile peppers, peanuts, sweet potatoes, cassava, maize, yams, watermelons, okra, and sesame seeds. Rice was first grown in Virginia by slaves, who were already familiar with rice growing in West Africa. While rice growing disappeared in Virginia due to the expansion of the more profitable tobacco crop, rice growing continued in the Carolinas and Georgia.

After the Civil War, Emancipation made it possible for former slaves to migrate north and west. Among the few professions open to them were those associated with food—they became cooks in restaurants or in the homes of the wealthy. African-Americans prepared and sold food on the streets of both southern and northern cities. Many African-Americans became professional cooks, and more than one observer has claimed that America's national cookery came from them. Many of the most famous American dishes did originate with African-Americans, including fried chicken, gumbo, barbecue, and the collection of dishes known as "soul food."

A NUTTY TALE

Before the Civil War, most of the peanut crop was fed to livestock. Enslaved people and poor whites ate them out of necessity. As slaves cooked the food in the antebellum South, they introduced the southern aristocracy to the culinary delights of peanuts. The most popular use was in peanut soup, which was being commonly consumed by southerners by the 1840s. Early peanut soup recipes frequently included oysters, which were so abundant at the time that anyone could acquire them in the Chesapeake.

When blockades were set up during the Civil War, drastically limiting the South's food supply, peanut consumption greatly increased throughout the South, and peanut oil became a crucial commodity used in place of whale oil, which had previously been imported. After the war, Thomas Rowland, a Virginian, was trying to figure out how to make a living in postwar Norfolk. Rowland bought peanuts from local farmers and shipped a small batch to commission men in New York. The nuts ended up with an Italian commission merchant, who sent out Italian peddlers with peanut roasters to sell the nuts. This venture was successful, and Rowland sent even more peanuts in the succeeding years. By the late nineteenth century, thousands of farmers in Virginia's Norfolk and Suffolk counties were raising peanuts, and thousands of Italian vendors were selling fresh-roasted peanuts on the streets of northern cities.

One such vendor, Amedeo Obici, bought a peanut roaster for $4.50 and went into business selling the nuts from a horse-drawn cart. Wishing to improve his product, Obici managed to find a way of blanching the red skins from shelled Virginia peanuts without splitting the kernel. In 1906, he formed the Planters' Peanut Company, which roasted and salted the larger Virginia peanuts. Feeling that his company needed to be closer to its point of supply, Obici opened a small peanut-processing factory in Suffolk County in 1914. By 1916, Obici had decided that a national advertising campaign was in order. In an effort to develop a trademark, he conducted a contest, offering a prize of five dollars for the best symbol. The winner was a fourteen-year-old boy named Anthony Gentile, who submitted a drawing of "a little peanut person." Obici hired a Chicago firm to draw several different caricatures based on the boy's drawing. The peanut person deemed most appropriate wore a top hat, monocle, cane, and the look of a raffish gentleman—Mr. Peanut was born.

★ **WHAT TO TASTE AND WHERE TO TASTE IT** ★

Regional Cuisine

LEMAIRE RESTAURANT

The Jefferson Hotel ★ 101 West Franklin Street ★ Richmond ★ (804) 788-8000

Richmond's pride in its past can be seen in the Jefferson Hotel, which opened in 1895 and has been part of Richmond's social life ever since. At the center of the hotel's Palm Court lobby is a life-size marble statue of Thomas Jefferson, which stands beneath a thirty-five-foot Tiffany stained-glass skylight. Next door is the Rotunda, an extraordinary room with a ceiling decorated with a reproduction of a Tiffany skylight. The Rotunda and the Palm Court are connected by the Grand Staircase, reputedly used as the model for the one in the movie *Gone with the Wind*. At the top of the staircase is the Lemaire restaurant, named for Etienne Lemaire, who was maître d' at the White House during Thomas Jefferson's tenure. The restaurant specializes in updated versions of traditional southern recipes: a classic Virginia spoonbread, oysters and clams on a bed of sautéed spinach, striped bass with cabbage and English peas, and honey-glazed roast tenderloin of pork.

Barbecued Pulled-Pork Sandwiches

MAKES 8 SANDWICHES

Prehistoric cave paintings depict wild boar hunts—which would make pork from wild boar one of our earliest meats. The first pork recipes come from China and are dated to about 500 B.C.; they describe a suckling pig roasted in a pit. The Spanish conquistador Hernando de Soto brought the first pigs to Florida in 1525. Today, the majority of pigs in the United States are raised in Iowa, Illinois, and Missouri.

3 pounds boneless pork butt
½ cup Worcestershire sauce
1½ cups of your favorite barbecue sauce
8 onion rolls, split
Minted Coleslaw (recipe follows), for serving (optional)

1. Preheat the oven to 350 degrees F. Line a medium roasting pan with aluminum foil.

2. Set the pork butt in the roasting pan and pour the Worcestershire sauce over it. Cook uncovered for 1 hour. Turn the pork over and continue to cook for another 1½ to 2 hours, until the meat reaches an internal temperature of 160 degrees F. When ready, the pork should be a dark golden brown and the meat should be very tender when pierced with a paring knife.

3. Remove the pork from the oven and let rest at room temperature until it is cool enough to handle.

4. In a large skillet over medium heat, combine the barbecue sauce and the pan juices from the roasting pan. With your fingers, shred the pork into thick strands and add to the pan. Simmer for 5 minutes or until the pork is piping hot. Add a few tablespoons of water if the sauce gets too thick.

5. Toast the onion rolls until lightly golden. To serve, place a generous mound of the pork on the bottom half of the toasted rolls. Top with the other half of the rolls and serve the sandwiches with Minted Coleslaw, if desired.

MINTED COLESLAW

MAKES 8 SERVINGS

1 small head cabbage, outer leaves discarded
1½ cups grated carrots
1 cup golden raisins
¼ cup chopped fresh mint
¼ cup chopped fresh parsley
¼ cup white vinegar
6 tablespoons sugar
¼ cup canola oil
Salt and freshly ground black pepper

1. Cut the head of cabbage into 4 wedges and cut out the core. In a food processor with the shredding blade attached, shred the cabbage. Place the cabbage into a large non-reactive bowl and add the carrots, raisins, mint, and parsley.

2. In a glass jar with a tight fitting lid, combine the vinegar, sugar, and oil. Shake well and season to taste with salt and pepper. Pour the dressing over the cabbage and toss the slaw until well coated. Cover and refrigerate for 1 hour before serving.

Mint is one of the most widely used of all aromatic herbs. There are about forty different species of true mint, but the two most important are spearmint and peppermint. Spearmint is thought to be the oldest and may be the type of mint described in the Bible. The name mint comes from an ancient Greek myth about a nymph called Minthe. She was kissing the god Pluto when Pluto's wife, Persephone, discovered them. Persephone, a goddess of considerable power, trampled Minthe into the ground. Pluto saw to it, however, that Minthe lived on in the sweet smell of the herb.

ABOUT CABBAGE

Cabbage is indigenous to western Asia and Europe. It is one of the oldest cultivated vegetables. German and Dutch settlers brought cabbage to America, where it was first grown and eaten mostly in New York, Pennsylvania, Wisconsin, and Michigan. The cabbage family, *Brassica*, also includes broccoli, Brussels sprouts, cauliflower, and kale. The most common type of cabbage that is good for cooking is Dutch or white cabbage, which also has a special place in coleslaw. Red cabbage is similar to white cabbage, but contains a red pigment that gives it a different color and flavor. Savoy cabbage, which has dark green crinkled leaves, is not quite as sweet as white cabbage, but is highly prized by French and Italian cooks. Chinese cabbage, or choy, has an elongated head and is much milder than either white or savoy cabbage.

Devil's Mess

MAKES 2 CUPS OR 4 SERVINGS

An historic Kullman diner is the home of Millie's. It was originally built in 1941 for neighborhood factory workers. Its signature dish is Devil's Mess.

4 tablespoons vegetable oil
1 small onion, finely chopped
1 green bell pepper, seeded and finely sliced
1 pound hot Italian sausage, pressed out of their casings
2 small cloves garlic, minced
1 tablespoon ground cumin
2 teaspoons curry powder
¼ to ½ teaspoon cayenne pepper
¼ teaspoon ground cardamom
1 cup dry red wine
¼ cup Worcestershire sauce
Salt

1. In a 12-inch skillet over medium heat, heat the oil. Add the onion and pepper and cook, stirring on occasion, for 5 minutes or until almost tender. Add the sausage, and sauté, uncovered for 5 minutes, stirring continuously to crumble the mixture. Add the garlic, cumin, curry powder, cayenne pepper, and cardamom and cook for a couple of minutes longer.

2. Add the wine and boil down until half remains. Add the Worcestershire sauce and 2 cups water and simmer for ½ hour or until about ½ cup of liquid remains in the bottom of the pan. Remove from the heat and season to taste with salt.

DEVIL'S MESS WITH SCRAMBLED EGGS
MAKES 2 SERVINGS

2 tablespoons butter
1 cup Devil's Mess
6 eggs, lightly beaten
2 cups shredded sharp Cheddar cheese
6 slices avocado

1. Preheat the broiler. In a 12-inch ovenproof skillet over medium heat, heat the butter. Add the Devil's Mess and cook for a minute to heat up the mixture.

2. Add the eggs to the pan and scramble them loosely. When the eggs are almost set, remove the skillet from the heat and sprinkle the cheese over the eggs. Transfer the skillet to the broiler and heat until the cheese is hot and melted, about 30 seconds.

3. Serve from the skillet; top each portion with 3 avocado slices.

★ WHAT TO TASTE AND WHERE TO TASTE IT ★

Diner Food

MILLIE'S DINER
2603 East Main Street ★ Richmond ★ (804) 643-5512

Millie's is a historic diner that has been on this site since 1941, when it was a favorite of neighborhood factory workers. The diner is packed with lovers of good food and good music—there is an excellent selection on the jukebox. We had Millie's original signature dish, Devil's Mess—peppers, onions, and hot Italian sausage, stewed with curry and scrambled eggs. For dessert, treat yourself to a vanilla ice-cream sandwich featuring homemade peanut butter cookies.

Cornbread-Stuffed Pork Chops with Peach Compote

MAKES 4 SERVINGS

Pork was one of the most important culinary traditions in the American colonies. This way of preparing it—stuffed with corn-bread—is a common way of preparing it in Virginia and other Southern states.

4 (7-ounce) bone-in center-cut pork chops, each about 1½ inches thick

4 tablespoons (½ stick) unsalted butter

¼ cup finely diced celery

¼ cup finely diced onion

¼ teaspoon dried thyme

¼ teaspoon dried sage

1 cup small cubes white bread

1 cup crumbled yellow cornbread

¼ cup chicken stock

Salt and freshly ground black pepper

1 tablespoon vegetable oil

4 ripe peaches, peeled and pitted, or 1 (10-ounce) package frozen peach slices, thawed

2 tablespoons brown sugar or honey

2 tablespoons apple or cranberry juice

⅛ teaspoon ground cinnamon

Pinch of ground allspice

Pinch of ground nutmeg

2 tablespoons brandy or additional apple or cranberry juice

1. With a sharp knife, make a 2-inch slit alongside the fat side of the pork chops. Working from that opening, carefully insert your knife into the pork chop and cut inside to create a pocket within the chop.

2. In a 9-inch skillet, melt 2 tablespoons butter over medium heat. Add the celery and onion and cook, stirring, for about 5 minutes or until soft. Add the thyme, sage, white bread, and cornbread, and cook for about 1 minute. Add the chicken stock and stir to combine. Season to taste with salt and lots of black pepper. Remove from the heat and let the stuffing cool to room temperature.

3. Preheat the oven to 350 degrees F. Stuff each of the chops with one-quarter of the stuffing. In a 10-inch skillet, heat 1 tablespoon butter and the oil over high heat. When hot, add the pork chops and cook them on each side for 2 to 3 minutes, until brown.

Transfer the pork chops to a baking pan and bake for 40 minutes or until completely cooked through.

4. Cut the fresh peaches into ½-inch wedges. In a nonreactive saucepan over medium heat, combine the peaches with the sugar, juice, spices, and brandy.

5. Reduce the heat to low and bring the ingredients to a simmer. Cover and cook for 5 minutes or until the fruit is tender. Uncover and simmer until almost all of the moisture has evaporated and you are left with a syrupy fruit mass. Remove from the heat and set aside until serving time.

6. Right before serving, reheat the compote until hot and whisk in the remaining 1 tablespoon of butter. Serve alongside or on top of the pork chops.

> Part of the art of pork cookery is to avoid overcooking. During the past few years, the pork producers have been working to produce a leaner cut of meat and reduce the older recommended cooking times. These days they recommend that the pork be cooked to an internal temperature of 160 degrees F for medium doneness. That will keep the meat tender and juicy while still reaching an adequate temperature for healthfully cooked pork.
>
> Peaches do not get sweeter once they are picked. They do get softer and juicier, but never sweeter. That is why it is important to avoid hard peaches that were picked when they were still green.
>
> A compote is a sweet, cooked preparation of fruit and sugar, usually more liquid in consistency than jams, jellies or preserves and often contain spices.

HAMMING IT UP

Hogs were (and still are) an important commodity in the South. Many farmers let them root for food in the forest, where they fattened on a flavor-enhancing diet of acorns and other nuts. In Virginia, the township of Smithfield became an early producer of ham; the Smithfield product was hand-rubbed with salt and other seasonings, smoked, and aged. After the Civil War, Smithfield also became a peanut-growing center. Peanut growers began to feed excess peanuts to their hogs, which gave the meat a unique, rich flavor. Hams from peanut-fed pigs became so famous at home and abroad that Queen Victoria had a standing order for six Smithfield hams every week. In 1926, the General Assembly of Virginia enacted a law defining a Smithfield ham as coming from a peanut-fed hog from Smithfield. Today, only two processors are permitted to use the Smithfield trademark.

Roast Pork with Black Pepper, Garlic, and Paprika

MAKES 4 SERVINGS

Pigs were carried by Columbus to the West Indies. Spanish explorers introduced them into Mexico, New Mexico, and Florida. English settlers brought pigs to Jamestown in 1608. Pigs thrived in America. Pork was easily preserved and it provided lard—which was the most important frying medium in America until World War II.

4 medium cloves garlic
½ cup chopped fresh flat-leaf parsley, plus several sprigs for garnish
2 teaspoons freshly ground black pepper
1 teaspoon hot paprika
1 tablespoon kosher salt
3 tablespoons extra virgin olive oil
1 (3½-pound) center-cut pork rib roast

1. Preheat the oven to 350 degrees F. Puree the garlic, parsley, black pepper, paprika, salt, and olive oil in a blender to a smooth paste. Paint the entire surface of the pork loin including the bones with the paste.

2. Set the roast, ribs down, in a roasting pan, and cook for 1 hour. After an hour, tip the roast so the bones point straight up, baste with any pan juices, and raise the heat to 450 degrees F. Continue to cook the roast for another 20 to 25 minutes, until the internal temperature of the pork reaches 155 to 160 degrees on a thermometer. The roast should be golden brown and firm to the touch.

3. Remove the pork roast from the oven and let it rest at room temperature, loosely covered with foil, for 10 to 15 minutes before slicing. Cut the roast between the bones, lay the chops on a warm platter, garnish with parsley sprigs, and serve.

Soft-Shell Crab Sandwich

MAKES 4 SERVINGS

Soft-shell crabs are common through the Atlantic and the Caribbean. But they have reached their peak of perfection in the Chesapeake Bay.

¼ cup mayonnaise
2 tablespoons prepared barbecue sauce
¼ teaspoon minced garlic
¼ cup all-purpose flour
Salt and freshly ground black pepper
4 soft-shell crabs (have your fishmonger clean them)
2 tablespoons vegetable oil
1 tablespoon unsalted butter
4 kaiser rolls, split in half
8 lettuce leaves, washed and dried
Slices of ripe tomato, optional

1. In a small bowl, combine the mayonnaise with the barbecue sauce and garlic. Set aside. In a shallow bowl or on a plate, combine the flour with salt and pepper to taste.

2. Pat the crabs dry with paper towels. In a 12-inch skillet, heat the oil and butter over medium heat. As the oil is heating up, dip the crabs in the seasoned flour on both sides, and shake off any excess.

3. Sauté the crabs, top side down, for 3 to 4 minutes, averting your face from the skillet as the crabs begin to cook because they spatter like a volcano (after a few minutes the sputtering settles down).

4. With tongs, turn the crabs over and cook for another 3 to 4 minutes, or until slightly red and firm. Spread the insides of both sides of each roll with barbecue mayonnaise, set a couple of lettuce leaves and slices of tomato (if desired) on the bottom, top it with a crab and other half of the roll.

Sweet Potato–Streusel Pie

MAKES 8 SERVINGS

There are two types of sweet potato: moist orange-fleshed and dry yellow-fleshed. The sweeter orange-fleshed varieties dominate the U.S. market. These moist-fleshed potatoes are often called "yams," but this is incorrect. The true yam is a large root vegetable grown in Africa and Asia and rarely seen in the western world. But common usage has made the term yam acceptable when referring to sweet potatoes.

1 (9-inch) ready-to-bake frozen pie shell

FOR THE FILLING
6 ounces (³⁄₄ of an 8-ounce package) cream cheese, at room temperature
3 large eggs
³⁄₄ cup sugar
1 (16-ounce) can sweet potatoes in light syrup, drained and rinsed in cold water
¹⁄₂ teaspoon salt
¹⁄₂ teaspoon ground cinnamon
¹⁄₂ teaspoon ground ginger
¹⁄₈ teaspoon ground nutmeg
³⁄₄ cup half-and-half

FOR THE STREUSEL TOPPING
¹⁄₃ cup quick-cooking oats
¹⁄₃ cup finely chopped pecans
¹⁄₃ cup all-purpose flour
¹⁄₂ teaspoon ground cinnamon
2 tablespoons sugar
2 tablespoons (¹⁄₄ stick) unsalted butter, melted
Vanilla ice cream or whipped cream, for serving (optional)

1. Preheat the oven to 375 degrees F. Set the pie shell on a baking sheet, prick the bottom, and bake it for 10 minutes. Remove and set aside to cool. (If the bottom balloons up a bit, just prick it with a fork and it will settle down.)

2. **TO MAKE THE FILLING:** In a mixing bowl, with a wooden spoon, blend the cream cheese with 1 of the eggs and ¹⁄₄ cup sugar. In a food processor, puree the remaining 2 eggs with the sweet potatoes, the remaining ¹⁄₂ cup sugar, the salt, ¹⁄₂ teaspoon cinnamon, ginger, nutmeg, and half-and-half.

3. Spread the cream cheese mixture on the bottom of the cooled pie shell, then spoon the sweet-potato filling on top. Bake for 30 minutes.

4. TO MAKE THE STREUSEL: While the pie is baking, combine the oats with the pecans, flour, ½ teaspoon cinnamon, and 2 tablespoons sugar in a bowl, and toss until blended. Drizzle the butter over the top and mix together with your fingers. Sprinkle this mixture over the pie and bake for 30 to 40 minutes longer or until the filling has set.

5. Remove the pie from the oven and cool to room temperature on a rack. If desired, serve with vanilla ice cream or whipped cream.

THE REAL FIRST THANKSGIVING

America celebrates many holidays, but Thanksgiving is the one most associated with American culinary traditions. Every real American knows the story of the first Thanksgiving: Seeking religious freedom, the Pilgrims established a colony at Plymouth, Massachusetts. Native Wampanoag taught them how to plant corn and hunt. When the crops were harvested, the Pilgrims celebrated the first Thanksgiving by gobbling up turkeys, saucing cranberries, mashing corn, and squashing pumpkins to make pies. It was such a memorable event that Americans have honored it ever since. No one would be more surprised by this modern-day rendition of the first Thanksgiving than the Pilgrims who settled in Plymouth in 1621. They did observe many days of thanksgiving, but these were solemn religious occasions celebrated with serious prayer to give thanks for specific events. Preparing a fancy meal was not on the day's agenda. Long after the Pilgrims were gone, New Englanders invented the "traditional" Thanksgiving—a family-oriented day featuring a turkey dinner replete with gravy, stuffing, potatoes, sauces, and pies. Of course, days of thanksgiving were celebrated by European explorers and colonists throughout the Americas. A plaque at Jamestown, Virginia, commemorates the fact that the real "first thanksgiving" celebrated by English colonists in America was held there in 1607—fourteen years before the Pilgrims were said to have first given thanks at Plymouth.

Spoonbread

MAKES 9 SERVINGS

Spoonbread is a southern dish that has recently become an all-American food. The first known recipe for it dates to 1906, but it is likely that spoonbreads had been around since colonial times.

Butter for baking pan
1½ cups yellow cornmeal
3 cups milk
½ cup (1 stick) unsalted butter, melted
1 teaspoon salt
½ teaspoon cayenne pepper, optional
4 eggs
½ teaspoon baking powder

1. Preheat the oven to 350 degrees F. Lightly butter a 1½-quart casserole or 9-inch square ovenproof pan.

2. In a 3-quart saucepan, whisk the cornmeal together with the milk, butter, salt, and cayenne pepper. Slowly bring this to a boil, whisking continuously. (When it comes to a boil it will get very thick, so whisk hard so the mixture does not lump.) After it thickens, transfer the mixture to a mixing bowl and cool it while you separate the eggs into yolks and whites.

3. Stir the baking powder into the cornmeal mixture and mix well, then add the yolks and whisk vigorously to incorporate them. Whip the egg whites until they form stiff peaks and fold this into the cornmeal mixture. Transfer the batter to the prepared pan and bake for 40 minutes or until a wooden toothpick, when inserted into the center, comes out clean. Cut and serve portions from the pan.

Peanut Butter Cookies

MAKES ABOUT 6 DOZEN COOKIES

Peanuts have been grown in the American South since the 1800s, and were used as a staple food by troops from both the North and South during the Civil War. Peanut butter was "invented" by John Harvey Kellogg, and it was distributed by vegetarians. By the early twentieth century, peanut butter was considered a "high-class" food that was served in tea houses. As the price of making peanut butter declined, it emerged as a popular spread during the Depression, and today it is a mainstay food in four out of five homes.

½ cup (1 stick) unsalted butter, plus more for the baking sheets
1 cup sugar
1 cup natural, unhomogenized peanut butter
1 large egg
½ teaspoon vanilla extract
1⅓ cups unsifted all-purpose flour
½ teaspoon baking soda
½ teaspoon salt

1. Preheat the oven to 375 degrees F. Lightly butter 2 baking sheets.

2. In a large bowl, beat the butter until soft. Gradually add the sugar and beat until creamy. Add the peanut butter, egg, and vanilla to the butter-sugar mixture and mix until incorporated.

3. Sift the flour with the baking soda and salt. Add to the peanut butter mixture and mix thoroughly.

4. Roll the dough into small balls about 1 inch in diameter, and place them on the cookie sheets. With a fork, flatten each ball, then make a mark with the tines of the fork perpendicular to the first marks to create a crosshatch pattern. Bake for 15 minutes. Let cool.

> The peanut is native to South America, but has been found around the world for over 500 years. The ancient Inca Indians of Peru had jars in the shape of peanuts. The United States produces only about 3 percent of the world's peanut crop. The largest producers are in India and China.

GREATER MIAMI and the beaches along the east coast of the Florida peninsula have been shaped by ocean waves, waves that formed barrier islands and that came in with hurricanes and rearranged the geography. But the most significant waves to arrive on these shores were waves of settlers. The first American Indians arrived about ten thousand years ago, followed (in good time) by Spanish explorers, northern retirees (many of them originally from eastern Europe), Cuban refugees, and further waves of immigrants; more than 40 percent of current Miami residents are foreign-born. Cuban, Nicaraguan, Haitian, Asian, Deep South, and Jewish cuisines collide, each retaining their unique traditions, while at the same time blending to create real American foods.

In 1513, Spanish explorer Ponce de Leon went in search of the Fountain of Youth. He landed on what he thought was an island. He saw

QUICK: WHAT'S THE FIRST SUCCESSFUL EUROPEAN COLONY IN AMERICA?

Ask most Americans what was the first successful European colony in what is today the United States, and many will answer Jamestown, Virginia, which was settled in 1607, or Plymouth, Massachusetts, which was settled in 1621. The right answer is St. Augustine, founded in 1565, forty years earlier than Jamestown. At one point, more than half of what is today the United States was controlled by Spain, from Florida to California. Hispanic heritage has greatly influenced the United States for over four hundred years, and this influence has been greatly felt in what Americans eat. Into what is today the United States, the Spanish introduced Old World animals—horses, cattle, pigs, and chickens—and plants, such as oranges, lemons, wheat, and rice, as well as many animals and plants from Mexico, such as domesticated turkeys, tomatoes, pineapples, chile peppers, avocados, casava, and sweet potatoes. When English settlements were established in the Carolinas and Georgia, they used orchards and fields planted by the Spanish, who had established forts and outposts northward from Florida.

lots of flowers, and hence named it "flowery," or *florida* in Spanish. Alas, poor Ponce. He didn't find the Fountain of Youth on his first voyage, so he returned five years later to explore the west coast of Florida. This time the explorers were met with a flight of arrows, one of which killed Ponce, who thereby achieved eternal rest if not the eternal youth he sought. But he and his fellow explorer, Hernando de Soto, did a lot for Florida and the rest of North America, especially in the culinary department. How's this for an accomplishment: They were the first to bring cattle, chickens, and pigs to the continent. The Franciscan missionaries who followed them brought spices, fruits, and vegetables from Mexico and Europe, as well as their all-important recipes for European and Latin American dishes. So the Spanish influence on the food of Miami goes back almost five hundred years.

RESORTING TO MIAMI

It wasn't until 1821 that the U.S. government got around to acquiring Florida from Spain, but even then nobody was particularly interested in settling at the southern end of the peninsula. For one thing, the Seminole Indians weren't too happy with settlers taking over their territory, and they stood their ground as best they could in three of the bloodiest Indian wars in American history.

It is only fitting that the Seminoles named the area *miami*, which meant "big water," probably referring to the Miami River. Despite the end of the Indian wars, no one but American Indians and traders were particularly interested in Miami

JUICED IN FLORIDA

Oranges and other citrus had been introduced to Florida by the Spanish, but these fruits were but a minor agricultural commodity until the railroads arrived in Florida during the late nineteenth century. At that time, most Americans ate oranges as a snack or breakfast fruit, or added them to fruit salads, and part of the orange crop went into marmalade. Few Americans drank orange juice until the 1920s, when the medical community proclaimed that oranges contained lots of vitamin C, which was touted as the wonder vitamin. Sales of Florida oranges increased threefold by World War II, with most of the increase due to the popularity of orange juice. Like many other frozen foods, orange juice concentrate was developed during the war. After the war, the Florida Foods Corporation began manufacturing frozen orange juice. The company named its major product Minute Maid. Florida remains America's number-one orange-growing state.

until multimillionaire Henry M. Flagler and his partner, John D. Rockefeller (also good for a small financial contribution), built a railroad along Florida's east coast, developing cities and resorts along the way. By 1896, the railroad had reached Miami, which at the time had fewer than four hundred residents, and Flagler built a resort hotel. Other resorts followed as wealthy northerners searched for a place to get away from the winter cold, and developers accommodated them with residential hotels.

The first of the really big spenders came to Miami during the early years of the twentieth century and settled in an area known as Coconut Grove. In 1916, James Deering, who had made his fortune selling farming equipment through International Harvester, built one of the most magnificent winter homes in the area. He called the estate

---

★ **WHAT TO TASTE AND WHERE TO TASTE IT** ★

Tropical French/Caribbean

ORTANIQUE ON THE MILE
278 Miracle Mile ★ Coral Gables ★ (305) 446-7710

Chef-partner Cindy Hutson blends French culinary discipline with the sprightly flavors of the Caribbean. For instance, she's created a salad of mango and hearts of palm with passion-fruit vinaigrette, topped with candied pecans. Hutson also marinates grouper in an orange liqueur–teriyaki sauce before sautéing the fish. For dessert, try the chocolate Tia Maria mousse and cinnamon cream rolled in a chocolate sponge cake and garnished with raspberries.

Jewish Deli

RASCAL HOUSE
17190 Collins Avenue ★ Miami ★ (305) 947-4581

Opened in 1954, Wolfie Cohen's Rascal House is a Miami Beach mainstay; when in the city, the Rat Pack would chow down there. The vinyl booths many not be attractive, but the menu boasts all the traditional favorites: corned beef and pastrami sandwiches, stuffed cabbage, brisket, and potato pancakes.

Vizcaya, which means "the high place." He was joined by flocks of fellow millionaires, who built themselves equally lavish estates. These days, Coconut Grove's attractions are shops, outdoor cafés, and excellent restaurants.

Miami Beach came into its own as a resort during the Roaring Twenties. Northerners hopped off the train ready to live it up, do a little gambling (which was illegal but tolerated by the local government), and drink a little alcohol (also illegal and tolerated by the local government). During Prohibition, so much whisky came into Miami from the Bahamas that Miami Beach was known as "the leakiest spot in America."

Miami Beach has also been associated with Jews coming down from the Northeast. They too left an extraordinary food heritage. You can revisit that heritage, circa 1950s, at the Rascal House, where the Rat Pack (Frank Sinatra, Dean Martin, and friends) tucked into matzo ball soup, corned beef, pastrami, stuffed cabbage, pea soup, and the best potato pancakes in town.

Coffee

NEWS CAFÉ
800 Ocean Drive ★ Miami Beach ★ (305) 538-6397

The News Café opened in 1988 as an ice-cream parlor and slowly grew to be the hottest hangout on the beach. Based on the idea of the European café, it's a spot where locals and tourists alike come in for coffee, a meal, or just a pleasant place to read the paper without being rushed. It's open twenty-four hours a day, every day of the year, and it's always an interesting place to see what's going on. News Café is one of the establishments that helped define the South Beach renaissance.

The Depression hit Miami particularly hard; after the stock market crash of 1929, conspicuous consumption was unacceptable (and pretty much impossible). As the Depression ended, World War II began, providing another reason for the sparkly set to dim their lights. The beautiful Art Deco buildings of the 1920s became the urban blight of the 1960s. As the city's resorts faded, Miami became a place for retirees to take refuge from the winter snows of the north. So many elderly people flocked to Miami that it came to be called "God's waiting room."

When Miami began to recover, many of the old buildings were slated to be torn down. Preservationists, however, prevailed, and some of the best Art Deco buildings were saved. Today, Miami's modern skyline blends easily with its salvaged past, the old folks mingle comfortably with fashion designers, bikini models, and Cuban émigrés, and the city that once had the highest murder rate in the country attracts 9 million tourists every year.

After a decades-long gastronomic dry spell, Miami and the beaches had a culinary renaissance during the 1990s. Cookbooks featuring Miami cuisine, such as Steven Raichlen's *Miami Spice: The New Florida Cuisine* and Caroline Stuart's *The Food of Miami:*

★ WHAT TO TASTE AND WHERE TO TASTE IT ★

Different

TANTRA
1445 Pennsylvania Avenue ★ Miami ★ (305) 672-4765

Want something unusual? Tantra is the place to go. It specializes in foods considered to be aphrodisiacs. Salmon is thought to be an aphrodisiac because the fish has a reputation for great sexual activity. It is served with caviar and truffles because they are rare . . . like true love. The Romans thought arugula would do the trick, so Tantra serves prawns on arugula. Chocolate is also on the menu.

BAMBU
956 Washington Avenue ★ Miami Beach ★ (305) 531-4800

Two stories high, with a minimalist Zen-like décor, Bambu was put together by a group that included the actress Cameron Diaz. The best place to base yourself is the upstairs VIP lounge for sakes or an Asian pear Martini. The pricey menu focuses on the foods of Japan, China, Vietnam, and Thailand: sushi with freshly grated wasabi, Shanghai noodle pad thai with shrimp, green curry chicken with lime juice and coconut milk. Bambu offers a nice assortment of teas, and for dessert, try a selection of ripe tropical fruits with a mint drizzle.

Authentic Recipes from South Florida and the Keys, reflect the shift from a culinary desert to a gustatory oasis. Chefs found Miami's semitropical climate and its easy access to tropical ingredients to be a launching pad for culinary excellence. Today, there are dozens of interesting restaurants in the area, and a lot of the food reflects Miami's singular character, especially the effects of ethnic migrations. Miami's unique blending of gastronomic influences gives it a "real" American cuisine like no other city.

HAVANA IN AMERICA

Half of Miami's population is of Hispanic heritage, and the city is peppered with Latin American flavors. But by far the largest immigrant group are the Cubans, who came to Miami during the 1960s in flight from Castro's communism. They were mostly talented professionals and successful businesspeople who were interested in re-creating the comfortable lifestyle they had left behind. They hit the ground running in Miami, immediately setting up the kinds of businesses they had owned back home. They also reproduced Cuban cuisine. Today, Miami boasts over two hundred major Cuban restaurants and thousands of small Cuban cafés.

Having breakfast in Little Havana, the most intensely Cuban neighborhood in the city, is a good introduction to Miami Cuban food. Choose from a variety of fried and baked goods including *croquetas* and *pastelitos*, which are light, flaky pastries filled with guava or cream cheese (or both). A heartier version is stuffed with meat. It's a version of the Cuban bread called *patines*, or "skates," so named because they resemble roller skates. Cuban food is filled with exotic ingredients, such as yuca and *boniato*, and the spices add zest. Codfish fritters are another breakfast delicacy, and the beverage of choice is *café cubano*. What makes it Cuban coffee? The way it's made: strong and sweet.

There are also a variety of sandwiches filled with prosciutto, salami, tomatoes—just about anything you'd like. They are built up into many-layered cake-like structures and then sliced into triangles; they're nice and filling. Other

THE KING OF BURGERS

Keith G. Cramer, owner of Keith's Drive-in Restaurant in Daytona Beach, Florida, heard about the McDonald brothers' fast-food restaurant and flew to San Bernardino, California, to observe their operation. As a result, he opened a restaurant called Insta-Burger-King in 1953. James McLamore and David Edgerton acquired the rights to franchise the operation and they opened an Insta-Burger-King restaurant in Miami. In 1958, they improved the machine that broiled the hamburgers and changed the name of the restaurant to Burger King. Miami is thus the original "Home of the Whopper."

sandwiches are pressed flat, such as the *cubano*, which consists of ham and roast pork marinated in *mojo* sauce (garlic, olive oil, and lemon or lime juice), dill pickles, mustard, and Swiss cheese on Cuban bread; the sandwich is pressed and grilled, so that the cheese is melted and the bread toasted. Another favorite sandwich, the *medianoche*, is similar but it uses a sweeter and lighter bread. Then there is the *frita cubana*, a patty of fried ground beef with spices, onions, and potatoes on a Cuban roll.

═ GATEWAY FROM AFRICA AND THE CARIBBEAN ═

Another major gastronomic influence in Miami came from the thousands of Africans who were taken to the New World to be slaves. Africans were first brought to Florida during the 1500s, and with them came some of their staple foods: eggplants, yams, rice, sesame seeds, watermelons, and okra. These days you can get a taste of the African influence at Ortanique in Coral Gables. An ortanique, by the way, is a citrus fruit indigenous to Jamaica; it's a cross between an orange, a tangerine, and a grapefruit. The food at Ortanique is described as "New World Caribbean cuisine."

Yet another immigrant group to flavor Miami's simmering pot is the Haitians. Many excellent small Haitian cafés can be found in Miami area, but Tap Tap is one of the few formal restaurants in town specializing in Haitian cuisine. So why is this dramatic

---

★ WHAT TO TASTE AND WHERE TO TASTE IT ★

Haitian

TAP TAP
819 Fifth Street ★ Miami Beach ★ (305) 672-2898

Haitian cuisine is traditionally a blend of African, French, and Middle Eastern influences. The emphasis is on spiciness. Some of the specialties at Tap Tap are pan-seared kingfish with herb sauce, goat chayote (a Caribbean stew), shrimp Creole with Haitian flavorings, and grilled chicken with watercress sauce.

West Indian

LC'S ROTI SHOP
19505 Northwest Second Avenue ★ Miami ★ (305) 651-8924

Roti is an unleavened Indian bread imported to Miami by West Indians. Many roti shops and stands dot Miami, but LC's is the place to go. While you're there, try their conch, goat, and chickpeas. While you can eat them without spice, the hot sauce and mango relish make for real West Indian food.

Barbecue

SHORTY'S BAR-B-Q
9200 South Dixie Highway ★ Miami ★ (305) 670-7732

Miami is a southern city, and what could be more southern than barbecue? A Miami tradition since 1951, Shorty's Bar-B-Q is a rustic shack that has been less than fully renovated. But what it lacks in décor it makes up for in fabulous barbecue: smoke-flavored and slow-cooked spareribs, brisket, and chicken. It still has customers lining up to eat off plastic plates with plastic cutlery and paper napkins. Shorty's serves the meat in a light sauce, but the sweet sauce is on the table and you can add it to your palate's content. And if you haven't eaten everything on your plate and aren't pretty well covered with sauce yourself, then you really haven't quite gotten the point of Shorty's.

and colorful dining destination called Tap Tap? In Haiti, a tap tap is a ramshackle bus—every inch of it painted with colorful images—that transports people, livestock, and produce from one end of country to the other. And Tap Tap Haitian Restaurant is about bringing Haitian cuisine to people who've never had the chance to try it.

BUILDINGS WITH EYEBROWS

Miami Beach is home to the largest concentration of Art Deco buildings in the world. The Art Deco movement began in Paris in the early in the 1900s. The objective was to take design elements used in industry and translate them into the decorative arts. During the 1920s and '30s, more than five hundred Art Deco structures went up in Miami Beach. Its oceanside location gave the architecture a special twist, and the style came to be known as Tropical Deco. It featured stucco and tile in bright pastels, and concrete awnings called "eyebrows" placed above windows for shade.

By 1990, however, these wonderful buildings were deteriorating. The Hotel St. Moritz, for instance, was spectacular when it was built in the 1920s, but by the early 1990s it had been shut down, run down, and appeared to have no future. Big developers wanted to demolish the St. Moritz and replace it with a new hotel that would cater to the convention visitor. Preservationists wanted the building returned to its original grandeur. Both groups got what they wanted in the Loews Hotels proposal, which included the restoration of the St. Moritz to its original Art Deco splendor and construction of a new hotel tower right behind it. It was the first major hotel to be built on Miami Beach in thirty years. Its restaurant, whose kitchen is headed by Chef Dwayne Adams, is known for its seafood.

Crispy Crab Cakes with Mango Salsa

MAKES 4 SERVINGS

Crab cakes are a tradition of East Coast America, but the mango sauce is a clear Caribbean influence that was added in Miami.

8 ounces finely chopped cooked shrimp

8 ounces cooked lump crabmeat, cleaned

2 teaspoons Dijon-style mustard

1/4 cup mayonnaise

2 tablespoons minced fresh parsley

2 teaspoons Worcestershire sauce

1/2 teaspoon Tabasco sauce

2 teaspoons prepared white horseradish

Salt to taste

Cayenne pepper to taste

1 egg

2 tablespoons dry bread crumbs

1/8 teaspoon Cajun spice mix, optional

2 cups crushed potato chips

2 tablespoons vegetable oil or more, for frying

Mango Salsa (recipe follows)

1. In a large bowl, combine all the ingredients but the potato chips and vegetable oil.

2. Form the mixture into twelve 2-inch round cakes. Pat the crushed potato chips on both sides of the crab cakes.

3. In a large nonstick skillet, heat the oil over medium heat. Sauté the crab cakes for 2 to 3 minutes on each side or until golden and hot throughout. Serve with Mango Salsa.

MANGO SALSA

MAKES 2 CUPS

2 ripe mangoes, peeled

2 scallions, thinly sliced

2 tablespoons chopped cilantro

1 tablespoon grated fresh ginger

Juice of 1 lime, strained

1/2 teaspoon low-sodium soy sauce

2 drops Tabasco sauce

1. Cut the flesh off both sides of each mango, as close to the large flat seed as possible. Trim any extra flesh from around the edge of the seed. Chop fine.

2. In a medium bowl, combine the mangoes and remaining ingredients. Refrigerate until ready to serve.

The mango has been called the "apple of the tropics" and it is certainly as widely appreciated in the warm parts of the planet as the apple is in the cooler zones. Mangoes have been cultivated for so long that no one is quite sure where they got their start.

All mangoes start out green, but as they ripen they change colors. A ripe mango can range in color from yellow to green to rose red. The best way to tell if a mango is ripe is to press the outside skin; it should yield to gentle pressure. Mangoes range in weight from about ten ounces to over four pounds. Considering the fact that they are not the easiest fruit in the world to peel and to clean off the inside stone, bigger is easier. Ripe mangoes are eaten as a fresh fruit and used in drinks, pies, ice creams, and uncooked relishes and salsas. The unripe mango is usually cooked into chutney.

Before you cut a lime, squeeze it or roll it on a hard surface. If you do that, you will get about twice as much juice out of it. Also, when you're zesting a lime, you want just the green outside surface. If you get the white connective tissue right under the skin, it will be bitter.

★ WHAT TO TASTE AND WHERE TO TASTE IT ★

Crab

JOE'S STONE CRAB
11 Washington Avenue ★ Miami Beach ★ (305) 673-4611

Joe's Stone Crab has been an institution in South Beach for more than ninety years. It occupies an entire city block, and is filled with locals, tourists, and celebrities. It has regularly been identified as the best restaurant in the Miami area. The famous stone-crab claw (medium, large, or jumbo), with its creamy mustard sauce, is what this restaurant is all about. You may have to wait more than two hours for a table. Key lime pie is a must for dessert.

Black Bean Soup

MAKES 8 SERVINGS

New World Beans were introduced to Europe in the sixteenth century by Spanish explorers returning from their voyages to the New World. From there they spread to Africa and Asia by Spanish and Portuguese traders. Beans are an inexpensive form of protein and an important staple in the cuisines of Mexico, Brazil, Guatemala, the Dominican Republic, and Cuba. Black beans are particularly favored in the Cuban cuisine of Miami.

1 pound dried black beans
10 cups chicken stock
4 tablespoons (½ stick) unsalted butter
2 ribs celery, finely chopped
2 medium onions, finely chopped
1 clove garlic, crushed
1½ tablespoons all-purpose flour
1 bay leaf
Salt and freshly ground black pepper
½ cup Madeira wine (optional)
Lemon slices, or chopped onion, chopped tomato, and cooked rice, for garnish

1. Wash the beans. Place in a large pot and add cold water to cover. Let soak overnight, or boil the beans in 6 to 8 cups of water for 2 minutes, then set aside for 1 hour.

2. Drain the beans and place them in another large pot. Add the chicken stock and bring to a boil. Reduce the heat to low and simmer for 1½ hours, adding water if the beans look as though they are drying out.

3. In a medium saucepan, melt the butter over moderate heat. Add the celery, onions, and garlic, and sauté until softened but not browned.

4. Stir in the flour and cook, stirring constantly, for 1 minute.

5. Stir the vegetable mixture into the beans. Add the bay leaf and pepper to taste. Cover and simmer over low heat, stirring occasionally, for 2 to 3 hours. Check occasionally and add water if the beans are not completely covered with liquid.

6. Remove and discard the bay leaf. Add salt and pepper to taste. Puree the soup through a food mill, food processor, or blender until smooth.

7. Return the soup to the pot and add the Madeira, if using. Reheat the soup and correct the seasoning. Garnish each portion with a lemon slice or serve with chopped onion, chopped tomato, and cooked rice.

Black beans are a very good source of cholesterol-lowering fiber, as are most other legumes. When combined with whole grains such as brown rice, black beans provide virtually fat-free high quality protein.

Bay leaves, which are also called laurel or bay laurel leaves, add a fragrant and delicate aroma and taste to a recipe. They have a sharp central spine which if eaten whole could become stuck in the digestive tract. They are great for seasoning but not for eating. Remove and discard bay leaves from all recipes before serving.

Sautéed Flounder with Shrimp

MAKES 6 SERVINGS

Flounder, a left-eyed flat fish, has been caught commercially by American fishermen since colonial times, but the fish did not become popular until the later part of the nineteenth century. The summer flounder off America's eastern shore is considered both an excellent game fish as well as a tasty eating fish.

2 pounds flounder fillets, cut into a total of 6 pieces, each about ½-inch thick
½ cup all-purpose flour
2 eggs, beaten
½ cup dry bread crumbs
5 tablespoons unsalted butter
2 tablespoons vegetable oil
2 tablespoons (total) mixed herbs and spices such as black pepper, cayenne,
*   dried basil, oregano, and thyme*
12 large shrimp, shelled and deveined

1. Lightly coat the flounder with the flour (shaking off any excess), then dip the fish into the eggs and finally into the bread crumbs.

2. In a sauté pan, melt 2 tablespoons of the butter with the vegetable oil over moderate heat. When almost smoking, add the flounder and sauté for 2 to 3 minutes on each side, until nicely browned. Remove the fillets to a serving dish.

3. In the same pan, heat the remaining 3 tablespoons butter and the herbs and spices until the butter begins to brown. Add the shrimp and sauté for 2 minutes. Place 2 of the cooked shrimp on top of each fillet. Pour the flavored butter sauce over the shrimp and fish and serve.

Clam Cakes with Black Bean Salad with Lime Tartar Sauce

SERVES 4

Everyone's heard of crab cakes, but clam cakes? In fact, clam cakes have been made along America's east coast and Gulf Coast for centuries. Recently, they have become popular nationally through food programs on television.

FOR THE CLAM CAKES

4 tablespoons salted butter
½ cup diced red bell pepper
½ cup diced green bell pepper
½ cup diced red onion
1 cup (two 6.5-ounce cans) canned clams, drained and minced
1 egg
½ cup mayonnaise
1 teaspoon Old Bay seasoning
½ teaspoon freshly ground black pepper
½ teaspoon salt
½ cup dried bread crumbs
2 tablespoons vegetable oil

FOR THE SALAD

2 ears of corn or 1 cup canned or frozen
1½ cups cooked black beans
2 pints cherry tomatoes, halved
2 tablespoons honey
2 tablespoons red wine vinegar
1 tablespoon sugar
Salt
Freshly ground black pepper

FOR THE LIME TARTAR SAUCE

½ cup mayonnaise
½ cup minced green bell pepper
2 tablespoons sour cream
2 tablespoons minced red onion
1 tablespoon minced capers
1 tablespoon fresh lime juice
Zest from half a lime

1. TO MAKE THE CAKES: In a large nonstick frying pan over medium-high heat, melt 2 tablespoons of the butter. Add the bell peppers and onion and sauté for 5 minutes. Empty the mixture into a large bowl and cool to room temperature.

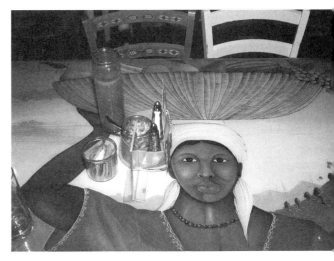

2. Add the clams, egg, mayonnaise, Old Bay, black pepper, and salt to the pepper and onion mixture and mix thoroughly. Fold in the bread crumbs. With your hands, form eight 2 ½-inch round cakes. Place them on a baking sheet, cover with plastic wrap, and refrigerate for 1 hour to allow cakes to set.

3. TO MAKE THE SALAD: Preheat the oven to 450 degrees F. Remove the silks from the ears of corn, leaving the husks intact. Soak the corn in cold water for 1 hour. (This will prevent the husks from burning in the oven.) Drain the corn and place in a roasting pan. Roast the corn about 30 to 40 minutes, or until the husks turn golden brown and the edges, dark brown. Remove the corn from the oven and cool to room temperature. Once cool, take the husks off and with a sharp knife, cut the kernels off the cob. Place the corn into a medium bowl and add the beans, tomatoes, honey, vinegar, and sugar. Mix together thoroughly. Season to taste with salt and pepper, cover and refrigerate until chilled.

4. TO MAKE THE TARTAR SAUCE: In a medium nonreactive bowl, mix together all of the ingredients. Cover with plastic wrap and chill until ready to use.

5. TO FRY THE CAKES: In a large nonstick frying pan over medium-high heat, melt the remaining 2 tablespoons of butter and the 2 tablespoons of vegetable oil. Add the cakes and sauté 2 minutes per side, or until the cakes are golden brown. (Cook in batches if necessary.)

6. TO SERVE: Place a mound of the bean and corn salad in the center of a serving plate. Rest two cakes on the sides. Top each cake with a dollop of tartar sauce and serve immediately.

Tropical Fruit with Mint Drizzle

MAKES 8 SERVINGS

Agriculture is an important economic force in Miami-Dade County, where more tropical fruit is harvested than any other county in the United States.

2 cups sugar

1 cup fresh mint leaves

2 tablespoons Chinese five-spice powder (a dry spice mix used in Chinese cooking, consisting of cinnamon, star anise, Szechuan pepper, clove, and fennel)

6 to 7 pounds ripe tropical fruits (such as mango, papaya, banana, carambola, lychee, caimito, sapote, kiwi, etc.), peeled and cut into bite-size pieces

2 limes, each cut into 4 wedges

1 Asian pear, peeled, cored and thinly sliced (optional)

Toasted black sesame seeds (optional)

1. TO MAKE THE MINT DRIZZLE: In a small saucepan, stir together 1 cup sugar and 1 cup water. Bring to a boil over medium-high heat and stir until the sugar dissolves to make a syrup. Remove from the heat and cool completely. In a blender, puree the mint leaves with the cooled syrup. Set aside.

2. In a small bowl, mix the remaining 1 cup sugar and the five-spice powder. Set aside.

3. When ready to serve, toss together the fruit and mint drizzle in a large bowl. Spoon the fruit and a bit of the mint drizzle onto the dessert plates and place a wedge of lime on each plate. Garnish each with a few slices of the Asian pear and sprinkle with the black sesame seeds, if desired. Serve each plate with a small bowl of the five-spice sugar on the side.

★ WHAT TO TASTE AND WHERE TO TASTE IT ★

Asian

NEMO

100 Collins Avenue ★ Miami Beach ★ (305) 532-4550

The most recent group of people to immigrate to Miami came from Southeast Asia, and they helped create something called fusion cuisine, which turns up in some of the city's most luxurious restaurants. Nemo is one. A representative fusion main course is wok-charred marinated salmon on four-sprout salad dressed with soy-lime vinaigrette. For dessert, try pastry chef Hedy Goldsmith's biscotti with fruit sorbets.

Key Lime Pie

MAKES 8 SERVINGS

The Key lime is in a class all its own. Much smaller than a regular lime, the Key lime is usually the size of a ping-pong ball or golf ball. Key limes have a distinctive aroma which makes them valuable to cooking. Not exclusive to the Florida Keys, Key limes were brought there years ago and became naturalized.

FOR THE CRUST

⅓ cup plus 1 teaspoon melted margarine
1¼ cups crushed graham crackers
¼ cup sugar

FOR THE FILLING

2 (14-ounce) cans sweetened condensed milk
5 egg yolks
Grated zest of 1 lime
1 cup fresh lime juice (5 to 6 limes)

1. TO MAKE THE CRUST: Preheat the oven to 350 degrees F. Coat the inside of a 9-inch pie pan with 1 teaspoon of the melted margarine.

2. In a mixing bowl, combine the crushed graham crackers, sugar, and the remaining ⅓ cup margarine. When the ingredients are fully combined, line the bottom and sides of the pie pan with the mixture. Bake for 10 minutes.

3. TO MAKE THE FILLING: While the crust is baking, in a medium mixing bowl, whisk together all the ingredients.

4. When the crust is baked, remove it from the oven and pour in the filling. Return the filled piecrust to the oven and bake for 10 minutes more. Let cool to room temperature before serving.

THE KEY TO PIE

Henry M. Flagler, who built the railroad to Miami, continued with his railroad-building career by completing it all the way to Key West, Florida. His railroad made it possible for development of the Florida Keys, where new residents found that the Spanish had planted lime trees on the Keys, but due to the climatic and soil conditions the limes were small and tart. Keys residents made use of them in various ways, particularly for flavoring custard pies. Chefs picked up this local dessert and it became a real American food. In 1926, a hurricane destroyed most of the limes in the Keys. Today, virtually all Key lime pie is flavored from limes grown elsewhere.

Flan

Flan is used in Spanish and Mexican cooking to describe an egg custard that is baked and flavored with caramel. The dish is inverted when served and the excess caramel is used as sauce. Flan is the Spanish version of crème caramel. The traditional flavoring is vanilla, but there are many variations. Florida was a Spanish colony for almost 250 years. The Spanish settlers brought flan with them and introduced it into Florida. Recent Latino immigrants have raised flan making to an art form.

FOR THE CARAMEL SAUCE

1 cup sugar

FOR THE FLAN

1 (14-ounce) can sweetened condensed milk
8 eggs
1 teaspoon vanilla extract

1. TO PREPARE THE SAUCE: Into a shallow 3-quart flameproof bowl or mold (stainless-steel is a good choice), put the sugar and 1 cup water. Place the pan directly on the burner and cook over medium-high heat until the sugar caramelizes to a dark brown color. This should take about 10 minutes. Much of the liquid will evaporate. Using pot holders, carefully remove the bowl from the burner and gently swirl the caramel sauce around the inside until all the sides are coated lightly. Set the bowl in a 9 x 13-inch baking pan and place that on a baking sheet.

2. Preheat the oven to 350 degrees F.

3. TO MAKE THE FLAN: In a blender, combine the condensed milk, 1¾ cup water, and the eggs. Blend until smooth. Add the vanilla and blend briefly. Pour the flan mixture into the caramel-lined bowl. Cover the bowl loosely with aluminum foil, gently crimping the edges to seal. The bowl will still be hot, so be sure to use a potholder when you touch it. Pour enough hot water around the bowl to go halfway up the outside of the bowl. Place the baking sheet holding the water bath and the covered flan bowl in the oven and bake for 1½ hours, until the custard is set.

4. After baking, carefully remove the flan from the oven and with potholders, lift the bowl out of the water bath and put the bowl onto a rack. Remove the foil cover. Let the flan cool at room temperature for 30 minutes, then refrigerate for 2 hours.

5. To serve, run a knife between the flan and the edge of the bowl. Set a plate over the top of the bowl, turn the whole thing over and give it a shake. The flan will unmold onto the plate. Spoon out any of the caramel sauce left in the bowl. Slice the flan into wedges and spoon the caramel sauce on top.

EAT TOO MUCH?

South Beach is a city on an island across from Miami. It has long been famous for its fashionable hotels, recreational areas, and good food. With all the good food in South Beach and Miami, it's no wonder that the city has also produced one of America's most popular diets. Miami cardiologist Arthur Agatston recommended reducing carbohydrates (bread, rice, pastas, and fruits) and increasing high-fiber foods, lean proteins, and healthful fats. His book *The South Beach Diet: The Delicious, Doctor-Designed, Foolproof Plan for Fast and Healthy Weight Loss* was a best seller, and his diet plan has swept the nation.

Sweetened condensed milk has an unlimited shelf life. It's a good idea to turn the can over every few months to keep the sugar well dispersed throughout the milk.

★ WHAT TO TASTE AND WHERE TO TASTE IT ★

Cuban

VERSAILLES
3555 Southwest Eighth Street ★ Miami ★ (305) 445-7614

Versailles has traditionally been rated as Miami's best Cuban restaurant. For thirty-five years, it has been a culinary landmark, serving a diversity of Latino foods but specializing in home-style Cuban cuisine. Its unpretentious décor includes a large dining room with mirrored walls—hence the name "Versailles." Its authentic Cuban fare includes *vaca frita* (flank steak marinated in mojo sauce), *criollo* (spicy braised pork stew), and *medianoche*. If you don't know Cuban food, order the Classico Combination. It is a large meal that consists of small portions of classic Cuban food. Versailles is packed with locals and tourists, even though it is far from the normal touristy hangouts. Be sure to end your meal with *café cubano* and try the flan or guava pastries.

ABOUT TWELVE THOUSAND YEARS AGO, massive walls of ice sheared off from retreating glaciers in North America, causing a catastrophic flood that created the Mississippi River. At the river's mouth, where it flowed into the Gulf of Mexico, the land was low and swampy, but that didn't stop the Choctaw and other Indian groups from settling there. When Hernando De Soto arrived in the sixteenth century, on a side trip from Florida, he took possession of the area with his usual pronouncement, "I plant this flag and claim this land for Spain!"—but the Spanish never got around to making good on the proclamation and establishing a colony.

The French, however, explored the mouth of the river, and in 1718 founded a settlement on the highest ground they could find. It was about a hundred miles upriver from the gulf, at a bend in the Mississippi. La Nouvelle-Orléans was named in honor of Phillipe, Duc de Orléans, the brother of Louis XIV (a.k.a. the Sun King). Louis got a considerably grander tribute when the entire territory was named Louisiana, and in those days it stretched up to Canada and across the Pacific Northwest. The colony at La Nouvelle-Orléans prospered and grew. It became the seaport for the extensive commercial trade that

---

★ WHAT TO TASTE AND WHERE TO TASTE IT ★

Cajun

BON TON CAFÉ
401 Magazine Street ★ New Orleans ★ (504) 524-3386
This family-owned restaurant serves the best Cajun food in New Orleans.
Try the crawfish étouffée and the crabmeat imperial.

---

moved up and down the Mississippi. In 1763, France lost the French and Indian War and Louisiana was handed over to Spain. At the same time, France also lost Canada to the British.

As the British took over French-speaking Canada, they demanded an oath of allegiance to the British Crown. But a group of French-speaking Catholics in Acadia (now Nova Scotia) refused to take the oath or give up their religion, which the oath also required. Though they were simple farmers and fisherman like their English forebears, the authorities saw them as a threat to the stability of the area and resettled them in small groups throughout North America. The great majority of the deported Acadians eventually found their way to southern Louisiana, where they were accepted by the French and Spanish Catholics who had settled the territory. Their descendants became known as Cadiens, or Cajuns. They remained farmers, fishermen, and trappers and still maintain a distinct culture quite different from the French Creoles, who descend directly from the original French and Spanish settlers of Louisiana.

As the United States expanded into the Midwest, the Mississippi River became a major transportation route. New Orleans grew rapidly, especially after a slave revolt in Haiti drove many French Creoles and their slaves out of the country. In 1795, Spain gave the United States the right to trade through New Orleans, and Americans flooded into the city.

The United States began to fear that during any future war the river might be closed to traffic, thus greatly disrupting American trade. After Napoleon convinced the Spanish to return Louisiana to France, the U.S. government became even more concerned. Luckily, Napoleon was broke and needed cash, so in 1803 he agreed to sell Louisiana to the United States for $15 million in cash. Those were the days when you could really get something for your money.

CARE TO MAKE A LITTLE PROGRESSO?

The Italian population in New Orleans wanted Italian food, so a Sicilian immigrant, Giuseppe Uddo, along with Vincent Taormina, started a business catering to Italian immigrants. They opened the Progresso Grocery store in the French Quarter of New Orleans. Just before World War I, they began selling tomato paste. Then they opened up a California cannery. But the factory produced more tomato paste than they could sell in New Orleans, so they decided to sell their paste to Italians in New York. Uddo teamed up with Frank G. and Vincent Taormina, distant cousins of his wife, to launch a major operation in New York. The company prospered, and they started importing and selling olive oil and peeled Italian plum tomatoes. Finally they decided to manufacture thick canned soups, like minestrone. They named their company Il Progresso. Although the company was eventually sold to Pillsbury, Michael Uddo has continued the family traditions through the G and E Courtyard restaurant in New Orleans.

Following the purchase, Americans made their way to Louisiana to see what was going on in the new territory. There was also significant immigration from Italy, Ireland, Germany, and Greece, and slaves were brought in from Africa. To make room for all those new arrivals, New Orleans expanded beyond the high ground that had originally been settled by the French. Swamps were drained and canals constructed—in fact, at one time New Orleans had more canals than Venice. Embankments were built along the Mississippi River and Lake Pontchartrain to protect the city from high water. When, in 2005, flooding caused by hurricane Katrina destroyed some of the embankments and inundated much of the city, the high-lying French Quarter—home to many of the city's most famous landmarks—was relatively unaffected.

Among those French Quarter landmarks are a number of the country's finest restaurants, the product of three hundred years of ingenious gastronomic adaptation and invention that has made New Orleans a city of food lovers. In no other American town is there a greater interest in food. It's the subject on everyone's lips (literally and figuratively),

Upscale Creole

BRENNAN'S RESTAURANT
417 Royal Street ★ New Orleans ★ (504) 525-9711

Brennan's is one of the great old restaurants of New Orleans. This French Quarter classic is made up of a series of charming, elegant, yet comfortable rooms that look out on a lush patio. It's run by Pip, Jimmy, and Ted Brennan, the great-grandsons of an Irish immigrant who arrived in New Orleans in 1840. Bananas Foster—composed of bananas, ice cream, brown sugar, cinnamon, and rum—likely was invented at Brennan's in 1951. While it is now possible to order this dish anywhere, why not do so at its point of origin? Brennan's is also one of the first restaurants to have built a worldwide reputation on its breakfasts, which Pip and Ted Brennan celebrated in their 1994 cookbook, *Breakfast at Brennan's and Dinner, Too.*

COMMANDER'S PALACE
1403 Washington Avenue ★ New Orleans ★ (504) 899-8221

Commander's Palace in the Garden District is a New Orleans institution. Founded in 1880, within twenty years the restaurant was attracting gourmets from around the world. Today, its décor and service are impeccable, and the food is among the best in America.

EMERIL'S NEW ORLEANS
800 Tchoupitoulas Street ★ New Orleans ★ (504) 528-9393

Emeril Lagasse, a Massachusetts native, came to New Orleans in 1983 to serve as executive chef at the legendary Commander's Palace (see below). Now he owns his own restaurant, which quickly became a hot spot in a town known for its great restaurants. Emeril's "New New Orleans" cuisine is derived from Creole cookery but also bears traces of the culinary heritage of such diverse places as Asia, Portugal, and the American Southwest. Emeril has opened additional restaurants in New Orleans and in other American cities, but this was his first and it is well worth visiting. Try his peanut butter pie.

the focus of the city's social activities, and the occupation of the culinary heroes (chefs like K-Paul Prudhomme and Emeril Lagasse).

There are two basic styles of cooking identified with New Orleans and southern Louisiana: Creole and Cajun. Creole (from the French Créole, derived from a Portuguese word used to describe a white person born in the colonies) refers to the elegant cuisine developed by the chefs of wealthy French and Spanish settlers in New Orleans. These European-trained chefs adjusted and adapted their classic French recipes to suit the local seafood, vegetables, fruits, and other ingredients they found in Louisiana.

Cajun cookery, the other main branch of New Orleans cooking, was largely developed in the surrounding bayous and prairies settled by the Acadian exiles. It's down-home country cooking that still shows

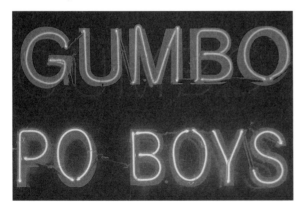

French origins but with ample contributions from African-American, Native American, and Spanish culinary traditions. Cajun food is hearty, often spicy, featuring game, crawfish, and every bit of the pig, from nose to tail.

JUMBO GUMBO

You can easily see how traditional European recipes were adapted to the New World by tracing the history of the dish called gumbo. French settlers had fond memories of bouillabaisse, a complex fish stew associated with Marseilles, and wanted to replicate the dish in Louisiana. Since the traditional fish and shellfish weren't available—they were Mediterranean species—the settlers substituted the fish and shellfish that came from the local lakes and rivers and the Gulf of Mexico.

Okra soup, introduced by enslaved African-Americans, was common in colonial America. One early-nineteenth-century recipe noted that "Gombo" (the Angolan word for okra was *n'gumbo*) was a celebrated dish prepared by stewing okra pods with ripe tomatoes, finely chopped onions, and spices. Somewhere along the line, sliced okra was added to the bouillabaisse (the original contains no vegetables except a little leek, onion, and tomato, as flavoring). Okra had been brought to the New World by African slaves, who hid the seeds of the plant in their hair. When okra is cut, it gives off a substance that thickens the liquid it's cooked in. There's also an alternative gumbo-thick-ening technique, adopted from the Choctaw Indians, who used dried, ground sassafras leaves, a powder the Creoles called filé. (Louisiana cooks use one or the other—never both.) Traditional bouilla-baisse is not thickened with anything. Over time, gumbos were devised that con-tained neither fish nor shellfish.

Gumbo had many admirers. Will Coleman, the publisher of Lafcadio Hearn's *La Cuisine Creole* (1885), described gumbo as the "great dish of New Orleans." There was, Coleman wrote, "no dish which at the same time so tickles the palate, satisfies the appetite, furnishes the body nutriment sufficient to carry on the physical requirements, and costs so little as a Creole gombo." It was a dinner in itself, the "*pièce de résistance*, entremet, and vegetables in one. Healthy, not heat-ing to the stomach and easy of digestion, it should grace every meal."

NOT POPEYE THE SAILOR MAN!

In 1972, Al Copeland opened a fast-food restaurant called Chicken on the Run in New Orleans. The old-fashioned fried chicken on the menu was nothing special, but when Copeland spiced up the batter with hot sauce, the crowds came flocking in. Copeland renamed the restaurant "Popeye's" after the character Popeye Doyle in the movie The French Connection. The first Popeye's franchise restaurant, located in Baton Rouge, Louisiana, opened in 1976. By 1996, the Popeye's chain had reached a thousand restaurants nationwide.

Buttermilk biscuits were added to the menu in 1985, Cajun crawfish in 1988, and Cajun popcorn shrimp in 1989. Popeye's has popularized Cajun and Creole foods across the United States and now worldwide, as the chain opens restaurants in other countries.

Today, gumbos may be based on chicken or game, or even greens (mustard greens, watercress, parsley, and so on), and are usually spiked with some form of hot pepper and served with or over rice. The recipe varies from cook to cook, from season to season, but the manifold interpretations of gumbo have one thing in common: The starting point is a roux, a pan-browned amalgam of fat and flour that is the basis of many great Louisiana dishes. Roux making is an art, and mastering that art is quite an accomplishment.

THE FRENCH CONNECTION

Many of the traditional dishes of New Orleans include rice, and Louisiana has been growing rice for more than two hundred years. Rice provides the base for many Creole and Cajun dishes, such as classic New Orleans jambalaya, a rice-based dish made with pork or shellfish or sausage or all of the above seasoned with herbs and spices. Jambalaya is a Louisiana adaptation of Spanish paella, in the same way that French bouillabaisse evolved into gumbo. Yet another Cajun dish is étouffée, a spicy Cajun stew traditionally made with crawfish, vegetables, and a dark roux—a combination of wheat flour and fat cooked at high heat. Étouffée is usually served over rice.

Although France has had little to do with New Orleans during the past two centuries, the French connection is still obvious in the architecture of the French Quarter and in the menus of the city's restaurants. Rémoulade sauce, for instance, is a classic accompaniment for shrimp in New Orleans. It's based on the standard French rémoulade, but enlivened with pungent Creole mustard and cayenne pepper. Like everything else that came to New Orleans from France, it's been jazzed up a bit.

★ **WHAT TO TASTE AND WHERE TO TASTE IT** ★

Classic French Creole

ANTOINE'S RESTAURANT
713 Rue Saint Louis ★ New Orleans ★ (504) 581-4422
Founded by Antoine Alciatore in 1840, Antoine's is one of New Orleans's best traditional restaurants. Diners at the restaurant have included presidents, royalty, and numerous entertainers. When Pope John Paul II visited New Orleans in 1988, Antoine's prepared his meals. Antoine's claims (as do other New Orleans establishments) to have invented Oysters Rockefeller and Baked Alaska; whether the "original" or not, they are dishes well worth trying here.

Two hundred million years ago, the southern part of the United States was completely covered with water. As the sea pulled back from the land in southern Louisiana, it left a huge concentrated deposit of natural salt. A few hundred thousand years later, the salt was again buried (by the ocean or by land). But at some point, an earth tremor forced a column of this salt up from the sea, and it become a sort of "island" among the marshes west of New Orleans. It's called Avery Island, and it's the site of America's first salt mine.

MONDAY, MONDAY

Louisiana tradition holds that red beans and rice is served on Mondays, which only makes sense: Monday was wash day, which left little time for cooking, and the beans could simmer away for hours unattended as the housewife dealt with the laundry. Also, many families could afford a substantial cut of meat (usually pork or ham) just once a week, for Sunday dinner. The thrifty cook wouldn't want a bit of that feast to go to waste, so the bone went into the pot on Monday to flavor the beans.

Now, if that weren't enough to endear Avery Island to American cooks, it's also the home of another of America's favorite seasonings. In 1868, a man named Edmund McIlhenny planted a few chile pepper seeds. When they were ripe, he picked the peppers, chopped them, and mixed them with the local salt and some vinegar to make a thin sauce. McIlhenny aged the sauce in wooden barrels for three years to let the sauce ferment and the flavors blend. When he felt it was ready, he siphoned the sauce into small cologne bottles and offered the sauce at the meals he served to friends and neighbors. When he was convinced of its appeal, McIlhenny gave the sauce a catchy name—Tabasco chile pepper. Now the McIlhenny Company turns out well over 100,000 bottles of Tabasco sauce every day. They ship the bottles to more than a hundred countries around the world. Tabasco sauce even goes into outer space in the astronauts' "spice packs."

Chicken and Sausage Gumbo

MAKES 6 SERVINGS

Okra is very popular throughout the American South, where it was introduced by black African slaves who brought the seeds from West Africa. Today okra is grown and eaten wherever black Africans were carried as slaves. When stewed, okra has a gelatinous texture, and acts as a thickener for gumbo that is a characteristic almost as important as the flavor imparted.

6 whole chicken legs with thighs, skinned
3/4 teaspoon kosher salt, plus more to taste
1/2 teaspoon freshly ground black pepper, plus more to taste
1/4 cup vegetable oil
1/2 pound andouille or kielbasa sausage, cut into 3/4-inch pieces
1 medium onion, diced
3 medium cloves garlic, minced
1 green bell pepper; stem, ribs, and seeds removed; chopped
1 red bell pepper; stem, ribs, and seeds removed; chopped
1/8 teaspoon cayenne pepper (optional)
6 cups chicken stock
1 1/2 cups coarsely chopped canned tomatoes with their juice
1 teaspoon ground coriander
1 teaspoon dried thyme, crushed
2 bay leaves
1/4 to 1/2 teaspoon crushed red pepper flakes
1/4 cup all-purpose flour
1/2 pound fresh okra, tops trimmed and pods sliced into rings,
  or frozen cut okra, thawed
Cooked white rice, for serving

1. Season the chicken with the 3/4 teaspoon salt and 1/4 teaspoon black pepper. Heat the oil in a large stewpot and brown the chicken over high heat, 7 to 10 minutes. Add the sausage and cook for 2 to 3 minutes longer, turning often. Remove the sausage and chicken and set them aside.

2. Drain all but 3 tablespoons of the fat from the pot and reserve the pan drippings for making a roux. Add the onion and garlic to the pot and fry over medium heat for 3 to 4 minutes, scraping up any browned bits from the bottom of the pot with a wooden spoon. Add the bell peppers, the cayenne (if using), and ¼ teaspoon black pepper, and cook for 5 minutes more or until the vegetables are softened. Return the meat to the pot, along with the chicken stock, tomatoes, coriander, thyme, bay leaves, and red pepper flakes to taste. Simmer the stew uncovered for 45 minutes. Skim any excess fat and scum that may come to the surface of the stew.

3. While the meat is stewing, make the roux. Heat the 3 tablespoons of reserved pan drippings in a small cast-iron skillet, and stir in the flour with a wooden spoon. Cook over medium heat, stirring constantly, until the roux is chocolate brown, 7 to 8 minutes. Carefully scrape the roux into a heatproof bowl; it is very hot and will continue to cook in the bowl. Set aside.

4. Add the okra to the stewpot. Continue to simmer over medium heat for 10 minutes, or until the okra softens. Whisk the roux into the stew and bring to a boil. Continue to simmer the stew for 15 minutes. Adjust the seasoning to taste with salt and pepper. Remove the bay leaves. Serve over the rice.

> Okra is a member of the hibiscus family. The finger-shaped pods grow on 3- to 4-foot-tall plants. When buying okra, look for 3-inch-long green pods that are clean and firm. Okra is sometimes, but rarely, red. It is a source of calcium, as well as phosphorus, potassium, iron, and vitamins A and C. Okra contains only 140 calories per pound.

★ **WHAT TO TASTE AND WHERE TO TASTE IT** ★

Turducken

K-PAUL'S LOUISIANA KITCHEN
416 Chartres Street ★ New Orleans ★ (504) 524-7394

For significant feasts during the Renaissance, chefs would bone pigeons, ducks, geese, chickens, and turkeys and then stuff the smaller birds inside the larger ones. Paul Prudhomme saw historical references to this, and invented his own version consisting of a boned chicken stuffed in a boned duck stuffed in a boned turkey with dressing layered between each of the birds. He called it the turducken. Today, turduckens can be found all over the United States, but the place to eat the best is still at K-Paul's in New Orleans, which serves it only on Thanksgiving Eve. For those unable to make it to K-Paul's, Prudhomme published his recipe in *The Prudhomme Family Cookbook.*

Shrimp Bisque

MAKES 6 SERVINGS

A bisque is a shellfish-based cream soup developed by French cooks, who may use crayfish, lobster, shrimp, or crab. Modern cooks have stretched the meaning of bisque and now make tomato and vegetable bisques, using the name whenever they thicken a soup with fresh heavy cream. The Cajuns of southwest Louisiana make a delicious crawfish bisque that includes cayenne pepper and whole crawfish floating in the broth.

4 tablespoons ($\frac{1}{2}$ stick) unsalted butter
1 carrot, chopped
1 leek, chopped
$\frac{1}{4}$ cup chopped shallots
1 rib celery, chopped
$\frac{3}{4}$ pound medium shrimp, peeled and deveined
$\frac{1}{4}$ cup brandy, optional
3 cups fish stock or 1$\frac{1}{2}$ cups bottled clam juice mixed with 1$\frac{1}{2}$ cups water
1 cup dry white wine
2 tablespoons tomato puree
4 sprigs fresh parsley
$\frac{1}{8}$ teaspoon dried basil
$\frac{1}{8}$ teaspoon dried oregano
$\frac{1}{8}$ teaspoon dried thyme
$\frac{1}{8}$ teaspoon dried tarragon
3 tablespoons raw long-grain white rice
$\frac{1}{2}$ cup heavy cream
Salt and freshly ground white pepper

1. In a stockpot or large saucepan, melt the butter over moderate heat. Add the carrot, leek, shallots, and celery; cook, covered, until softened, about 5 minutes. Stir in the shrimp and cook for about 2 minutes, just until the shrimp turn pink.

2. Add the brandy, if desired. Add the fish stock, wine, tomato puree, parsley, and 1 cup water. Crush the dried basil, oregano, thyme, and tarragon in the palm of your hand and add them to the pot. Bring to a simmer. Add the rice and simmer, uncovered, for about 20 minutes, until the rice is very tender.

3. Puree the soup in a food processor or blender until smooth.

4. Return the soup to the pot and stir in the heavy cream. Season to taste with salt and white pepper. (If using clam juice, season carefully as it is quite salty.) If the soup is too thick, thin with a little white wine, fish stock, or water.

Brandy is an alcoholic liquor distilled from grape wine or the fermented juice of apples, cherries, pears, or other fruits. The distillation process consists of heating the wine or fruit juice to vapor, passing the vapor through metal tubing, and then cooling it back to a liquid state. The "spirit" of the wine is captured in the brandy, which is placed in oak barrels and left to age for several years. The aging process gives brandy a distinctive color, taste, and smell.

Brandy is a large generic term that encompasses many different types. Cognac and Armagnac, which are made from wine, and Calvados, made from apple cider, are the most famous brandies of France.

BOIL AND SETTLE

New Orleans is famous not only for gumbo, an adaptation of bouillabaisse, but also for its bouillabaisse proper, the traditional fisherman's stew that originated in Marseilles. The word bouillabaisse (some say) comes from the Provençal bouiabaisso, which means "boil and settle," indicating that the stew should be brought to a boil only briefly. Bouillabaisse was made from a variety of local seafood—rascasse, John Dory, whiting, eel, and spiny lobster, among others—all easily available in the Mediterranean coast of France. The French brought the recipe to Louisiana, and according to New Orleans lore the famous British author William Makepeace Thackeray is reported to have said, "In New Orleans you can eat a Bouillabaisse, the like of which was never eaten in Marseilles or Paris." Surprising, when you consider that Thackeray never visited New Orleans. But he surely loved the dish; in 1855, he published "Ballad to Bouillabaisse," which included these immortal lines:

This Bouillabaisse a noble dish is—
A sort of soup, or broth, or brew,
Or hotchpotch of all sorts of fishes,
That Greenwich never could outdo;
Green herbs, red peppers, mussels, saffron,
Soles, onions, garlic, roach and dace.

Mini Crab Cakes with Rémoulade Sauce

MAKES ABOUT 30 SMALL CAKES

Crabs were once common along America's eastern shore and the Gulf Coast. The first crab cakes were likely based on fish cake recipes that had been made by Europeans for centuries. During the early twentieth century, crab cakes became popular around the Chesapeake Bay and in New Orleans.

2 tablespoons unsalted butter
2 scallions, white and green parts minced
1 rib celery, minced
1 medium clove garlic, minced
1 pound lump crab meat, cleaned and picked over to remove any bits of shell
2 large eggs, lightly beaten
2 teaspoons fresh lemon juice
2 tablespoons whole-grain mustard
2 tablespoons minced fresh flat-leaf parsley
1 teaspoon kosher salt
½ teaspoon freshly ground black pepper
Pinch of freshly grated nutmeg
⅓ cup cracker meal, plus more for dredging
⅔ cup vegetable oil, for frying
Rémoulade Sauce

1. In a medium skillet, heat the butter; add the scallions, celery, and garlic, and cook over medium heat until the vegetables are translucent, 3 to 4 minutes.

2. In a medium bowl, combine the cooked vegetables with the crab, eggs, lemon juice, mustard, and parsley. Season with the salt, pepper, and nutmeg. Add the cracker meal and stir well to combine thoroughly. Form heaping tablespoons of the crab mixture into 1½ inch-round cakes. Roll the cakes in additional cracker meal and place them on a baking pan. Refrigerate for at least 30 minutes before cooking.

3. When ready to serve, heat a large skillet. Pour the oil into the skillet to a depth of ½-inch. Heat the oil over medium heat, keeping the oil at a low simmer; cook and brown the cakes for 1 to 2 minutes on the first side and about 1 minute on the second side, or until they are cooked through and golden brown. Transfer the cakes to paper towels to drain. Serve the cakes warm, with the Rémoulade Sauce.

RÉMOULADE SAUCE

MAKES ABOUT 1 CUP

⅔ cup mayonnaise

2 scallions, white and green parts chopped

2 tablespoons finely minced fresh flat-leaf parsley

2 tablespoons minced fresh dill

1 teaspoon fresh lemon juice

2 tablespoons drained white horseradish

4 tablespoons whole-grain mustard

1 tablespoon ketchup

1 teaspoon Worcestershire sauce

1 tablespoon sweet paprika

½ teaspoon kosher salt

⅛ teaspoon freshly ground black pepper

Tabasco sauce to taste

In a small bowl, whisk all of the ingredients together and refrigerate until ready to serve.

★ **WHAT TO TASTE AND WHERE TO TASTE IT** ★

Oysters

CASAMENTO'S RESTAURANT

4330 Magazine Street ★ New Orleans ★ (504) 895-9761

Established in 1919 by Joe Casamento, this restaurant serves excellent oysters.
If you are not an oyster fan, try the soft-shell crabs, fried shrimp, and trout.

Shrimp Creole

MAKES 4 SERVINGS

Shrimp is an important part of culinary life along the Gulf Coast, and many dishes using it have been derived from Cajun and Creole sources. Shrimp Creole was likely prepared in New Orleans for many years, but it wasn't until the mid-twentieth century that the dish was popularized throughout the United States.

FOR THE CREOLE SAUCE:

2 tablespoons vegetable oil

1 onion, chopped

2 bell peppers (red or green), chopped

3 cups diced tomatoes

3 ribs celery, chopped

2 cups tomato puree

1 teaspoon cayenne pepper

2 tablespoons chopped garlic

1 tablespoon chopped fresh parsley

1 cup chicken stock

Salt and freshly ground black pepper, to taste

4 drops Tabasco sauce

FOR THE SHRIMP:

½ cup unsalted butter

24 large shrimp, shelled and deveined

A few sprigs fresh parsley

Cooked rice

1. TO MAKE THE SAUCE: Heat the vegetable oil in a large saucepan. Add the onion, bell peppers, and tomatoes. Cook and stir for 1 minute. Add the celery. Stir and add the tomato puree. Simmer for 5 minutes.

2. Stir in the remaining sauce ingredients. Reduce the heat and simmer for 7 minutes.

3. Melt the butter in a large sauté pan over moderate heat. Add the shrimp and parsley and sauté for 4 minutes.

4. Stir in the Creole Sauce and serve over the rice.

Muffalettas

CENTRAL GROCERY CO.
923 Decatur Street ★ New Orleans ★ (504) 523-1620

Central Grocery is, in fact, a grocery store filled with the aromas of spices, cheese, and charcuterie, but it also serves food. It is touted as the point of origin for muffaletta sandwiches, which are served in the Central Grocery sandwich shop.

Brennan's Bananas Foster

MAKES 4 SERVINGS

Bananas Foster is a flaming dessert sauce that is spooned over ice cream. It was developed at Brennan's restaurant in New Orleans in 1950. In the late 1940s, New Orleans was the nation's largest banana port. There were bananas all over the French Quarter. Owen E. Brennan, Sr. commissioned his chef Paul Blange to create a dish using bananas. The dish Blange developed is named after Richard Foster, a New Orleans businessman who was a regular customer and friend at Brennan's.

4 tablespoons (½ stick) unsalted butter
1 cup brown sugar
Pinch of ground cinnamon
4 bananas, peeled and halved lengthwise
¼ cup rum
Vanilla ice cream

1. In a sauté pan combine the butter, sugar, and cinnamon over moderate heat. and cook for about 3 minutes, until the sugar dissolves.

2. Add the bananas to the mixture and cook for 30 seconds. Stir in the rum. Cook for 1 minute. Very carefully, use a long match to ignite the sauce. Shake the pan until the flames subside.

3. Spoon the sauce over vanilla ice cream.

ICE CREAM HISTORY

Ice cream was a hot commodity in early America. George Washington owned a "cream machine for making ice" and Thomas Jefferson's recipe for making ice cream is still used today. In 1846, Nancy Johnson took a wooden bucket, filled it with ice and salt, and fitted within it a metal can equipped with beaters powered by a crank. Unfortunately for her, Nancy didn't patent her invention and imitators proliferated. German immigrants spread their love of ice cream in the 1880s and 1890s when they began opening candy stores, soda fountains, and ice cream stores across the United States.

Creole Praline Candies

MAKES ABOUT 2 DOZEN PIECES

A praline is a candy made from caramelized sugar and almonds or pecans. American Creoles imported the recipe from France, where it was invented by the chef of the French diplomat César, comte du Plessis-Praslin, who believed that sugar and nuts aided digestion. He may not have been right about that, but pralines are delicious, and are still extremely popular in New Orleans.

1 cup granulated sugar
1 cup packed light brown sugar
½ cup heavy cream
2 tablespoons (¼ stick) unsalted butter
1 cup pecan pieces

1. In a large heavy saucepan, combine the sugars, heavy cream, and butter. Cook, uncovered, over medium heat until the mixture boils and registers 238 degrees F on a candy thermometer, or until a sample of the mixture forms a soft ball in cold water.

2. Take the pot off the heat and stir in the pecans. Beat for about 3 minutes or until creamy and somewhat cooled.

3. Drop the mixture by tablespoonfuls onto a double thickness of wax paper. The pralines will harden in about 15 minutes and be ready to eat.

Peanut Butter Pie

MAKES ONE 8-INCH PIE, 6 TO 8 SERVINGS

Peanuts originated in South America. They were exported to Africa shortly after Europeans arrived in the New World and the slave trade introduced them into North America, where they thrived in the South. Peanut Butter Pie is an American tradition that reached the pinnacle of success in New Orleans.

FOR THE CRUST

1½ cups finely ground graham cracker crumbs
6 tablespoons (¾ stick) unsalted butter or margarine, melted
2 tablespoons superfine sugar
2 teaspoons unsweetened cocoa powder
2 tablespoons peanut butter

FOR THE FILLING

1 (8-ounce) package cream cheese
¼ cup peanut butter
½ cup granulated sugar
¼ cup chopped unsalted roasted peanuts
1 teaspoon vanilla extract
¾ cup heavy cream
Whipped cream, chocolate syrup, and chopped peanuts, for garnish (optional)

1. TO MAKE THE CRUST: Preheat the oven to 300 degrees F. Combine the graham cracker crumbs with the butter, superfine sugar, cocoa, and peanut butter. Mix until completely blended. Press into an ungreased 8-inch pie pan and bake for 15 minutes. Cool completely.

2. TO MAKE THE FILLING: Using an electric mixer, beat the cream cheese, peanut butter, and granulated sugar together until light. Add the peanuts and vanilla and continue to beat until well blended.

3. In a separate bowl, with clean beaters, whip the heavy cream until stiff peaks form. Fold about one-third of the whipped cream into the cream cheese mixture to lighten it, then add the remaining cream and fold in carefully and quickly, so as not to deflate the whipped cream.

4. Fill the cooled pie shell with filling. Chill at least 2 hours in the refrigerator. If desired, garnish each slice with whipped cream, chocolate syrup, and/or chopped peanuts.

Chocolate Bread Pudding

MAKES 4 TO 6 SERVINGS

This recipe includes both chocolate and vanilla—both of which originated in the New World. When chocolate arrived in Europe it was considered a "food of the gods," and vanilla was just as well received. This recipe includes pecans, which are one of the traditional foods of New Orleans.

2 cups whole milk
2 cups half-and-half
6 ounces semisweet chocolate, chopped
1 teaspoon vanilla extract
1/2 teaspoon ground cinnamon
4 large eggs
1 cup light brown sugar
2 tablespoons (1/4 stick) unsalted butter, melted
6 cups (1-inch pieces) quality French bread, left out overnight to dry
1/2 cup chopped pecans
1/2 cup heavy cream
2 tablespoons confectioners' sugar
1 tablespoon dark rum

1. In a medium saucepan, bring the milk and half-and-half just to a boil. Remove the pan from the heat and add the chocolate, vanilla, and cinnamon. Whisk briskly until the chocolate is melted.

2. In a medium bowl, whisk together the eggs and brown sugar. Slowly whisk the chocolate-flavored milk into the eggs.

3. Preheat the oven to 325 degrees F. Lightly brush an 8-inch round, 4-inch deep baking dish or casserole with some of the melted butter. Put the bread into the baking dish and cover with the custard; stir in the remaining butter. Let the pudding sit for 30 minutes, occasionally pressing the bread cubes into the liquid to saturate them, until the bread absorbs most of the custard.

4. Sprinkle the top of the bread pudding with the pecans. Cover with foil and bake for 40 minutes. Remove the foil and continue to bake for another 20 minutes or until the pudding is set. Remove from the oven and cool slightly.

5. Whip the cream in a chilled bowl until the cream holds soft peaks; don't overwhip the cream or it will be grainy. Fold in the confectioners' sugar and rum. Serve the bread pudding warm, with a dollop of the whipped cream.

SAN ANTONIO
Texas

O N January 17, 1690, Spanish explorers heading north from Mexico crossed an uncharted river; because it was St. Anthony's Day, they named it the San Antonio. But it wasn't until 1718, when the Spanish established a fort at the river head, that San Antonio became the first permanent settlement in Texas. Franciscan missionaries founded the San Antonio de Valero mission near the fort so they could minister to the local American Indians. The settlement wasn't much—its total population, including the Indians, probably numbered no more than two thousand—but it was the capital of Spanish Texas, which was part of Mexico. Much of the settlers' food had to be imported from Mexico, and luxuries were scarce. To pay for what they needed, San Antonio ranchers raised beef, which was an important part of the cuisine of northern Mexico.

Spain closed the San Antonio mission in 1793, and it became a military outpost called the Alamo. No one knows for sure how the Alamo acquired its name, but most likely it was because the soldiers stationed there were from El Alamo in Coahuila, Mexico.

When Mexico gained its independence from Spain in 1821, there were only two small towns in Texas, San Antonio and Goliad, and the entire territory had no more than five thousand inhabitants. San Antonio suffered during the Mexican war for independence from Spain, and again when Texas fought for its own independence, particularly during the famous 1836 battle of the Alamo. The United States annexed Texas in 1845, much to the joy of many Texans. Fifteen years later, the same Texans didn't like the ways things were going, so they seceded from the United States and joined the Confederacy. Unlike most other southern cities, San Antonio came through the Civil War almost untouched.

After the war, the city began to grow, and a number of different immigrant groups arrived, notably a large contingent of Germans, who brought their culinary traditions with them. They enjoyed particular types of meat and meat dishes, like Wiener schnitzel. They kept up the German tradition of great breads and sweet baked goods like pfeffernüesse and stollen. By 1877, people of German heritage were the largest group in San Antonio. Their interaction with the Mexicans and Anglos of the city would create a unique cuisine.

INNOCENT STRANGERS

San Antonio began as a Mexican community, and the strongest influence on its foodways still comes from northern Mexico. In the early years, San Antonio's central plaza teemed with open-air tables offering traditional Mexican foods: tamales, tortillas, chiles rellenos, beans, enchiladas, and many more.

Some distinctive Mexican-derived dishes were born in San Antonio. One was chili con carne, a thick, stewlike dish of chopped or shredded beef seasoned with hot peppers, onions, and garlic. The term itself was an Americanization. The proper

---

★ WHAT TO TASTE AND WHERE TO TASTE IT ★

Mexican

LIBERTY BAR
328 East Josephine Street ★ San Antonio ★ (210) 227-1187
Constructed in 1890, the building housing the Liberty Bar has rested askew atop its foundations since a 1921 flood. This eclectic restaurant offers excellent chicken dishes, pot roast, homemade breads, and southern desserts, and features mesquite-grilled meats. Chef Oscar Trejo also dishes out top-flight Mexican foods.

ROSARIO'S CAFÉ AND CANTINA
910 South Alamo Street ★ San Antonio ★ (210) 223-1806
Owner and chef Lisa Wong prepares excellent enchiladas and unusual dishes like "Mexican Caesar" salad. On Friday evenings there is live music from local bands, but be prepared for crowds.

Mexican term for the dish is *carne con chiles*, emphasizing the meat and not the chile. An Anglo visitor to San Antonio, describing this local specialty, wrote, "The innocent stranger who conspicuously takes a mouthful of chile con carne never inquires what the other ingredients are. His only thought is how to obtain the services of the fire department to put out the fire in the roof of his mouth." Despite its fiery chile seasoning—or perhaps because of it—chili con carne became a popular dish in Texas and throughout the American Southwest. By the 1890s, this dish had penetrated as far north as New York City. In Chicago, a San Antonio chile stand was set up on the grounds of the Columbian Exposition in 1893. Some Mexicans were irked by the presentation of chili con carne as an authentic Mexican dish; Francisco J. Santamaria, author of *El diccionario general de americanismos*, declared it "a detestable dish identified under the false title of Mexican." Today, chili con carne, more often called simply "chili," is one of the core dishes of Tex-Mex cuisine, and a nationwide favorite.

CHILEHEADS

Before Texas became a state, most Americans had never tasted hot chiles. As chili con carne and other Mexican-style dishes made their way though the United States, chile peppers took on more significance. In an effort to supply the ready market for chiles and Mexican foods, a number of Texas companies began packaging them for distribution. The first known manufacturing of Mexican food in this country occurred in the 1870s, when an Anglo-Texan began selling his canned Montezuma Sauce, which was filled with chiles and goat meat. It was not the overwhelming success he had hoped it would be.

★ WHAT TO TASTE AND WHERE TO TASTE IT ★

Tamales

TÉLLEZ TAMALES & BARBACOA
1737 South General McMullen Street ★ San Antonio ★ (210) 433-1367

Tamales were a common food in Mexico in pre-Columbian times. They were made in various ways, but were generally composed of cooked beans encased in cornmeal dough. The tamales were wrapped and tied in cornhusks, and then boiled. Mexican Indians brought tamale making to San Antonio in the seventeenth century, and it has thrived there ever since. Today, tamales may be filled with beef, pork, or chicken along with beans. The best tamales in San Antonio are served at Téllez Tamales & Barbacoa, where they have been handmade in the traditional way for the past forty years.

TASTING CHILES

Chile peppers (capsicums) get their heat from capsaicin, the family name of a group of eight alkaloids. The main difference among the alkaloids is the speed with which each reacts with moisture in the mouth to cause a burning sensation. Small-fruited types of chiles, such as habaneros, are generally hotter than large peppers. The heat factor of peppers is measured in Scoville heat units. A jalapeño has 80,000 Scoville heat units, while habaneros from Jamaica or the Yucatán and Scotch bonnet peppers have been found to have 550,000 heat units. There are hundreds of varieties of chiles. Below we've grouped a few common chiles based on their heat.

MILD
BELL: These look identical to sweet bell peppers but they are mildly hot.
CAYENNE: Slender, deep-red peppers often used in Cajun recipes.
POBLANO: Mild, large, and frequently used for stuffing.

MEDIUM
ANAHEIM: Medium to hot pungency; commonly used in salsas and for stuffing.
BIRD'S EYE: Small, may be dark or light green depending on the variety.
JALAPEÑO: These thick-fleshed little peppers are usually sold green in the United States.

HOT
HABANERO: May range from yellow to red; used in making blistering hot sauces.
SCOTCH BONNET: Almost indistinguishable from the habanero, but are slightly smaller; popular in the Caribbean.
SERRANO: Bright red or green, slightly smaller than habaneros, and extremely hot.

Another entrepreneur who thought there was money to be made in packaged Mexican foods was a German immigrant named William Gebhardt. In around 1885, he settled in New Braunfels, Texas, just thirty-five miles from San Antonio. Gebhardt opened a café where the dishes were spiced with chiles imported from Mexico. To keep his staple seasoning on hand for ready use, Gebhardt borrowed a traditional way of preserving chiles: He dried them and crushed them into powder. Unlike previous makers of chile powder, he bottled and sold it. In 1890, his business expanding, he opened a factory in San Antonio. To make more useful seasoning, Gebhardt combined the powdered chiles with dried and ground garlic, oregano, and cumin. This chili powder eliminated the need to handle fresh chiles (which can burn skin and eyes), so any housewife or cook could easily prepare chili con carne and other Mexican dishes. Gebhardt launched a sales campaign promoting his chili powder throughout the Midwest, and he trademarked the name "Gebhardt's Eagle Brand Chili Powder." The powder was perceived to be such an essential ingredient that cookbooks specified it by name in Mexican-style recipes.

When Gebhardt began marketing chili powder north of the Texas border, he ran into a serious stumbling block: Non-Texans had little idea what to do with the stuff. So in 1908 Gebhardt produced a thirty-two-page cookery pamphlet introducing basic Tex-Mex dishes. This little booklet was the first Mexican-American cookbook printed in English in the United States. It proved so successful that updated editions were regularly published through the 1950s.

Gebhardt sold his company to his brother-in-law, who expanded the product line to include canned beans and tamales. During the 1920s, the company introduced Gebhardt's Original Mexican Dinner Package, consisting of cans of chili con carne, Mexican-style beans, shuck-wrapped tamales, deviled chili meat, and a bottle of chili powder—all for the price of one dollar. By the 1930s, Gebhardt products were being sold throughout the United States and Mexico.

While Gebhardt was the first successful packager of chile products in the United States, he was followed by many others. Chile beans became a common food in mainstream America, and chiles were added to many other traditional American recipes. As chile peppers became more popular in the United States, fresh chiles, mainly jalapeños, began to appear in supermarkets. So did dozens of other chiles, from the mild Anaheim chiles to the extremely hot habaneros. In the late twentieth century, other chile-heavy cuisines, such as Szechwan and Thai, became popular, and a wider variety of fresh, dried, and powdered chiles—as well as expanded lines of Mexican groceries—took their places in the supermarket.

★ WHAT TO TASTE AND WHERE TO TASTE IT ★

Caribbean and Latin American

AZUCA
713 South Alamo Street ★ San Antonio ★ (210) 225-5550

Chef Rene Fernandez and his partner, Pierre Kranzle, describe their menu as "nuevo Latino," which means that the exotic foods on the menu are cooked Latin-style, with plenty of fresh and unusual ingredients like taro, yuca, and white yams. Appetizers include crab cakes and coconut shrimp. The *parillada mixta* is a mixed grill of beef, chicken, pork, and sausage in chimichurri sauce (jalapeño peppers, garlic, oregano, parsley, wine vinegar, and olive oil). For dessert, try the caramelized banana crêpes. On Thursday evenings there is flamenco music; on Friday and Saturday nights it's salsa and merengue bands.

During the late twentieth century, chile consumption developed a cultlike following. Serious aficionados, self-described "chileheads," competed in chili cook-offs throughout America. There is even a magazine, *Chile Pepper*, devoted to hot peppers. Chili is so important in Texas that the state legislature voted it the Texas state dish.

WHERE'S THE BEEF?

The Old West is a treasured part of America's heritage—cattle ranches, cowboy hats, chuckwagons, and bucking broncos. We can thank the Spanish and Mexicans, who introduced cattle into Texas, for these traditions. In the early days, beef was a major food source (and income source) around San Antonio, and it still is. The first cattle drives began in San Antonio, heading south to Saltillo, Mexico. After American annexation of Texas, cowboys began driving cattle north to feed urban populations in the Midwest and beyond.

In Texas, beef is served in many ways, including some that are particularly identified with the state: barbecue, chicken-fried steak, fajitas, and chili con carne. While the early history of barbecue is murky, traditional Texas-style barbecue is slow cooking of large cuts of meat—sometimes half a steer—in pits heated with smoldering mesquite and covered with earth. This ancient cooking method, which dates back to pre-Columbian times in the Americas, turns even tough beef into a tender, smoke-infused delicacy.

Although not peculiar to San Antonio, a favorite Texas beef dish is chicken-fried steak (a.k.a. country-fried steak), affectionately known as CFS. Chicken-fried steak may have been a creation of German immigrants who ate something similar, Wiener schnitzel (a Viennese specialty of pounded veal scallops, breaded and fried). "Chicken-fried" refers to the fact that the steak—often a cheap, tough piece of beef that has been pounded to tenderize it—is coated with egg and flour and then fried. After the steak is cooked, gravy is made from the pan drippings and milk. Although the earliest published recipe for chicken-fried steak dates only to 1949, the dish had been around for generations before that time. CFS is common throughout much of the South and parts of the West and Midwest, and many Texans consider it the unofficial state food. It's always on the menu at roadside dinners, where you can tell the quality of the CFS by the number of pickup trucks parked out front.

═══ HOW MEXICAN FOOD WAS NATURALIZED ═══

Chili con carne is, of course, just one dish in the wide selection of Tex-Mex dishes. Two other Tex-Mex specialties are margaritas and nachos. The margarita, now known around the world, is a cocktail served in a salt-rimmed glass. The components are tequila, orange liqueur (Triple Sec or Cointreau), and lime juice. While the exact date and place of origin of the margarita is unknown, it became extremely popular in bars throughout America during the 1960s. It is a staple in Mexican restaurants in the United States, but in Mexico you'll find margaritas mostly in places catering to the tourist trade, as no self-respecting tequila aficionado would sully the good stuff by mixing it with other ingredients. Since its initial popularity, the margarita has been subject to many variations, some intended to disguise the flavor of tequila, which some Americans don't appreciate. It's believed that Mariano Martinez, Jr., assembled the first frozen margarita in 1971 at Dallas's El Charro Bar.

Another favorite Tex-Mex food in America are nachos, another dish with a mysteri-

---

★ WHAT TO TASTE AND WHERE TO TASTE IT ★

Puffy Tacos

RAY'S DRIVE INN
822 Southwest 19th Street ★ San Antonio ★ (210) 432-7171

Mexican tacos are basically any food rolled, folded, or fried into tortillas that are consumed by hand. The various fillings for tacos include chili sauce, beef (shredded or ground), chicken, pork, chorizo or other sausage, egg, tomato, cheese, lettuce, guacamole, onions, and refried beans. Mexican tacos are usually soft-shelled, unlike the U-shaped crisp fried tortillas served in many American Mexican restaurants and fast-food outlets. What's characteristic about Tex-Mex tacos is that they're puffy, and there is no better place to taste puffy tacos than at Ray's Drive Inn.

Southwestern

BIGA ON THE BANK

203 South St. Mary's Street ★ San Antonio ★ (210) 225-0722

Chef Bruce Auden is a San Antonio star who has created an elegant restaurant with a creative menu. Appetizers include smoked-salmon nachos and chicken-fried oysters. Other unusual dishes include foie gras served with a maple waffle. Featured dishes change nightly, but always include his signature dishes like phyllo-wrapped sea bass with creamy mustard leeks.

ous past. A man named Ignacio (Nacho) Ahaya claimed to have created them and put his name on them. As the story goes, Ahaya was asked to prepare a snack for Anglo officers' wives while the cook was out. He "grabbed a bunch of fried tortillas, put some yellow cheese on the tortillas, let it heat a little bit, then put some sliced jalapeños on top." Wherever they originated, nachos quickly spread throughout Texas, where they were served at a concession at Dallas's State Fair in 1964. Within two decades, nachos could be found in bars, football stadiums, airports, and fast-food establishments all over the country.

THE CHIP THAT LAUNCHED A THOUSAND SNACKS

In Mexican homes, leftover tortillas never go to waste, and one way to make them more appealing is to cut them in pieces and fry them into crisp chips. Different people made them in different ways. In San Antonio, residents made *friotes* from fried masa (corn flour). According to legend, Elmer Doolin sampled some, liked what he ate, and purportedly bought the recipe for one hundred dollars. He had three problems. The first was that the fried tortilla chips were too big to put into the small waxed paper packages then available, so Doolin reduced their size. Then the tortilla chips were bland, so he added plenty of salt and other flavorings. Then he needed a name that would help sell his new product, so he came up with "Fritos." In the midst of the Depression, he launched America's first corn-chip business. Potato chips had been around for decades, but they had just become commercially viable with the invention of packaging that kept them fresh. Doolin used this new technology for his corn chips, and his market expanded as far as St. Louis. A world-changing event took place in 1945 when Doolin met Herman W. Lay, then a prominent potato-chip manufacturer. Lay agreed to distribute Fritos nationally, and the "Frito-Lay" partnership was born. Lay bought Doolin's company in

1949, but because Fritos had been such a marketing success, he made "Frito-Lay" the name of the newly expanded company. Though the Frito-Lay Company eventually moved to Dallas, San Antonio can be said to be the home of the American corn chip.

An early advertising figure used to sell the corn chips was the Frito Kid. In 1963, the company tried replacing the Kid with Frito Bandito, which appalled the Mexican-American community; the Frito Bandito quickly became history. At about this same time, the Frito pie came into fashion. This homemade favorite is created by pouring a portion of hot chili into a partially opened bag of Fritos, then topping this with grated cheese and chopped onions. Today, Frito pie gourmets make them in a dish, not in the bag.

The success of corn chips went hand-in-hand with the growing popularity of salsas, which in the United States are generally uncooked dipping sauces based on tomatoes (or tomatillos) and chile peppers. Salsalike mixtures have been around since Aztec times. The first known commercial producer of salsa was Pace Foods of San Antonio. Dave Pace experimented with bottling salsa in 1947, getting the formula precisely to his taste the following year. Pace's initial market was regional, but the fresh-salsa market exploded during the 1980s and continued to increase during the following decade. By the 1990s, salsa had become a real American food, with sales approaching and occasionally surpassing that of America's traditional king of condiments, ketchup.

ATTENDING CHURCH'S

In 1952, George W. Church, Sr., a retired incubator salesman, launched Church's Fried Chicken to Go in downtown San Antonio. It was a low-overhead operation that sold only take-out, but what was distinctive about Church's was that it served larger chickens than its competitors did. At first, Church's only sold fried chicken; French fries and jalapeños were added in 1955. When George Church died in 1956, four outlets had been opened. Family members took over the operation, and by 1962 the chain had grown to eight locations in San Antonio. The company began an expansion beyond San Antonio. The Church family sold the company in 1968, and the following year Church's Fried Chicken, Inc., became a publicly held company. In addition to its chicken, Church's also serves commercial versions of real American foods—fried okra, coleslaw, mashed potatoes, corn on the cob, and honey-butter biscuits.

HUNGERING FOR SAN ANTONIO

Today, San Antonio is the second-largest city in Texas and the eighth-largest city in the United States. While the majority of people in San Antonio trace their heritage to Mexico, the city boasts many different ethnic strains. New immigrants from Latin America and Asia have made San Antonio their home, and this diversity has contributed to the city's vibrant culinary life. Visitors to San Antonio can satisfy their hunger at German delis, Mexican, Latin, and French restaurants, barbecue joints, and southwestern eateries. Fiesta San Antonio, an annual ten-day celebration in late April, includes many events and plenty of multicultural food. Along the Riverwalk, a revitalized one-mile stretch along the San Antonio River, you'll find cafés, restaurants, and shops catering to tourists.

★ WHAT TO TASTE AND WHERE TO TASTE IT ★

German

SCHILO'S DELICATESSEN
424 East Commerce Street ★ San Antonio ★ (210) 223-6692

Established more than eighty years ago, this deli, located on the Riverwalk, offers a variety of traditional German foods. There are hearty, filling soups (split pea with ham is excellent) and sandwiches—try the Reuben or one made from the imported and fresh-made deli meats and sausages. They also have house-made root beer and a wide selection of German beers. Don't miss the sweet strudels for dessert.

Huevos Rancheros

MAKES 4 SERVINGS

Huevos Rancheros is a breakfast dish of Mexican origins common in San Antonio restaurants. Most American recipes for it have been modified to suit American sensibilities. If you want the real thing, add plenty of spicy salsa.

4 corn tortillas
2 tablespoons corn oil
8 large eggs
1 to 1½ cups Enchilada Sauce (recipe follows)
1 cup grated Monterey Jack or sharp Cheddar cheese (about ¼ pound)
Salsa, sour cream, chopped cilantro for garnish (optional)

1. Preheat the oven to 400 degrees F. Wrap the tortillas in foil and set them in the oven.

2. Heat 2 large skillets, preferably nonstick, over medium heat. Add 1 tablespoon corn oil to each skillet. When the oil is hot, fry the eggs for 2 minutes, then cover the skillet and cook for 30 seconds to 1 minute, until the tops are opaque. Remove the skillets from the heat.

3. Remove the tortillas from the oven, unwrap them and lay them flat in a baking pan. Leave the oven on, or preheat the broiler. Spread 2 tablespoons of enchilada sauce over each tortilla. Then with a spatula, gently transfer 2 fried eggs to each tortilla and sprinkle the eggs with ¼ cup of cheese. Broil or bake until the cheese begins to melt, about 30 seconds.

4. Transfer each tortilla to a warmed plate and spoon about ¼ cup of enchilada sauce around the edge of each tortilla. If you wish, top each portion with salsa, sour cream, and cilantro. Serve immediately.

HOW CHEDDAR CHANGED ITS NAME

Cheddar cheese gets its name from the English town where it was originally produced. During the Revolutionary War, Americans did not want to eat a cheese named after a city in enemy territory. So they renamed it American cheese.

ENCHILADA SAUCE

MAKES ABOUT 4 CUPS

*4 ounces whole dried pasilla chile peppers or 2 ounces pasillas combined with 2
     ounces New Mexican or ancho chiles*

½ cup rice vinegar

3 tablespoons corn oil

1 medium onion, finely chopped

2 tablespoons sesame seeds

4 medium cloves garlic, minced

¼ teaspoon ground cloves

½ teaspoon ground cinnamon

1 (14.5-ounce) can whole tomatoes, drained and chopped

1 teaspoon unsweetened cocoa powder

1 corn tortilla, cut into shreds

1 teaspoon salt, or to taste

1. With scissors, cut off the chile stems and slice the peppers open lengthwise. Discard the seeds. Cut the chiles in half and set them in a heatproof bowl.

2. Bring 4 cups water and the vinegar to a boil, pour over the chiles and let them steep for 30 minutes, until softened.

3. In a heavy 4-quart saucepan, heat the oil over high heat. Add the onion and sauté, stirring frequently, for about 5 minutes or until golden brown. Add the sesame seeds and garlic and sauté for a minute, stirring, until the sesame seeds begin to turn color. Stir in the cloves and cinnamon, then immediately add the tomatoes and the chiles with the liquid in which they were steeping. Bring to a simmer, cover, and simmer over low heat for 30 minutes. Stir in the cocoa powder and tortilla, and remove from the heat. Let cool for 30 minutes.

4. In a blender, in batches, puree the sauce until smooth. Season with salt to taste.

The flavor and amount of "heat" depends on the type of chile peppers you use. If you like your sauce less fiery, mix the pasillas with milder New Mexican or ancho peppers. Handle the chile peppers with surgical gloves and keep your hands away from your face.

Rice vinegar is as tangy as regular vinegar, only it is made from fermented rice rather than apple cider or grape wine. Rice vinegar is preferred in Asian dishes because of its unique flavor. Substitute a light cider vinegar if absolutely necessary, but avoid wine vinegars for recipes that call for rice vinegar.

Mexican-Style Chicken Appetizers

MAKES 30 APPETIZERS

Mexican colonists introduced chickens and their cookery into Florida and the American Southwest. This recipe is an American creation based upon Mexican culinary traditions.

6 skinless, boneless chicken-breast halves

FOR THE MARINADE

3 cloves garlic, crushed
1/2 teaspoon freshly ground black pepper
1/2 teaspoon ground allspice
1 tablespoon chopped fresh oregano, or 1 teaspoon dried
1/2 cup red wine vinegar
1/2 cup orange juice
1/2 cup grapefruit juice
1/2 cup olive oil
Salt, to taste

FOR THE ONION GARNISH

2 medium red onions, julienned
1/2 cup red wine vinegar
1/2 cup orange juice
1/2 cup grapefruit juice
1/3 cup olive oil
3 cloves garlic, crushed
1 teaspoon freshly ground black pepper
Salt, to taste

Tortilla chips, crackers, pitas, or bread

1. Place the chicken breasts in a baking dish. Combine all of the ingredients for the marinade and pour over the chicken. Marinate for 2 hours in the refrigerator.

2. Meanwhile, place the onions in a mixing bowl. Add the remaining garnish ingredients. Allow the onion mixture to marinate for 2 hours.

3. Preheat the oven to 350 degrees F. Remove the chicken from the marinade and place into a roasting pan. Bake the chicken for 45 minutes, brushing with the marinade as needed. Let cool. Cut into bite-sized pieces.

4. Top the tortillas with the chicken mixture and garnish with the marinated onions.

Tortillas

MAKES 15 TORTILLAS

Historically, tortillas were prepared by soaking maize in lime-water until the outer skin came off. Then the softened kernels were rubbed into a paste on a *metate* (stone mill). The resulting corn dough would then be hand flattened and cooked on a hot stone or griddle. Tortillas are one of the major building blocks of Mexican cookery. Hardened tortillas were used as plates to hold food and as spoons to convey it to the mouth. When the food was consumed, the plate and spoon were then consumed, and there were no dishes or utensils to clean up!

1½ cups masa harina (corn flour), and more if needed
1 cup plus 2 tablespoons water
Vegetable oil to grease the griddle

1. Place the masa harina in a large bowl and form a well in the middle. Add the water to the well and slowly incorporate the masa harina until the dough is formed. Knead the dough until smooth, adding additional flour or water if necessary. Roll the mixture into walnut-sized balls. Cover with plastic.

2. TO FORM THE TORTILLAS: Lay a piece of plastic wrap on the bottom plate of a tortilla press, then place one walnut-sized ball of dough on top. Cover the dough with another piece of plastic, close the press, and push the handle down firmly. Open the press and lift off the top section of plastic. You should have a flat round tortilla ready for the griddle. Repeat process with the rest of the balls of dough.

3. TO COOK THE TORTILLAS: Heat a griddle over medium heat. Lightly grease the griddle with oil. Place a tortilla on the griddle and cook each side for 30 seconds. Repeat process with the rest of the tortillas. Cooked tortillas can be stored in the refrigerator for two weeks or frozen up to six months.

SALSA ROJA

MAKES 1 CUP

1 clove garlic
Pinch of salt
1 ripe, large tomato, roasted, peeled, cored and roughly chopped
3 serrano or 2 jalapeño chiles, stems removed. For a milder salsa, seed and devein the chiles

1. In a mortar, with a pestle, grind the garlic and salt into a smooth paste. Add the chopped tomatoes and chiles. Mix and season to taste with salt.

Alamo Burgers

MAKES 4 SERVINGS

Alamo Burgers are named after the most visited site in San Antonio.

1 pound ground beef chuck
¼ cup taco sauce
4 pita breads
Refried beans, warmed
½ head iceberg lettuce, finely sliced
1 cup shredded Cheddar or Monterey Jack cheese (about ¼ pound)

1. Prepare an outdoor grill or preheat the broiler.

2. In a bowl, mix the beef with the taco sauce. Shape the meat into 4 patties. Grill or broil to the desired doneness.

3. Slice 1 inch off one side of each pita bread and open the pocket. Coat one side of the inside of the pita with some of the warm refried beans.

4. Put the cooked burgers into the pita pockets and stuff with lettuce and cheese.

Most people prefer hamburgers made with a mixture of beef that is 75 percent meat and 25 percent fat. Beef chuck has this ratio naturally and is ideal as a cut for hamburgers. Handle the meat as little as possible during the preparation. The more ground meat is handled, the more juice is lost. For the same reason a hamburger should not be pressed down to the cooking surface. The pressure pushes out the meat's natural juices.

Pita bread, also known as pocket bread, is made from white or whole-wheat flour and is the staple food of Middle Eastern countries. It is round, flat, only lightly leavened, and hollow inside. People in the Middle East believe that pita bread is a gift from God. They eat it with every meal, often tearing it into finger-size pieces to scoop food from platters. Fresh pita bread warmed in an oven or over a flame swells up like a pouch.

Pecan-Breaded Chicken

MAKES 8 SERVINGS

Chicken dipped in butter-mustard and then coated with ground pecans delivers nutty textures and flavors.

6 tablespoons (¾ stick) unsalted butter, plus more for the pan
4 whole boneless, skinless chicken breasts, split in half
Freshly ground black pepper
¼ cup plus 2 tablespoons Dijon-style mustard
2 cups finely ground pecans
2 cups sour cream

1. Preheat the oven to 400 degrees F. Lightly butter a baking pan.

2. Flatten the chicken breasts and lightly pepper them.

3. In a saucepan, melt 6 tablespoons butter and remove the pan from the heat. Whisk in ¼ cup of the mustard. Dip the chicken into the butter-mustard mixture and then into the ground pecans to coat thoroughly.

4. Place the chicken in the prepared baking pan. Bake for about 15 minutes, until golden and cooked through. Remove the chicken from the pan and set aside to keep warm.

5. Pour the pan drippings into a bowl, add the sour cream and the remaining 2 tablespoons mustard, and mix thoroughly.

6. Place 2 tablespoons of the sour cream-mustard mixture on each dinner plate and cover with a chicken breast. Serve immediately.

When storing raw poultry in the refrigerator, be sure that it is tightly wrapped, to prevent the meat or its juices from coming into contact with any other surfaces. Assume that all raw chicken has some salmonella bacteria that could cause food-borne illness. Wash raw chicken thoroughly with cold water. Wash any surface that the raw poultry comes in contact with before anything else touches it. After you have touched raw poultry, wash your hands before you touch any other foods or surfaces.

Make sure the internal temperature of cooked poultry reaches at least 180 degrees F before serving. Never eat partially cooked poultry.

Don't store poultry—cooked or raw—with stuffing inside. The densely packed stuffing promotes bacterial growth. If you are going to hold stuffed chicken or other fowl for more than a few minutes, remove the stuffing after the bird is cooked and refrigerate it separately.

BBQ-Rubbed Sweet Potatoes

MAKES 4 SERVINGS

Sweet potatoes originated in the tropical areas of the Americas and they were widely distributed throughout the Caribbean in pre-Columbian times. European explorers exported sweet potatoes to Europe, where they became popular enough to be mentioned by Shakespeare in the *Merry Wives of Windsor*. Europeans also introduced sweet potatoes into Africa, where they were quickly adopted due to their similarity to the yam. It is through the slave trade that sweet potatoes and yams were introduced into the American South, where they were commonly grown by slaves and poor whites. It wasn't until after the Civil War that the sweet potato became popular throughout the United States. This recipe for "BBQ-Rubbed Sweet Potatoes" is a real American creation fusing traditions from Africa with those of barbeque.

2 teaspoons paprika
2 teaspoons chile powder
2 teaspoons BBQ spice
1 teaspoon garlic powder
1 teaspoon ground cumin
1 teaspoon poultry seasoning
1 teaspoon salt
1 teaspoon dried oregano
1/2 teaspoon onion powder
4 medium sweet potatoes
4 tablespoons salted butter
4 tablespoons light brown sugar

1. Preheat the oven to 375 degrees F. Line a baking sheet with aluminum foil.

2. In a medium bowl, mix together the paprika, chili powder, BBQ spice, garlic powder, cumin, poultry seasoning, salt, oregano, and onion powder.

3. Wash each sweet potato thoroughly under cold running water. Carefully pierce each potato 4 to 5 times, with the tip of a small knife or the tines of a fork. With the sweet potatoes still wet, dredge each potato into the spice rub and place on the prepared baking sheet.

4. Bake the sweet potatoes for about 1 hour 20 minutes, or until they are very tender when pierced with a fork. To serve, split each potato open, lengthwise, and dollop each with 1 tablespoon of butter and 1 tablespoon of brown sugar.

NEW ORLEANS CLOCKWISE FROM ABOVE: Mardi Gras float ★ Mardi Gras band ★ Mardi Gras float ★ King Cake ★ Pralines

NEW ORLEANS ABOVE: Classic car parked by Creole food signs ★ LEFT: Oysters with Tabasco sauce

SAN ANTONIO ABOVE LEFT: Melons ★ ABOVE RIGHT: Classic San Antonio cocktails

SAN ANTONIO CLOCKWISE FROM ABOVE: Dyed eggs for the Fiesta Tejano ★ Coleslaw ★ Texas pride sign ★ Indian corn ★ Chili peppers

LOS ANGELES CLOCKWISE FROM
ABOVE: Produce at the market ★ Olive trees
★ Fresh tomatoes ★ Gladstone's Seafood Joint
★ Pink's Hot Dog Stand

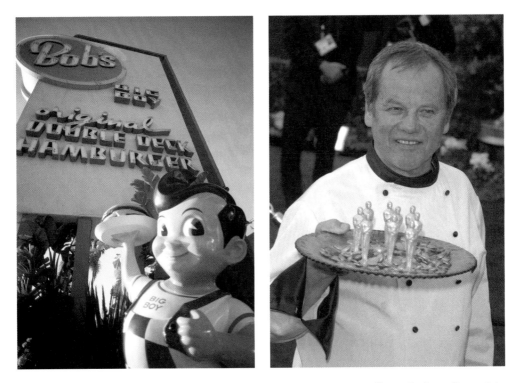

LOS ANGELES ABOVE LEFT: Bob's Big Boy ★ ABOVE RIGHT: Wolfgang Puck on Oscar night
★ BELOW: Grand Central Market

SAN FRANCISCO CLOCKWISE FROM
ABOVE: Napa Valley grapes ★ Boudin Bakery
★ Chinatown market ★ Chicken with olives ★
Ghirardelli

SAN FRANCISCO ABOVE LEFT: The Buena Vista Café ★ ABOVE RIGHT: Chinatown street

CHICAGO BELOW LEFT: Hot Dog sign ★ BELOW RIGHT: Mr. Beef

CHICAGO CLOCKWISE FROM TOP LEFT: Bakery window ★ Cakes ★
Swedish Cardamom Cake ★ Street sign

Chile con Carne

MAKES 6 SERVINGS

Chile con Carne is a real Texan creation, based on northern Mexican culinary traditions. It was first noted in the mid-nineteenth century, and it became a food fetish in the late twentieth century with books published on how to make it and contests trying to establish who makes the best.

2 tablespoons vegetable oil
2 pounds lean beef round, cut into 1-inch cubes
2 cloves garlic, minced
2 cups chopped onions
2 cups beef stock
2 cups canned tomatoes with their juice
2 tablespoons chile powder
1 teaspoon dried oregano
1 teaspoon ground cumin
½ teaspoon cayenne pepper
Salt and freshly ground black pepper
4 cups cooked pinto beans, drained
2 tablespoons finely ground cornmeal

1. In a large deep skillet or sauté pan, heat the oil over medium heat. When the oil is hot, add the beef and cook, stirring, until the cubes are brown on all sides, about 5 minutes.

2. Add in the garlic and cook, stirring occasionally, for 3 minutes. Add the onions and cook, stirring, for another 3 minutes. Add the stock, 1 cup water, the tomatoes and their juices, and the seasonings. Mix well and simmer for 1½ hours. Add additional water if the chile begins to become dry during the cooking time.

3. Add the beans and the cornmeal and simmer for 30 minutes more.

Cornmeal is available in two colors: yellow and white; the color is the only difference, other than fineness of grind. In cooking, yellow and white are interchangeable: If a recipe calls for yellow cornmeal, you can use white. Generally, yellow cornmeal is used in down-home–style foods and white cornmeal is used when a more refined presentation is desired.

Pecan Pie
MAKES 6 SERVINGS

The pecan is a member of the hickory nut family and America's native nut. George Washington planted pecan trees at Mount Vernon and is said to have carried pecan nuts in his pockets throughout the Revolutionary War. Thomas Jefferson grew pecans in his gardens at Monticello. Pecans are now grown mainly in our southern states, and Texas is one of the largest producers.

FOR THE DOUGH

1 cup all-purpose flour, plus more for rolling
½ teaspoon salt
1 tablespoon sugar
2 tablespoons (¼ stick) chilled unsalted butter, cut into cubes,
    plus more for greasing the pie plate
4 tablespoons vegetable shortening, chilled
About 2 tablespoons ice water

FOR THE FILLING

2 cups coarsely chopped pecans
4 tablespoons (½ stick) unsalted butter, melted
¾ cup sugar
¾ cup light corn syrup
3 eggs, lightly beaten
1½ teaspoons vanilla extract

1. **TO MAKE THE DOUGH:** In a food processor, combine the flour with the salt and sugar. Add the cold butter cubes and shortening, and pulse the machine 15 to 20 times, until the butter and shortening have been cut into the flour in pieces about the size of oatmeal flakes. Add the water and process, pulsing the machine on and off, for a few seconds longer until the dough comes together. Transfer the dough to the counter and, if it is still dry, sprinkle it with a teaspoon or so more water and work the water into the dough; if the dough is too wet, dust with flour and work it in. Flatten the dough into a disk, cover with plastic wrap, and chill for at least 2 hours or preferably overnight, to relax the gluten and make sure the dough isn't tough.

2. Lightly butter a 9-inch pie plate, preferably made of ovenproof glass. Lightly flour the counter and the rolling pin and roll the dough into a 10-inch round about ⅛-inch thick. Lift the dough into the prepared pie plate and lightly press it in. With your thumb and index finger, pinch the edge of the dough at 1-inch intervals to create a fluted rim. Refrigerate the dough for at least 2 hours.

3. Preheat the oven to 325 degrees F.

4. TO MAKE THE FILLING: In a mixing bowl, combine the pecans, butter, sugar, corn syrup, eggs, and vanilla. Pour the mixture into the chilled pie shell.

5. Set the pie on a baking sheet and bake for 1½ hours, or until the filling is set. Cool on a wire rack.

> Pecans, like all nuts, are a good source of protein. The oil in pecans is high in poly-unsaturates, and the nut is very low in sodium. You can buy pecans in the shell, shelled in halves, and shelled crushed. Shelled pecan nuts can easily be ground in a food processor or blender, or smashed with a rolling pin. Once shelled, and especially if ground, pecans are very perishable. They keep best tightly covered in the refrigerator or freezer.

THE REAL AMERICAN PIE

In pre-Columbian times, relatively few foods were domesticated in North America. The staples—corn, squash, and beans—originated in Central or South America and diffused northward thousands of years ago. The pecan is one of the few foods native to Texas. American Indians used pecan nuts as thickeners for their soups and stews. Anglos ate them right from the shell and used them in desserts and confections, notably pralines. The pecan pie was a late-nineteenth-century invention, and its birthplace may well have been San Antonio. In 1898, eighteen-year-old Huldah Haynes worked as a nanny for a German hotel owner in San Antonio. She submitted her recipe for "Texas Pecan Pie" to the *Ladies Home Journal*, which published it in 1898, and it remains the earliest such recipe. Nothing more is known of Huldah Haynes, but shortly after her recipe appeared in print, pecan pie recipes began to appear in virtually every cooking magazine and cookbook published in the United States. Unlike apple pie, which has forebears in Europe, pecan pie is a truly American dessert.

LOS ANGELES

Los Angeles is in the same state as San Francisco, but there's a world of difference between the two. San Francisco was in its glory days during the nineteenth century. At the time, there was no particular reason to expect that the sleepy little community of El Pueblo de Nuestra Señora de Ora la Reyna de los Angeles de Porciúncula, as Los Angeles was originally called, would become one of the nation's largest and most ethnically diverse cities. Los Angeles had no natural harbor, relatively little fresh water, a small population, and, worst of all, it had no gold. It did have rich, fertile soil, a good growing climate, and plenty of land, but these were of little use without some way of transporting crops to distant markets. Lacking the wealth and population of San Francisco, Los Angeles was slow to mature as a center of culinary interest.

In the 1870s, this began to change. When the Southern Pacific Railroad started planning its route to California, the city of Los Angeles took the opportunity to offer the railroad company an assortment of substantial subsidies if it would make Los Angeles the railroad's terminus. The railroad saw the light at the end of the line and decided to terminate in Los Angeles. Having secured a way of sending agricultural products to the rest of the country, Los Angeles began to prosper. While prospectors found no gold in the mountains around Los Angeles, they did find another kind of gold in the soil—orange gold. Citrus fruit became one of the area's most important crops, and train-loads of California oranges were shipped across the country.

But Los Angeles didn't have enough workers to pick the fruit and other crops, so farmers and real-estate agents advertised southern California's attractions throughout the rest of the nation, stressing its year-round pleasant climate, excellent employment prospects, and cheap land. Americans flocked to the "dreamland" and were eventually joined by others—from Mexico, Japan, China, Italy, and Korea. After a man-made port was created, goods could easily be exported and immigrants welcomed.

DON'T EAT THE TAMALES

At Los Angeles's culinary core was Mexican food. In the nineteenth century, a vast array of traditional dishes were adapted to include California's produce. At the time, most Americans limited themselves to fairly bland foods, so these recipes, with their chile, garlic, onions, and pungent spices, did not appeal to most Anglos in Los Angeles. In fact, Kate Sanborn, an early Anglo-Californian, advised visitors, "whatever other folly you may be led into, let me implore you to wholly abstain from that deadly concoction, the Mexican tamale," which she described as "a curious and dubious concoction of chicken hash, meat, olives, red pepper and I know not what, enclosed in a corn-husk, stewed until furiously hot, and then offered for sale by Mexicans in such a sweet, appealing way that few can resist the novelty." Sanborn warned that the effects of eating such dishes were "serious."

To attract Anglo-Americans to their establishments, Mexican restaurateurs in Los Angeles learned to tone down their spicier dishes, and some of these denatured recipes found their way into local cookbooks. Other dishes—enchiladas, refried beans, Spanish

---

★ WHAT TO TASTE AND WHERE TO TASTE IT ★

Mexican

BORDER GRILL SANTA MONICA
1445 4th Street ★ Santa Monica ★ (310) 451-1655

The Border Grill is owned by Susan Feniger and Mary Sue Milliken, of Food Network *Too Hot Tamales* fame. New York's *Newsday* has identified them as Mexican food's "pre-eminent American translators."

LA SERENATA DE GARIBALDI
1842 East First Street ★ Los Angeles ★ (323) 265-2887

Probably the most notable and best-known Mexican restaurant in town is La Serenata de Garibaldi, located on a great stretch of east L.A.—right across from Mariachi Square, where Los Angeles began.

---

rice, tamales, and tacos—survived as street food to become central to Cal-Mex food today. Constant infusions of Mexican immigrants have strengthened the Mexican culinary influence, and today Los Angeles is a great town for Mexican food. A good place to start is downtown, where the city began. Olvera Street has tried to retain Los Angeles's Mexican heritage; Olvera Street's La Golondrina Café was one of the first restaurants in the city to serve authentic Mexican food. Close by is La Serenata de Garibaldi, probably the most notable and best-known Mexican restaurant in Los Angeles.

FUSION CONFUSION

Los Angeles is a hotbed of fusion cuisine. The earliest example is Cal-Mex cooking, a marriage of Mexican flavors and Anglo sensibilities. Some dishes have undergone transformations that would make them unrecognizable in Mexico. The American taco (the hard taco), for instance, has little to do with the tacos eaten in Mexico, which are small dishes that make up a light meal or snack. The California taco consists of a tortilla deep-fried to form a U-shaped shell, then filled with ground beef occasionally mixed with other ingredients, American cheese, shredded iceberg lettuce, and tasteless tomatoes. Sauces are optional. It's basically a cheeseburger in a foreign costume. The Taco Bell fast-food chain, not surprisingly, thrived in the Los Angeles suburbs. Rest assured, though, that real Mexican tacos have survived in Los Angeles, and you can find them at modest taco stands around the city. Perhaps unique to the Cal-Mex tradition is the seafood taco. There are a number of other foods and recipes that are based in Mexican traditions but are really adaptations. The burrito, which means literally "little burro," is a tortilla stuffed with beans, rice, meats, and other ingredients, and most likely originated during the 1930s in Los Angeles's famed El Cholo Spanish Café, which still survives.

The Mexican community also introduced the avocado and promoted the development of avocado orchards. During

HOW TO MAKE A FORTUNE

Chinese immigrated to Los Angeles and settled in Chinatown, which became an important part of the city's cultural mosaic. Chinese restaurants were common in Los Angeles, but it was not the Chinese community in Los Angeles that created the fortune cookie. A Los Angeles preacher, Baker David Jung, is credited with doing so around 1916. His fortune cookies enclosed strips of paper bearing Biblical passages, which he handed out. He later launched the Hong Kong Noodle Company, which produced cookies with sayings purported to be ancient Chinese aphorisms. Fortune cookies were adopted in Chinese restaurants all over the country, and are clearly a real American food.

SUPER MARKETING

During the early twentieth century, most Americans shopped for food daily at neighborhood grocery stores. These were full-service establishments, where clerks would pick the desired items from the shelves and pack them into bags and boxes. The customer carried the groceries home or had them delivered. With the widespread adoption of the automobile in the 1920s, it became possible to shop farther from home and carry home a much larger supply of groceries. Los Angeles, with its relatively cheap land and its great dependence on the automobile, is the city where the supermarket was born. These large stores, offering low prices based on high volume, were self-service: Customers walked around the store, collecting their choices in baskets and then proceeding to checkout stands. Once supermarkets became successful in Los Angeles, the idea was quickly adopted throughout the United States. Supermarkets greatly increased the variety of products that Americans could buy, and lowered the cost of food. Today, Americans spend less of their disposable income on food than do people in other countries, thanks in part to supermarkets.

the early twentieth century, avocados became a hallmark of California cuisine. Guacamole, which has become the most popular way to serve avocados, was a novelty then, and Angelenos took a while to standardize their spelling of its name: As late as the 1930s it appeared as "wakimoli." Mexicans used guacamole as a sauce, but in California it became a salad, consisting of chunks of avocado and minced onion, dressed with olive oil; the mixture was served on a bed of lettuce and eaten with a fork. This very basic guacamole was elaborated upon as the years went by, and is now one of the signature dishes of the Cal-Mex repertoire.

The first known recipe titled "guacamole" in an English-language cookbook appeared in *Fashions in Foods in Beverly Hills*, published by the Beverly Hills Woman's Club in 1930. The recipe was contributed by Ramon Novarro, who had been born Ramon Samaniegos in Durango, Mexico. Novarro is best remembered for his lead role in the 1926 film version of *Ben Hur*. His guacamole recipe calls for avocados, green chiles, and seedless grapes—the last ingredient was meant to replace pomegranate seeds, which the actor claimed were the traditional garnish. When tortilla chips became popular in the 1960s, guacamole became a fixture at Mexican-American restaurants and a favorite at Super Bowl festivities.

Italian

SPAGO BEVERLY HILLS
176 North Canon Drive ★ Beverly Hills ★ (310) 385-0880

The newer Spago Beverly Hills, which opened in 1997, is the place for fine dining and celebrity spotting.

CICADA
617 South Olive Street ★ Los Angeles ★ (213) 488-9488

At this gourmet restaurant in an Art Deco location—a former haberdashery inside the historic Oviatt Building in downtown Los Angeles—you can sample any Italian pasta, but try the unusual items, such as duck ravioli or shiitake gnocchi. Great for dining before or after an evening of entertainment at the nearby Music Center or Walt Disney Concert Hall.

HOLLYWOOD: LAND OF SALADS

That guacamole and other recipes were popularized by Hollywood actors and actresses comes as no surprise. Then, as now, movie fans were interested in every facet of the stars' lives, including what they ate. Figure-conscious movie actresses doted on green salads, and their fans around the country followed their lead. California's abundant fresh produce made it easy for Angelenos to toss or compose appealing combinations of lettuce, cucumbers, bell peppers, celery, tomatoes, grapefruit, and fresh herbs. For those not counting calories, there were salads featuring cream cheese or Cheddar, and dressings lavishly enriched with whipping cream or mayonnaise.

Among the Los Angeles restaurants that catered to Hollywood's elite was the Brown Derby. In true California vernacular style, the building was actually constructed in the shape of a derby hat. The restaurant was opened near the famous intersection of Hollywood and Vine by Robert Cobb in 1926. About ten years later, according to Walter Scharfe, later president of the Brown Derby Restaurants, the now famous Cobb salad was created "quite by accident. One evening . . . Cobb went to the icebox and found an avocado, which he chopped with lettuce, celery, tomatoes, and strips of bacon. Later he embellished it with breast of chicken, chives, hard-boiled egg, watercress, and a wedge of Roquefort cheese for dressing, and the salad was on its way to earning an international reputation." Cobb salad has enjoyed a recent revival, although today's chefs can't seem to resist substituting more exotic ingredients for Cobb's basics. Then again, Cobb himself apparently "noodled" with his creation quite a bit before he considered it successful.

Another salad whose star still shines brightly is the Caesar salad: romaine lettuce and garlic-toasted croutons in a zesty vinaigrette flavored with Parmesan cheese. Its invention is usually credited to Cesar Cardini, an Italian immigrant who ran a series of restaurants in Tijuana, Mexico, just across the border from San Diego. In 1924, Cardini composed the salad as a main course, arranging the crisp romaine leaves on a plate to be eaten with your fingers. Later, Cardini would tear the leaves into bite-sized pieces so that the salad could be prepared and tossed at tableside. This salad was very popular with the

Hollywood movie crowd who visited Tijuana, and it began appearing on menus in Los Angeles restaurants. Cardini, way ahead of his time, insisted that only Italian olive oil and imported Parmesan cheese be used. He also required the salad to be subtly flavored, but somewhere along the line anchovies were added. A version of the salad, called "Garlic Salad Tia Juana," appears in *The Palatists Book of Cookery*, published by a Hollywood-area charity in 1933. A teaspoon of Worcestershire sauce (which contains anchovies) is among the ingredients.

Cardini's restaurant in Tijuana and the Brown Derby at Hollywood and Vine are long gone, but the salads that originated in these establishments have become true American classics. They were among the first salads to be considered a complete meal.

HAUTE CUISINE

Angelenos certainly don't subsist only on ethnic foods and salads. But serious restaurants in the city got off to a rocky start. In 1852, the first L.A. restaurant opened, La Rue's. According to a contemporary account, La Rue's had a mud floor, a half-dozen wooden tables, and dirty tablecloths; the food was poorly cooked but generously portioned. In the twentieth century, this culinary picture slowly changed. Restaurants such as La Rue's and, later, Perino's, targeted the culinary elite; although both of these establishments were Italian owned, they both served classic French food. While perhaps not on a par with French restaurants in New York or San Francisco, they did introduce some Angelenos to haute cuisine, and many who tried it wanted more.

DRIVE-INS AND HAMBURGERS

Los Angeles grew in a very different way from other American cities. Because there was so much inexpensive land around, Los Angeles simply spread out, swallowing the surrounding acreage rather than putting up taller buildings on tightly packed city blocks. Luckily for Los Angeles, the automobile came along to bridge the gaps in its sprawling metropolitan area. Los Angeles became more dependent on the car than any other city in America, and automobiles helped to shape the way Californians ate. While drive-in dining may have originated elsewhere, it reached its peak in Los Angeles, where wacky architecture, bold colors, and blazing neon lights caught the attention of passing motorists, who were served their meals on a tray by perky carhops.

Hamburger drive-ins remain a Los Angeles tradition. Bob's Big Boy in Burbank is a perennial a hot spot, particularly on Friday nights, when restored vintage cars assemble in the parking lot. Other classic hamburger establishments include the Original Tommy's, launched in 1946 by Tommy Koulax, and Father's Office in Santa Monica.

Despite their German-sounding name, hamburgers are a truly American food. The first references to hamburger sandwiches are to be found in Los Angeles newspapers—predating the St. Louis World's Fair of 1904, which popularized hamburgers, by over a decade. Hamburger stands dotted Los Angeles from the 1890s on. One was the enterprise of two brothers who had come to Los Angeles to pursue a career in movies.

FRIED IN L.A.

Deep-fried potatoes, which probably originated in France, were made in a variety of shapes and sizes, but they did not become an important American food until almost the mid-twentieth century. Short-order joints tried serving them with hamburgers during the 1930s, but customers didn't show much interest. Then came World War II: Beef was rationed, but potatoes were abundant. At White Castle and other fast-food chains, French fries became a standard "side," and by the war's end, burgers and fries were inseparable. Dick and Maurice McDonald, proprietors of McDonald's hamburgers in San Bernardino, California, recognized the importance of a top-quality French fry. They carefully selected the type of potatoes, determined the best shape and size of the cuts, and selected the right equipment and the proper fat for frying. Many aficionados believe that the early success of McDonald's was mainly due to their French fries. Today, virtually every major fast-food chain uses the same potatoes (grown to their specifications), employs similar equipment, and follows the same procedures as McDonald's. Although still called French fries, these are a real American food—especially when slathered with all-American tomato ketchup.

Hamburgers

BOB'S BIG BOY
4211 West Riverside Drive ★ Burbank ★ (818) 843-9334

The first Bob's Big Boy was launched by Bob Wian in 1936, where the Big Boy himself—a huge figure of a cherubic child in red-checkered pants—advertised the original double-decker burger. The Bob's Big Boy Car Hop Coffee Shop in Burbank, with its seventy-foot-tall neon sign, has been restored to its 1950s grandeur and declared an architectural landmark by the State of California. Try the classic Big Boy combo with a "silver goblet" milkshake and a hot fudge sundae for dessert.

THE ORIGINAL TOMMY'S
2575 West Beverly Boulevard ★ Los Angeles ★ (213) 389-9060

One hamburger joint that survived the fast-food onslaught is Tommy's, opened by Tommy Koulax in 1946 as a ramshackle little stand on the corner of Beverly and Rampart Boulevards in downtown Los Angeles. Tommy's specialty, now as then, is the chili burger. While Tommy's has franchised its operation and you can find other Tommy's outlets around the city, the original stand is the place to go.

FATHER'S OFFICE
1018 Montana Avenue ★ Santa Monica ★ (310) 393-2337

Father's Office serves great hamburgers and French fries, and hundreds of beers to wash them down. The place is often crowded, and reservations are not accepted, so you may have to wait in line for a table.

KETCHUP ICE CREAM?

In 1945, Irvine Robbins opened the Snowbird Ice Cream Store in Glendale, California. Robbins advertised that it served twenty-one flavors of ice cream. At the same time, his brother-in-law, Burt Baskin, opened an ice-cream parlor in the Los Angeles area called Burton's. The two formed a partnership in 1946 to create Baskin-Robbins, which sold premium ice cream. They began to franchise their operation, and within three years the chain had grown to eight stores. In 1953, the company advertised that its stores served thirty-one flavors of ice cream; this number was selected so that a customer could consume a different flavor every day of the month. The company also regularly created new treats that celebrated holidays or special events, like the landing on the moon in 1969, when the company released a Lunar Cheesecake. One franchise even tried ketchup ice cream, but it wasn't a great success, even for ketchup aficionados.

Like countless others, they were soon looking for other employment, and opened up a hot dog stand near the Santa Anita racetrack. They gradually expanded their business, adding hamburgers to their menu and carhops dressed like cheerleaders to their staff. After World War II, the brothers became disenchanted with the carhops: Their salaries ate into profits, and they attracted the wrong type of customers—teenage boys. The brothers wanted a family-oriented self-service eatery that would attract suburban families. In 1953, Richard and Maurice McDonald finally realized their dream in San Bernardino, California, one hundred miles east of Los Angeles. When they started franchising their operation, McDonald's hamburger stands began appearing all over Los Angeles—and, eventually, the world.

THE CANNED AND THE RAW

Starting in the 1800s, Los Angeles was a fishing port, and one of the most prized catches was tuna. But few Americans ate tuna until the early twentieth century. The change was due in part to Albert P. Halfhill, who came to Los Angeles in the 1880s. Halfhill was a commercial fisherman who went out for cod and salmon, but by 1903 these had been fished almost to extinction. Halfhill sought another species, this time

A CHIP OFF THE OLD SPUD

Potato chips, which were also called Saratoga chips (after their birthplace, the upstate New York spa), were being served in fancy restaurants by the mid-nineteenth century. By the turn of the century, potato chips were packed into barrels and sold in grocery stores. Once the barrel was opened, however, the crisp chips absorbed moisture and went limp and soggy. They could be restored to their original crispness by heating them in the oven just before serving, but commercial potato chips were not a success. This changed in 1926, when Laura Scudder began making potato chips in Monterey Park, a suburb of Los Angeles. She cut and folded sheets of waxed paper and then ironed them to form bags. After the chips were packed in, the tops of the bags were sealed with the iron. The chips stayed fresh and crisp in these sealed packages, and potato chips were on their way to becoming a favorite American snack food.

for commercial canning. Large tuna were abundant in California waters, but at the time there were objections to its meaty flesh: Most people thought it was a scavenger, and its flavor was considered too strong for the fresh-fish market. Albacore tuna, however, consisted mainly of white meat, and Halfhill thought consumers would accept its milder flavor. He experimented with canning tuna, eventually perfecting a process that removed the oil that many people found objectionable. Halfhill put 250 cases of his canned tuna on the market in 1908. Others began to follow his lead, but consumer acceptance was slow. Then a marketing genius realized that white albacore tuna resembled chicken breast meat, and Chicken of the Sea–brand tuna was born. As tuna fishing grew as an industry, canned tuna became cheaper; during the Depression, low-cost, high-protein tuna became an American staple, rather than a delicacy. Although sport fishermen still fish for tuna along the California coast, the large-scale tuna fleets have left Los Angeles. Today there's a very different tuna specialty on Los Angeles menus.

Japanese restaurateurs began opening establishments in Los Angeles in the early days of the twentieth century, but most catered only to Japanese Americans or Japanese tourists. It seemed unlikely that Anglos would ever sit down to a meal of raw seafood, the beautifully crafted sushi and sashimi that hold such an honored place in Japanese dining. In the 1970s, Japanese chefs had an idea: Maybe they could get Americans to eat "sushi" that did not contain raw fish. The California roll was the answer—avocado and cooked crab rolled up in sticky rice. The California roll was an immediate success in the United States and even found its way to Japan, where traditionalist restaurateurs still refuse to serve this American invention. For many Americans, the California roll

Japanese Fusion

MATSUHISA INTERNATIONAL

129 North La Cienega Boulevard ★ Beverly Hills ★ (310) 659-9639

One of the finest Japanese restaurants in Los Angeles is Matsuhisa International, launched by chef Nobu Matsuhisa in 1987. Trained in Peru, Chef Matsuhisa created an Asian fusion menu that was so successful he subsequently opened the Nobu chain of restaurants in other cities. Matsuhisa International's sushi bar serves unusual dishes, such as lobster ceviche and sashimi sparked with cilantro or garlic. For those eating at the restaurant for the first time, the omakase tasting menu is recommended.

opened the door to "real" sushi and sashimi, and it turns out that millions of Americans do love to eat raw fish after all. And one of the choicest fish for sushi and sashimi is tuna. During the 1990s, a thick, rare-cooked tuna steak became a mainstay of fine restaurants in Los Angeles, and the formerly humble tuna became a high-class culinary sensation.

LOS ANGELES TODAY

When Michael McCarty opened Michael's restaurant in 1979, Los Angeles was on the verge of becoming a world-class restaurant town. The restaurant featured fresh local ingredients with unique flavor combinations, characteristics that later became associated with the California culinary revolution that has swept America. Assisting in the revolution was Austrian-born, French-trained chef Wolfgang Puck, who made a splash serving French cuisine at Ma Maison in 1981. He later opened Spago, an innovative Italian restaurant, above Sunset Strip in the Hollywood Hills. Puck took

Korean

WHARO KOREAN BBQ

4029 Lincoln Boulevard ★ Marina del Rey ★ (310) 578-7114

This traditional Korean restaurant employs charcoal pots for cooking. Its barbecued meats include Kobe and Kalbi beef, pork, and shrimp. It offers modern interpretations of Korean culinary traditions.

Eclectic

SONA

401 North La Cienega Boulevard ★ West Hollywood ★ (310) 659-7708

Chef David Myers features dramatic dishes with seasonal items. His wife, Michelle Myers, creates such desserts as "chocolate bread pudding swimming in hot chocolate with malted ice cream and caramelized bananas."

THE ORIGINAL PANTRY CAFÉ

877 South Figueroa Street ★ Los Angeles ★ (213) 972-9279

With the exception of a few nights during World War II, this often crowded, noisy spot has been open twenty-four hours a day since 1924. Don't plan to eat here unless you're really hungry. All meals are oversized, but the breakfasts are particularly enormous. The Pantry is noted for what we now call comfort foods: traditional steaks and daily specials such as macaroni and cheese. This restaurant is a throwback to L.A. during the 1920s, and it's worth a visit just for a taste of history. Be sure to bring cash, as the Pantry doesn't take credit cards. The proprietors have made one concession, though— they've installed an ATM.

his classic French training in new directions, becoming known for his brick-oven pizza with inventive toppings.

High-quality ethnic restaurants have also blossomed in Los Angeles. In addition to excellent Mexican, Chinese, and Japanese cuisine, the city is also known for its excellent Korean food, of which Wharo Korean BBQ in Marina Del Rey is one of the best. Fusion cuisine remains top on the agenda of many Los Angeles restaurants, including Matsuhisa International, launched by the Peruvian-trained Japanese chef Nobu Matsuhisa in 1987.

Los Angeles has come a long way from its sleepy beginnings. During the past quarter century, it has gone from a culinary backwater to a culinary oasis.

Guacamole

MAKES ABOUT 2 CUPS

While the avocado is native to Central and South America, more avocados come from California than from any other part of the world. Their peak season is from January through April.

2 ripe avocados
2 tomatoes, cored, seeded, and chopped
1 medium onion, chopped
2 serrano chilis or green chilis, trimmed, seeded, and minced
2 sprigs cilantro, stems discarded, chopped
½ teaspoon salt
Tortilla chips

1. Cut the avocados in half and discard the pits. With a spoon, scoop the flesh into a bowl. Mash with a fork.

2. Stir in the tomatoes, onion, chilis, cilantro, and salt.

3. Serve at room temperature with tortilla chips. If you refrigerate it, let it come to room temperature before serving.

Avocados are highly digestible and provide vitamins A, C, and E, and several B vitamins. There is a good amount of iron in avocados as well, and they are low in sodium. Avocados, however, are rich in fruit oil, which is a saturated fat. If you are on a low saturated fat diet (a good idea for most people), limit your intake of avocados.

Leaving them in a sunny spot can ripen firm avocados at home. Or you can close them up in a paper bag and keep them in a warm spot. Check their progress daily.

Avocados bruise easily, so store them carefully and avoid buying any that are bruised; the quality of the flesh will be affected.

If preparing guacamole ahead of time, place a sheet of plastic wrap directly on the surface to prevent the browning that occurs when avocado flesh comes in contact with air. A light coating of lemon juice on top of the finished guacamole will help hold its color.

Caesar Salad with Garlic Croutons

MAKES 6 SERVINGS

The invention of Caesar Salad is usually credited to Cesar Cardini, an Italian immigrant who ran a restaurant in Tijuana, Mexico, just across the border from San Diego. This salad was very popular with the Hollywood movie crowd who visited Tijuana, and it began appearing on menus in Los Angeles restaurants in the 1930s.

FOR THE DRESSING

1 egg
1 tablespoon anchovy fillets, rinsed, drained, and minced
1 clove garlic, finely chopped
¼ cup fresh lemon juice
2 tablespoons Dijon mustard
1 teaspoon Worcestershire sauce
¾ cup olive oil
Salt and freshly ground black pepper

FOR THE SALAD

3 to 4 hearts of romaine lettuce, separated, washed, and dried, but left whole
¼ cup chopped mixed fresh herbs such as parsley, basil, chives, and rosemary
¼ cup freshly grated Parmesan cheese
Garlic Croutons (recipe follows)

1. TO MAKE THE DRESSING: In a small pot, bring enough water to a boil to cover the egg. Add the egg and boil for one minute. Drain and immediately crack into a small bowl.

2. In a large salad bowl, stir the anchovy and garlic together with a whisk, add the egg and mix well. Whisk in the lemon juice, mustard, and Worcestershire sauce, and add the oil in a slow steady stream while whisking constantly. Season with salt and pepper to taste.

3. TO MAKE THE SALAD: Toss the romaine leaves, herbs, and cheese with the dressing. Divide the greens onto 6 salad plates, garnish with the garlic croutons and serve immediately.

Parmesan is a hard grating cheese that is made in and around the Italian city of Parma. True Parmesan cheese comes from the Emilia-Romagna region and by Italian law is labeled Parmigiano-Reggiano. Parmesan cheese is made from cows' milk and is aged 2 to 3 years. It is made in huge wheels that can weigh as much as 88 pounds. Parmesan is a sharp, salty, tangy cheese; when young, it is delicious as a table cheese.

It is best to buy whole chunks of Parmesan and grate it yourself as you need it. Grated Parmesan should be kept in the refrigerator and allowed to come to room temperature before serving. Keeping a whole chunk of Parmesan fresh is easy. Wrap the cheese in a lightly dampened cheesecloth or other thin muslin cloth. Wrap that in aluminum foil and keep it in the refrigerator.

GARLIC CROUTONS
MAKES 2 CUPS

3 cloves garlic, finely minced
⅓ cup olive oil
6 slices bread, crusts removed, cut into ½-inch cubes or strips

1. In a small bowl, combine the garlic and oil. Cover and let marinate for 3 hours or longer.

2. Preheat the oven to 400 degrees F.

3. Place the bread pieces in a single layer in a sauté pan or baking pan. Pour the garlic and oil mixture over the bread and stir to coat.

4. Bake for 10 minutes or until golden brown.

Garlic heads (bulbs) should be firm, with plenty of dry papery covering. Garlic heads that have signs of sprouting are past their prime. A single bulb of garlic contains between ten and twenty cloves. Do not confuse cloves with whole bulbs.

GARLIC AND THE VAMPIRES

During the 1300s, the bubonic plague claimed the lives of one in three Europeans. Yet one group of people went largely untouched by the plague: they were the garlic vendors, who ate more garlic than anyone else and wore garlic bulbs around their necks. The common belief was that the plague was spread by vampires. It was therefore assumed that vampires were afraid of garlic, and avoided the vendors. In fact, in normal quantities garlic acts a very mild antibiotic, but in the large quantities eaten by the vendors, it was apparently strong enough to protect many of them from the plague. The myth persists that garlic can be used to ward off vampires.

Mexican-Style Chicken in a Bag

MAKES 4 SERVINGS

Tomatoes originated on the coastal areas of eastern South America and spread to ancient Central America where they became very popular. When Spanish conquistadors ran into them in Mexico, they brought them back to Europe. Tomatoes were quickly adopted in Spain and Italy, but in England they remained a decorative plant; that continued for hundreds of years. Tomatoes were introduced into Los Angeles by Spanish missionaries in the eighteenth century. Tomatoes grew well in California, and today the state produces 80 percent of the tomatoes consumed in the United States.

1 (4-ounce) can chopped green chilis, drained
1 (15-ounce) can tomato sauce
1 tablespoon Worcestershire sauce
1 tablespoon cider vinegar
½ tablespoon dry mustard
1 teaspoon cayenne pepper
3 cloves garlic, minced
1 tablespoon ground cumin
½ teaspoon ground cloves
4 pieces skin-on, bone-in chicken (about 2½ to 3 pounds)

1. In a mixing bowl, combine all the ingredients except the chicken. Mix well.

2. Lay out 4 pieces of parchment paper, each approximately double the size of a piece of chicken. Lay the chicken skin side down on half of each parchment piece. Paint the chicken with the sauce. Turn the chicken skin side up, and paint with the remaining sauce. Fold the parchment over the chicken and fold the edges to seal tightly. Place the pouches in a steamer basket over simmering water and steam for 45 minutes. (This can also be baked in a preheated 350-degree F oven on a cookie sheet for 45 minutes.) Make sure the chicken is fully cooked.

3. Serve each pouch on a plate, and let your guests open them at the table.

Worcestershire sauce is an anchovy-based, meaty-tasting condiment that has its roots in an ancient Roman condiment called garum. The modern version was developed by two English druggists, John Lea and William Perrins, who were given a recipe for a sauce by the British governor general of Bengal. They hated the sauce and poured it into a wooden barrel in their basement. Several years later they rediscovered the barrel, tasted the sauce, and found they now liked it. They named it Worcestershire because it was made in the English district of Worcester. Lea & Perrins Worcestershire sauce is still made the same way. Anchovies, soybeans, tamarind, vinegar, garlic, shallots, molasses, and spices are mixed and aged for 2 years in wooden vats. The sauce is pressed out, strained, and put in bottles.

Tilapia with Lemon Sauce

MAKES 4 SERVINGS

Capers are unopened flower buds that have been pickled. They are picked from a bush that we think originated in North Africa but now grows throughout the countries that border on the Mediterranean Sea. Recently we have begun to grow them in the southern part of the United States.

$\frac{1}{4}$ cup fresh lemon juice
1 teaspoon chopped shallots or onions
Salt and freshly ground black pepper
1 tablespoon chopped capers
$\frac{1}{4}$ cup sliced pitted black olives
$\frac{1}{2}$ teaspoon chopped lemon zest
$\frac{3}{4}$ cup plus 1 teaspoon vegetable oil
3 tablespoons chopped Italian parsley
4 boneless, skinless tilapia fillets or other firm, white-fleshed fish
Salt and freshly ground black pepper
Cooked asparagus, baby cherry tomatoes, and chopped parsley, for garnish

1. In a bowl, combine the lemon juice, shallots, salt and pepper to taste, capers, olives, and lemon zest. Slowly whisk in $\frac{3}{4}$ cup of the oil until the sauce is emulsified. Stir in the parsley. Set aside.

2. Season the fish with salt and pepper to taste. Pour the remaining 1 teaspoon oil into a large nonstick skillet, and heat over medium-high heat. When hot, add the fillets and cook for about 2 minutes on each side, depending on thickness of fish.

3. Put the fillets on a serving plate, garnish with the asparagus and tomatoes, the lemon sauce, and a sprinkle of parsley.

As a general rule, the smaller the caper, the better the quality. The best are the tiny nonpareils. The larger capers are tasty but stronger in flavor. It's a good idea to chop up larger capers before you use them in a recipe.

Pizza with Smoked Salmon and Caviar

MAKES FOUR 8-INCH PIZZAS

The following recipe has been adapted from the recipe I videotaped with Wolfgang Puck at Spago.

20 ounces pizza dough, divided into 4 equal pieces
Flour, for the baking sheets
¼ cup olive oil
½ medium red onion, very thinly sliced
½ cup sour cream
4 ounces smoked salmon
4 tablespoons black caviar
Fresh dill, for garnish

1. Preheat the oven to 500 degrees F.

2. Roll or stretch the dough into four 8-inch rounds. Place the pizzas on 2 lightly floured baking sheets. Brush each pizza crust to within 1 inch of the edge with 1 tablespoon olive oil and sprinkle with one-quarter of the red-onion slices. Bake for 8 to 10 minutes or until the crust is golden brown.

3. Spread each crust with 2 tablespoons sour cream. Divide the salmon among the pizzas, arranging it decoratively on top. Place 1 tablespoon of the caviar in the center of each pizza and garnish with fresh dill. Serve immediately.

Do not open caviar until ready to serve. Remove from the refrigerator 10 to 15 minutes before use. Caviar is very fragile so be gentle with it; always serve with a nonmetal spoon. Cover and refrigerate leftover caviar immediately.

Lemon Soufflés with Chocolate Ice Cream

SERVES 6

Soufflé is a French word literally meaning "to puff up." The French experimented with dessert soufflés during the eighteenth century, and recipes for them were first introduced into the United States through French cookbooks and immigrant chefs. The first American recipe for a lemon soufflé appeared in a cookbook published in Philadelphia in 1828. The recipe has been greatly revised over the years, and this recipe with chocolate ice cream is a true American dish.

1 cup milk

½ cup sugar, plus more for dusting the molds

4 strips lemon zest, each about 1 inch long and ½ inch wide

4 large egg yolks

3 tablespoons cornstarch

6 egg whites

1 tablespoon grated lemon zest (about 2 lemons)

½ cup chocolate ice cream or sliced fresh strawberries

1. In a 1-quart, nonreactive saucepan, over low heat, combine the milk with 2 tablespoons of the sugar and the lemon zest and bring the milk to a simmer, stirring often. Remove from the heat and discard the lemon strips.

2. In a large bowl, whisk together 2 tablespoons of sugar with the egg yolks until well blended, then fold in the cornstarch. Slowly pour the hot milk into the yolk mixture, whisking all the while. Return the mixture to the saucepan and over medium-high heat bring it to a boil, stirring constantly so the mixture doesn't stick to the bottom of the pan. When the mixture comes to a boil it will thicken. Over low heat cook for 1 minute after it comes to the boil, whisking continuously and reaching into the corners of the saucepan where the pastry cream tends to stick and burn.

3. Transfer the mixture to a clean bowl or to the bowl of a stand mixer fitted with a paddle attachment. Beat for a few minutes until no more steam rises from the surface of the pastry cream. Set a piece of plastic wrap flush on the surface of the pastry cream so that it doesn't form a skin and refrigerate it if baking the soufflés at a later time.

4. Preheat the oven to 400 degrees F. Butter the inside of six ½-cup soufflé molds or ceramic ramekins then lightly coat the inside with sugar. Set the molds in a 2-inch deep baking pan.

5. Whip the egg whites until soft peaks form, then slowly add the remaining ¼ cup of sugar and whisk until the peaks are stiff. With a wide-blade flexible spatula fold one-fourth of the whipped egg whites into the pastry cream to lighten it, then fold in the remaining whipped egg whites. Fill each ramekin. Place in the oven securely on a rack, then pour very hot water into the baking pan so it reaches three-quarters of the way up the sides of the ramekins. Bake for 40 to 45 minutes or until the soufflés are golden brown.

6. Remove the soufflés from the pan and if you wish, set each on a plate lined with a doily. To serve, break open the center and bury a small spoonful of chocolate ice cream or berries in the center of each soufflé. The ice cream melts and creates a sauce for the soufflés; the berries add a different flavor and texture. Serve immediately.

MILLIONS OF YEARS AGO, the tectonic plate under the Pacific Ocean banged into the tectonic plate under what is now California. The Pacific plate began to slide under the California plate. They also started grinding against each other, producing a great deal of heat, pressure, the Sierra Nevada mountains, and a series of volcanoes that sent mineral-filled rock to the surface. One of the minerals in the rock was gold, which turned out to be the single most important ingredient in the gastronomy of California. The best place to take a look at the impact of gold on California's (culinary) plate is San Francisco.

In 1849, San Francisco was one of the settlements that the government of Mexico had established along the coast. Each of these settlements consisted of a Franciscan mission accompanied by a military fort and a small civilian colony, but they were isolated from Mexico and considered insignificant. The food of the coastal region was basically the same as that of western Mexico: Olives supplied the basic cooking oil; figs, dates, citrus fruits, chiles, and tomatoes were grown; chicken, sheep, and turkeys were raised; corn and eventually wheat were planted, as were grapes, which were essential for making the wine used by the church.

Almost every major city in America was shaped by a group of people with similar religious ideas, similar traditions, and a similar desire to build a new community—Puritans in Boston, Mormons in Salt Lake City, Catholics in New Orleans. The one great exception is San Francisco. San Francisco as we know it today is primarily the result of 225,000 guys showing up around 1849 to find gold. They were not interested in agriculture, or craftwork, or building a community. They were interested in getting as rich as they could, as fast as they could. And as soon as they got any money, they wanted to spend it on eating and drinking.

HOW GOLD CHANGED TO GREEN

About 75 percent of the miners who rushed in to find gold came from the eastern United States; the rest came from Europe, China, Japan, Australia, and Hawaii. The new arrivals overwhelmed the small Spanish-Mexican population and quickly changed the way everyone ate.

To meet the needs of the immigrants flooding in, modest hotels and boardinghouses were opened. At first the restaurants were simple and rather crude, but while real prospectors didn't cook, they had money to spend on food, so to meet their demands the quality of the restaurants of San Francisco soon improved.

Many of the trading ships that stopped in San Francisco came from the northern Italian port city of Genoa. When the sailors heard that there was gold in the hills, they jumped ship and headed for the mines. They also sent word back home about the gold, which meant that thousands more Italian men came to San Francisco. The voyage from Italy took five months, and the newcomers arrived to find that all the promising claims had been taken. But California seemed to offer more opportunities than the old country—

the land was good for farming, the sea was filled with fish, and it was easy to make a new life in a new land. The thwarted prospectors settled in and sent to Italy for their families. During the 1880s, there was a second wave of Italian settlers, this time from southern Italy and Sicily. They built their community in an area called North Beach, which is still a center of Italian society in San Francisco. It is filled with Italian restaurants, bakeries, and coffeehouses.

★ WHAT TO TASTE AND WHERE TO TASTE IT ★

Old San Francisco

TADICH GRILL
240 California Street ★ San Francisco ★ (415) 391-2373

Tadich's is the oldest restaurant in San Francisco, with a long wood bar, intimate walnut booths, white tablecloths, and bentwood chairs. While it's famous for its seafood—rex sole, salmon, sea bass—the restaurant is more about atmosphere and tradition than gastronomy. It's always crowded, but that's part of its appeal.

Mexican

MAYA
303 Second Street ★ San Francisco ★ (415) 543-2928

Professional service, an elegant, spacious, and soothing interior, a definitive collection of tequilas, and excellent food: Richard Sandoval and his chefs are masters at presenting the complex and varied dishes of Mexican cuisine. Richard was my teacher when I was learning about Mexican cheeses. If his quesadillas stuffed with Oaxacan cheese and zucchini blossoms or his chile relleno (a roasted poblano chile split and stuffed with scallops, squid, and shrimp, topped with Oaxaca cheese, and baked) are on the menu, you owe yourself a taste of each.

LA AQUARIA
2889 Mission Street ★ San Francisco ★ (415) 285-7117

Fast and inexpensive, La Aquaria claims to have "The Best Tacos & Burritos in the World," and many San Franciscans agree. Perfectly grilled beef, pork, and chicken fill freshly made tortillas. Burritos packed with rice, beans, and salsas of varying degrees of heat are also available. The restaurant is primarily for take-out, but has a few tables.

French ships heading for Asia came into San Francisco to pick up fresh water and provisions. When the sailors heard about the gold rush they too jumped ship and rushed to the hills. If they struck it rich, they came back to town and lived it up—eating and drinking the best of what was available. If they didn't find gold, they came back to town and opened a restaurant. A French chef opened the Poule d'Or in 1849. The name means "Golden Chicken," but few miners spoke French so they renamed it the Poodle Dog; it was famous for frogs' legs and other French delicacies.

The French and Italian immigrants influenced the early cooking of San Francisco, but the biggest impact came from the Chinese. At the time of the gold rush, China was in total chaos. The Manchu dynasty was falling apart and unable to govern. There was widespread starvation and the peasants were in rebellion. Thousands of Chinese left their homeland in search of their golden opportunity, which they believed was buried in the mountains just outside of San Francisco. Originally the Chinese community in San Francisco was almost entirely male. They lived in rooming houses and took their meals in small restaurants that catered to Chinese tastes. They built their own town within a town. The first Chinese restaurant in America, the Maco & Woosung, was opened in San Francisco during the gold-rush years by immigrant Norman Asing. Today, San Francisco's Chinatown is the oldest and one of the largest Chinese communities outside of Asia, and some of its restaurants serve the finest Chinese food in the world.

SERVING UP A REVOLUTION

Starting in the early 1970s, restaurants in and around San Francisco started developing a style of cooking that became known as California cuisine. Its original practitioner was Alice Waters, who opened her restaurant Chez Panisse in Berkeley. Like Julia Child, Waters had spent time in France, and at first served simple French food with a particular emphasis on the traditions of Provence. As time passed, she began experimenting with local ingredients and organized local farmers to grow produce and raise animals according to her specifications. She changed her menu daily, focusing on the freshest and best seasonal ingredients; her preparations flattered the food without overwhelming it.

The restaurant served a number of dishes that came to be identified with California cuisine: grilled fish and vegetables, green salads topped with grilled meat or warm goat cheese, and grilled pizza with nontraditional toppings. Many of these innovations have been attributed to Jeremiah Tower, one of the first chefs at Chez Panisse. In 1982, Waters hired Paul Bertolli as chef. He was a native Californian who had worked in restaurants in Florence, Italy. Bertolli brought Italian flavors, like roasted garlic, olive oil, and red peppers, to the Chez Panisse table. Waters was one of the first American

DRESSING UP

One place where commercial salad plants grew easily was California. So it is no surprise that a late-nineteenth-century visitor to California found it to be the "land of salads." In the early 1920s, the British actor George Arliss was a hit in William Archer's play *The Green Goddess* when it played in San Francisco. He frequently ate at the Palace Hotel (now the Sheraton Palace), and in his honor a chef at the hotel invented Green Goddess dressing, composed of mayonnaise, anchovies, spinach, scallions, vinegar, and spices.

★ WHAT TO TASTE AND WHERE TO TASTE IT ★

California Cuisine

HAWTHORNE LANE
22 Hawthorne Street ★ San Francisco ★ (415) 777-9779

Hawthorne Lane features an elegant atmosphere and a sophisticated bar. A few years ago I tasted my way through the menu in preparation for a segment on my television program and thoroughly enjoyed the California cuisine with its Asian accent.
The tables are perfect for a business meeting at lunch, while the booths are just what you want for a romantic dinner.

restaurateurs to partner with local farmers, ensuring them a market for the finest ingredients they could produce. She has become an outspoken advocate of sustainable agriculture, a key factor in the continued success of California cuisine.

Chefs from Chez Panisse went out on their own and made many additional contributions to American cooking. Jeremiah Tower launched Stars in San Francisco. His 2003 book, *California Dish*, describes the California culinary revolution and its impact on America. Former Chez Panisse chef Mark Miller launched the Coyote Café in Santa Fe, New Mexico, and then published *The Coyote Café Cookbook*, which popularized southwestern cuisine.

WINING THROUGH CALIFORNIA

As far back as the sixteenth century, Spanish missionaries in Mexico were cultivating European vines without major problems. In 1769, the Franciscans moved north, and within a decade missions as far north as the San Francisco Bay were producing wine. California's Mediterranean-like climate was generally free of the fungal diseases that plagued grapevines in the eastern United States. The mission vineyards were small but successful, though commercial production of wine would not begin until the missions were secularized.

BATHING IN CHARDONNAY

During the 1700s, French royalty living in Paris believed that taking a bath in a cask of Chardonnay wine reduced the negative effects of aging. The more they bathed in it, the more they drank—and the more they drank, the more they believed it worked. However, the French Revolution had a generally negative effect on the aging of French royalty. In fact, most of them just stopped aging, and the Chardonnay bath was forgotten. The nearest thing available today is the Chardonnay massage offered at the Meadowood Spa in Napa—though the Chardonnay is presently blended into a body lotion rather than used to fill a barrel.

The gold rush had been good to a few people, but by the end of the rush most of the prospectors were looking for new ways to earn a living. Agoston Haraszthy, a Hungarian immigrant who had been a county sheriff, gold assayer, and state representative, believed that northern California was ideal for growing wine grapes and began importing hundreds of European vines. The Buena Vista vineyard, which he founded in 1857, is still operating. Later immigrants from France and Germany established the first commercial vineyards with vines they brought from their home countries.

During the 1870s, the California wine industry centered itself around San Francisco Bay, making it the leading

★ WHAT TO TASTE AND WHERE TO TASTE IT ★

Wine

LONDON WINE BAR
415 Sansome Street ★ San Francisco ★ (415) 788-4811

While California wine can be tasted in many wine bars in San Francisco, one of the best places to do so is at the London Wine Bar, which has a wide selection.

wine-producing area in the United States. California wine was sold at Philadelphia's Centennial Exposition in 1876, and was again marketed at the 1893 World's Fair Columbian Exposition in Chicago, but these promotional campaigns didn't create much of a response. Larger firms were buying up smaller vineyards, and the state's first large-scale industrial wineries were being established. Despite the rapid development of the wine industry in the state, however, there was little demand for the wine even in California.

America was not a wine-drinking country, and the wine industry almost disappeared during Prohibition and the Depression. This changed beginning in the 1930s, when Frank Schoonmaker, an American wine authority, began publicizing the best California wines, especially those of Napa and Sonoma Counties. Previously, California wines had been marketed with French names. Schoonmaker urged winemakers to call the wines by the varietal names of the grapes, such as Zinfandel or Cabernet Sauvignon.

California finally developed a worldwide reputation, and exports were beginning to grow. Wine making became big business, and wine makers were struggling to find the fastest, cleanest, most efficient ways of growing, harvesting, making, and marketing their product.

The search for efficiency sparked a renaissance in wine-making technology. The California firms, with an insatiable need for qualified staff to run their wine-making operations, funded the Department of Viticulture and Enology at the University of California at Davis. That department, in turn, became a center of innovation for wine-making technology, doing research on the climate of California and developing high-yield grape varieties and new fermentation and aging techniques. Davis provided the wine makers with the technology and personnel they needed.

During the late 1960s and early 1970s, hundreds of small boutique wineries were founded in California's Napa Valley and neighboring Sonoma County. In the process, California became synonymous with premium American wine making. The new generation of Napa Valley wine makers had been a wealthy one to begin with, but during the late 1970s and the 1980s even more money poured into the area. Celebrities bought vineyards and wineries, and larger concerns hired star architects to design major new winery buildings. Some vintners had built up excellent reputations, and by the 1980s California wines were competing successfully with the best French wines.

Most of the wineries in Napa and Sonoma have tasting rooms and offer tours of their facilities. A one- or two-day visit is well worth the time. Just make sure that you have a designated driver.

MILK'S LEAP TOWARD IMMORTALITY

The only unfortunate interruption in the history of California wine making was a totally misguided and highly destructive experiment by our federal government, known as the National Prohibition Act. From 1919 to 1933, the government tried to keep citizens from drinking anything that contained alcohol. Many of the great California wineries were forced to close. But there was one positive benefit to Prohibition: A number of wineries realized that much of the technology used to ferment grape juice into wine could be used to ferment milk into cheese.

The first significant demand for dairy products came from the gold rush prospectors. Many of the families who rushed west searching for gold traveled across the country with their family cows. When they reached California, the men started prospecting; the women started milking and making butter and cheese. Finding gold was an iffy business; trading dairy for gold, however, was very reliable. Successful prospectors paid big bucks for fresh milk, butter, and cheese. These early farmers became the nucleus of the California dairy industry. Cheese was first commercially produced in California in 1857.

Two of the most famous cheeses originating in California are Teleme, a soft cheese with a tangy aftertaste, and Monterey Jack, first manufactured by David Jacks in 1882. During the 1870s, David Jacks acquired sixty thousand acres of land in Monterey and Salinas Valley. He also bought fourteen dairy farms in Mon-

DAIRY MAIDS

The traditional division of labor in dairying goes back thousands of years. Men would herd the sheep, goats, and cows, while women did the milking and made butter and cheese.
In colonial America, making cheese became a skill that was passed from mother to daughter, and selling their cheese gave farm women an independent source of income. Rural women also set up small factories to produce cheese for urban markets. The profits from the cheese enterprises helped cheese-making families educate their daughters. In the last thirty years, a number of American women have started small cheese-making companies in California that offer a superior product.

Cheese

COWGIRL CREAMERY ARTISAN CHEESE
One Ferry Building #17 ★ San Francisco ★ (415) 362-9354

A good place to sample California cheese is the Cowgirl Creamery Artisan Cheese in the Ferry Building, which has hundreds of local and imported cheeses. The company also has a shop in Point Reyes. In addition to an outstanding selection of cheeses, they stock cheese books, cheese knives, cheese boards, and special condiments to accompany their cheeses. A good selection for a tasting would be:

BELLWETHER FARMS

Bellwether Farms specializes in young, tangy cheeses made with 100 percent Jersey cow milk. They are the only producers of Crescenza, an Italian-style creamy soft-ripened cheese, and they are noted for their ricotta. Their other signature cheese is called Carmody.

MARIN FRENCH CHEESE

Marin French is the oldest continually operating cheese plant in the United States. They've been making Schloss, a washed-rind classic, since the 1930s. Their cheeses ripen in the unique microclimate of a subterranean aging room. Recently, they took a silver medal in London for their brie, a category typically dominated by Europeans.

FISCALINI FARMSTEAD

John Fiscalini and cheese maker Mariano Gonzalez continue to win awards for their Bandage cheddar and for the recently released San Joaquin Gold.

COWGIRL CREAMERY

Sue Conley and Peggy Smith continue to draw new consumers to their soft-ripened cheeses, their fresh cheeses (cottage cheese and fromage blanc), and to their weekly booth at the Ferry Building Farmers Market, where they offer the wares of other American artisanal cheese makers in addition to their own.

VELLA CHEESE COMPANY

Vella Cheese has remained a California standard of quality cheese making for more than seventy years. Vella's Dry Jack is known the world over, and the producer's Italian-style cheeses are especially good.

Sourdough Bread

BOUDIN AT THE WHARF

160 Jefferson Street ★ San Francisco ★ (415) 928-1849

An early maker of sourdough bread in San Francisco was Isidore Boudin, who, in 1849, tried to make French bread using sour dough. Today, Andre-Boudin Bakeries still survives and is still using the original mother dough starter, which they have perpetuated for over 150 years. Their "Original San Francisco Sourdough French Bread" is considered one of the best in the San Francisco Bay area. While the bread is available through many restaurants and stores, the best place to acquire it is at the demonstration bakery at Boudin at the Wharf: You can watch the breads being made, and then you can taste them at the bakery's café at Fisherman's Wharf. Boudin's San Francisco sourdough bread freezes well, so you can bring home as much as your freezer will hold.

WHO'D WANT OLD SOUR BREAD?

Sourdough breads have been consumed since antiquity. The word sourdough goes back to Middle English, and recipes for such breads appear in English cookbooks beginning in the seventeenth century. Sourdough bread is made with wild yeast and bacteria that give a slightly sour taste to the bread. What makes sourdough bread taste different in one part of the world than it does in another is the local wild yeast that grows in the area. The wild yeast in San Francisco is so specialized that it is known as lacto bacillus San Francisco. Of course, you could buy sourdough starter in San Francisco and bring it home to any city in the world and make sourdough bread. But it would never taste the same as it does in San Francisco because your local wild yeast would add itself to the starter and change everything.

terey and Big Sur. In partnership with Swiss and Portuguese dairymen, he dominated the dairy business throughout Monterey. Jacks was able to get his buddies in the railroad business to run a line from Monterey to San Francisco so he could make regular cheese shipments by train. Jacks's cheeses were soft, white, and based on an old California mission recipe. When Jacks shipped his cheese, he put it in a box and stamped it with his name and the cheese's origin, "David Jacks from Monterey, California," which is where we get the name *Monterey Jack*.

During World War I, Monterey Jack took on a second form. A San Francisco cheese wholesaler had left a surplus shipment of Monterey Jack sitting in his warehouse. When he finally opened the crates, he discovered that the cheese had aged quite nicely. It had lost most of its moisture, and was as hard as Parmesan or

Italian

DELFINA
3621 18th Street ★ San Francisco ★ (415) 552-4055

The menu changes daily, the food is delicious, the wine list is well chosen, and the service is friendly and efficient. The space is small and the décor is in keeping with the aluminum tables. This place is all about good food.

TOMASSO'S
1042 Kearny Street ★ San Francisco ★ (415) 398-9696

At Tomasso's, everyone eats family style at long community tables in cozy booths. The fare consists of traditional southern-Italian dishes and Neapolitan pizza from the oldest brick oven in San Francisco.

---

pecorino Romano. It had also acquired a nutty flavor—but that was all just fine. The war had cut off the supply of cheese from Italy, and the large Italian community in San Francisco needed a replacement. Dry Jack was quickly accepted by Italian-American cooks.

Today, California has the largest dairy industry in the United States, producing nearly 4 billion gallons of milk each year, almost half of it going into cheese. Most of California's dairies are located near the cheese makers. The milk that goes into the cheese is usually less than twenty-four hours old, which gives many of the cheeses a fresh milk flavor.

Chocolate

GHIRARDELLI CHOCOLATE SHOP & CAFFE
GHIRARDELLI SQUARE CAFFE
900 North Point Street ★ San Francisco ★ (415) 474-1414

One of the oldest chocolate manufacturers in the United States—and many say the best—is Ghirardelli in San Francisco. The company has been making chocolate since 1852, and they're good at it. Today, you can buy Ghirardelli chocolate in many places in America, but the best place is still their Ghirardelli Square Manufactory in San Francisco, where you can watch and smell it being produced.

Fast Food

TAYLOR'S REFRESHER AT FERRY MARKET
One Ferry Plaza ★ San Francisco ★ (866) 328-3663

For me, this is the perfect fast-food restaurant. I first heard about it from one of the world's leading wine authorities, who described it as having the best fast-food hamburger in the country. My favorite is the blue-cheese burger. The shakes, onion rings, and French fries are also excellent.

Until recently, California has relied on large production facilities that mass-produce cheese, but specialty cheese making is on the rise. Today, California boasts more than fifty cheese makers who produce more than 150 types of cheese in a wide range of textures and styles, from brie to cheddar. Flavored cheeses, like those spiced with jalapeño chiles, have been growing in popularity. California has increased its cheese production since 1993, overtaking Wisconsin.

The counties just above San Francisco make up the oldest dairy district in the state. The cool ocean air and fog that comes in off the Pacific give the region an even temperature throughout the year. The soil is ideal for the clovers and grasses that dairy cattle feed on, and the long rainy season lengthens the time that the cattle can feed on natural pasture.

Crab

PPQ DUNGENESS ISLAND
2332 Clement Street ★ San Francisco ★ (415) 386-8266

The Dungeness crab inhabits eelgrass beds and water bottoms off San Francisco. The crab season opens in November, which is the best time to taste freshly caught Dungeness crab. Many places in San Francisco serve Dungeness crab, and many restaurants at Fisherman's Wharf, where the crabs are unloaded, have cauldrons full of crabs out front and are well worth trying. One unusual restaurant that specializes in preparing it is PPQ Dungeness Island, a Vietnamese restaurant, where the crab is served with garlic and garlic noodles. The only way to eat them is with plastic bibs. Crab season ends in late spring.

Irish Coffee from the Buena Vista Café

MAKES 1 SERVING

The staff at Buena Vista claim that the whiskey is added only because it helps hold up the cream.

2 sugar cubes or 1 teaspoon sugar
Freshly brewed coffee
1 jigger Irish whiskey
Heavy cream, lightly whipped

1. Warm a heatproof glass with hot water. Pour out the water.

2. Place the sugar in the glass.

3. Fill the glass to the three-quarter mark with hot coffee and stir to dissolve the sugar.

4. Stir in the whiskey.

5. Hold a spoon on the surface of the coffee and pour the cream into the spoon until it spreads out and covers the coffee in a 1/4-inch layer.

★ WHAT TO TASTE AND WHERE TO TASTE IT ★

Irish Coffee

BUENA VISTA CAFÉ
2765 Hyde Street ★ San Francisco ★ (415) 474-5044

The Buena Vista Café is a popular and usually crowded bar with more tourists than residents. In addition to stiff drinks and a great view of the bay, the café serves an ample breakfast and good sandwiches; but its real claim to fame is the Irish coffee.

Beef with Broccoli

MAKES 4 SERVINGS

In addition to introducing Chinese food to the miners of San Francisco, the Chinese community introduced Chinese cooking equipment. The most common stove throughout Chinese history was in the shape of a small box with a round hole in the top. The wok was developed to sit over the opening without falling into the fire inside the box. The sides of the wok slope so the heat at the bottom can radiate evenly up the sides, but the slope also causes the ingredients to fall back into the center where the heat is concentrated. It is an extraordinarily efficient design. The wok is the basic, all-purpose utensil of Chinese cookery, and since its introduction in California, it has become a staple in the American home kitchen.

Broccoli was first made popular by the Italians around Naples. It was brought to England and the colonies in the eighteenth century. The wave of Italian immigration to the United States in the 1920s increased its popularity. Most of the broccoli we eat now is grown in California.

2 cups fresh broccoli florets
½ cup vegetable oil
1 pound boneless lean beef, cut into bite-sized strips
3 cloves garlic, chopped
1 tablespoon chopped peeled fresh ginger (optional)
½ cup chopped scallions, green and white parts
1 red bell pepper, cored, seeded, and cut into strips
½ cup very thinly sliced peeled carrots
1½ cups sliced mushrooms
1 cup drained canned sliced bamboo shoots
3 tablespoons oyster sauce or black bean sauce
2 teaspoons soy sauce, or more to taste
Cooked white rice, for serving

1. In a wok or large sauté pan, bring 2 cups water to a boil over high heat. Add the broccoli and cook for 2 minutes. Plunge the broccoli into cold water to stop the cooking. Drain and set aside.

2. Return the wok to medium-high heat. Pour in the oil and heat until it begins to shimmer. Add the beef strips and stir-fry until the beef changes color, about 1 minute. Remove the beef with a slotted spoon and set aside. Pour off all but 2 tablespoons of the oil.

3. Add the garlic and ginger, if using, to the pan and stir-fry for 1 minute. Add the cooked broccoli, scallions, bell pepper, and carrots and stir-fry for 1 minute. Add the mushrooms and bamboo shoots and stir-fry for 1 minute. Return the beef to the pan and add the oyster sauce and soy sauce. Stir-fry for 1 minute, or until the beef is cooked through. Serve at once with white rice.

> Broccoli is an intensely green sprouting member of the cabbage family. We eat the flowering head of the plant before it flowers and turns yellow. Any yellow florets or open buds on your broccoli mean that the plant is too mature and may be bitter and tough.
>
> Broccoli is one of the most nutritious vegetables: It is a good source of vitamins A and B, calcium, iron, and potassium, and has more vitamin C than an equal volume of oranges. A full cup of broccoli is high in fiber and has only 40 calories. Broccoli is best and most nutritious when it is still bright green and crunchy. Overcooking makes it soggy and destroys the vitamins.

★ WHAT TO TASTE AND WHERE TO TASTE IT ★

Chinese

YANK SING
Rincon Center ★ 101 Spear Street ★ San Francisco ★ (415) 957-9300 and
49 Stevenson Street ★ San Francisco ★ (415) 541-4949

Dim sum means "point to your heart" and suggests that the little Cantonese dishes served (traditionally for lunch) at a dim sum tea parlor will allow you to eat to your heart's content. Yank Sing is the oldest tea parlor in San Francisco and considered by many residents to be the best. You will be surrounded by rolling carts with small portions of about fifty different foods, such as steamed buns, roast pork, fried shrimp. Each dish has a specific price, and you will be charged according to what you have chosen. The courteous, efficient, English-speaking staff facilitates the meeting of East and West.

TON KIANG
5821 Geary Boulevard ★ San Francisco ★ (415) 387-8273

The specialty is the rustic Hakka cuisine of southern China: clay-pot dishes, salt-baked chicken, excellent seafood, stuffed bean curd, and many wine-flavored dishes. Friendly service, a pristine environment, and excellent food have made the place extremely popular—stop in during the week or at off-hours, or be prepared to wait in line and remember that patience is a virtue.

Mandarin Chicken Salad

MAKES 4 TO 6 SERVINGS

San Francisco's Chinatown is the oldest and one of the largest Chinese communities outside of Asia, and some of its restaurants serve the finest Chinese food in the world. Most of the cooking is of the Mandarin style.

Mandarin cooking is the cuisine developed by chefs in Beijing, China's Imperial City. The word comes form the Chinese word mandar, which means to govern, and was often used to describe people in positions of power. Beijing is a port city located on the northeast coast of China. As the seat of government and the center of culture in China, many of the best cooks migrated there. Beijing became the culinary capital of China and Mandarin cooking became the most influential style in the country.

3 chicken breasts, poached and cooled, skin and bones removed
2 cups fresh bean sprouts
2 tablespoons soy sauce
1 tablespoon white wine vinegar
1 tablespoon sesame oil
½ teaspoon chili oil
½ teaspoon sugar

1. Coarsely shred the chicken.

2. In a medium saucepan, boil the bean sprouts in water to cover for 2 minutes. Drain, refresh under cold water, and drain again.

3. In a small mixing bowl, combine the dressing ingredients.

4. Place the shredded chicken in a serving bowl and add the bean sprouts and the dressing. Stir together. The longer the salad marinates in its dressing, the better it tastes.

Minestrone Soup

MAKES 6 TO 8 SERVINGS

San Francisco's Little Italy was originally settled by sailors from Northern Italy who jumped ship to join the gold rush. When the rush was over, they stayed on as farmers, shopkeepers, and restaurateurs, putting their community together in an area known as North Beach. This recipe is a good example of their traditional Minestrone Soup.

Soup in Italy is served and enjoyed as often as pasta, and minestrone is the most popular. Often pasta, rice, or crusty country bread is added. Freshly grated Parmesan or Romano cheese is sometimes sprinkled on top, which greatly enhances the nutritional value of the soup. For best results, cut the vegetables into similar sizes so they will cook evenly.

¼ cup olive oil
1 large onion, chopped
2 ribs celery, diced
2 large carrots, peeled and diced
1 clove garlic, minced
2 medium potatoes, peeled and diced
1 cup fresh Italian plum tomatoes, peeled, seeded, and chopped
1 large zucchini, diced
½ cup cooked chickpeas
½ cup cooked cannellini (white beans)
½ cup cooked red kidney beans
Salt and freshly ground black pepper
1 tablespoon chopped fresh parsley
½ teaspoon dried oregano
½ teaspoon dried basil

1. In a stockpot or large saucepan, heat the oil over moderate heat. Add the onion, celery, and carrots, and sauté until the onion is translucent, 3 to 5 minutes. Stir in the garlic, potatoes, tomatoes, and 7 cups water. Bring to a boil. Reduce the heat and simmer for 45 minutes.

2. Add the zucchini and simmer for 30 minutes.

3. Add the chickpeas and beans; season with salt and pepper to taste. Crush the herbs and add to the soup. Bring to a boil and reduce the heat. Simmer for 15 minutes.

Chicken with Citrus Sauce and Raisins

MAKES 6 SERVINGS

Raisins are grapes that have been dried to a point that prevents the development of enzymes that cause spoilage. In 1873, a California grape grower had his entire crop scorched by the hot sun. Instead of throwing out the dehydrated grapes, he brought them to a local grocer and convinced the grocer that he was selling "raisinated grapes," a rare Persian delicacy. That was our first California raisin crop.

6 skin-on, bone-in chicken breast halves
Salt and freshly ground black pepper to taste
2 sprigs fresh rosemary, chopped, or 1 teaspoon dried
3 small cloves garlic, thinly sliced
3 shallots, thinly sliced
4 tablespoons olive oil
½ cup pine nuts
¼ cup dry white wine
1 tablespoon red wine vinegar
¼ cup fresh lemon juice
½ cup fresh orange juice
⅔ cup chicken stock
½ cup golden raisins

1. Rub the chicken with salt, pepper, rosemary, garlic, shallots, and 1 tablespoon of the olive oil in a glass or ceramic dish and store, covered, in the refrigerator for 1 hour or longer. It tastes best if you marinate it overnight.

2. Preheat the oven to 350 degrees F.

3. Remove the chicken from the marinade and scrape the solids back into the dish. In a large flameproof casserole over medium heat, cook the remaining 3 tablespoons olive oil and the marinade ingredients for 5 minutes. Add the chicken skin side down, and cook until the skin is lightly golden. Add the pine nuts, wine, vinegar, lemon juice, orange juice, stock, and raisins. Simmer uncovered over medium heat for 3 to 4 minutes to concentrate the flavor and thicken the sauce.

4. Transfer the casserole to the oven and bake uncovered for 20 minutes or until the chicken is cooked through. Remove the chicken to a platter and cover with foil to keep warm. Over high heat, boil the pan juices until thick. Season with salt and pepper to taste. Serve the chicken with spoonfuls of sauce, nuts, and raisins over the top.

Cold Noodles with Asparagus & Ginger

MAKES 4 SERVINGS

Handmade egg noodles have been made in Chinese restaurants in America since the mid-nineteenth century, but it wasn't until the 1970s that they became popular outside the Chinese-American community.

FOR THE DRESSING

1 1/2 teaspoons kosher salt
1/2 teaspoon freshly ground black pepper
2 tablespoons rice vinegar
1 tablespoon Chinese black or balsamic vinegar
2 teaspoons soy sauce
4 teaspoons finely minced peeled fresh ginger
1/2 teaspoon finely minced orange zest
1/3 cup vegetable oil
1 tablespoon dark Chinese or Japanese sesame oil

FOR THE NOODLES

1/2 pound Chinese egg noodles
1/2 pound asparagus
4 radishes, thinly sliced
1 scallion, white and green parts, thinly sliced
2 tablespoons minced cilantro, plus sprigs for garnish

1. TO MAKE THE DRESSING: In a large bowl, whisk together the salt, pepper, vinegars, soy sauce, ginger, and orange zest. Slowly whisk in the vegetable and sesame oils.

2. TO MAKE THE NOODLES: Bring a medium pot of water to a boil, salt the water, and cook the noodles until al dente, according to the package directions. Drain the noodles into a colander and rinse them under cool water. Shake the noodles free of excess water. Add the noodles to the dressing, toss to coat, and set aside.

3. Peel the bottom part of the asparagus stalks with a vegetable peeler and trim the tough ends. Cut the asparagus on the bias into 1/4-inch-thick slices about 1 1/2 inches long. Steam the asparagus and radishes in a steamer basket or bamboo steamer over boiling water for 2 minutes. Remove the steamer tray and rinse the vegetables under cold water to stop the cooking.

4. Toss the noodles with the cooked asparagus, radishes, scallions, and minced coriander. Place in a serving bowl and garnish with sprigs of cilantro.

Monterey Jack Corn Fritters

MAKES ABOUT 14 FRITTERS

Monterey Jack or Jack cheese is a firm, cooked, semi-soft whole-milk or skim-milk cheese made from cow's milk. When aged or dry, it resembles Cheddar, but when soft and not aged, it is similar to Muenster in flavor. Monterey Jack originated in Monterey County, California. The "Jack" comes from a Scottish immigrant named David Jacks who made the cheese and shipped it out of Monterey, with his name on the shipping crate. Eventually, customers in northern California began asking for Monterey Jack cheese.

Monterey Jack is a modern version of a queso blanco, the white cheese that was made by Spanish missionaries in California. Monterey Jack works well in Mexican recipes.

1 cup yellow cornmeal
1 (8-ounce) can creamed corn
½ cup buttermilk
½ cup vegetable oil
1 cup shredded Monterey Jack cheese (about ¼ pound)
¾ teaspoon baking soda
Salt
2 teaspoons finely chopped jalapeño pepper
1 egg
3 scallions, green part only, finely chopped
Unsalted butter

1. In a mixing bowl, blend together all the ingredients except the butter. The batter should be slightly thicker than pancake batter.

2. Place a griddle over moderately high heat until hot. Lightly butter it and, using about ¼ cup of the batter at a time, pour rounds of batter onto the griddle. Cook until bubbles come to the surface. Flip the fritters and cook for a few minutes more. Serve immediately.

Ricotta Cheesecake

MAKES 8 SERVINGS

Ricotta cheesecake is a favorite tradition in San Francisco's Italian community.

FOR THE CRUST

1½ cups amaretti cookie crumbs
5 tablespoons unsalted butter, melted

FOR THE FILLING

¼ cup amaretto
½ cup chopped dried apricots
3 cups whole-milk ricotta cheese
¼ cup all-purpose flour
⅔ cup sugar
⅛ teaspoon ground mace
1 teaspoon vanilla extract
4 large eggs, separated
Salt

1. TO MAKE THE CRUST: Combine the crumbs with 4 tablespoons of the butter. Brush a 10-inch springform pan with the remaining butter and cover the bottom with the crust. Refrigerate while you prepare the filling.

2. Preheat the oven to 350 degrees F.

3. TO MAKE THE FILLING: In a small pan, heat the amaretto with the apricots to plump the fruit. Set aside.

4. In a food processor, pulse the ricotta until it is creamy. Remove from the processor and mix it in a bowl with the flour, sugar, mace, vanilla, egg yolks, and soaked apricots.

5. In a stainless-steel bowl, whisk the egg whites with a pinch of salt to soft peaks. With a rubber spatula, fold one-third of the egg whites into the ricotta filling to lighten the batter. Fold in the remaining egg whites.

6. Pour the filling into the chilled crust and bake for 1 hour or until the filling is golden brown and set. Remove from the oven and cool on a rack.

Ricotta is a fresh cheese similar to cottage cheese. It has a very mild flavor and delicate consistency, and heats well. It is made from whey or buttermilk, and comes in regular and part-skim varieties. At 4 and 2 % fat, both are considered low-fat cheeses. It is the basis for the great cheesecakes of Italy.

CHICAGO
Illinois

TWELVE THOUSAND YEARS AGO, the middle of the North American continent was covered by a huge glacial lake. As it receded, it left wide prairies and the Great Lakes with swampy shores. The marshlands at the southwest corner of what we now call Lake Michigan were overgrown with wild onions—onions that gave off a very strong odor. The native tribes who lived nearby called the place Checagou, which means "great strength." Today we call it Chicago, and it's stronger than ever.

The first permanent settler in the area was Jean Baptiste Point DuSable, the son of a French-Canadian merchant and an African-American slave. In 1779, he set up a trading post on what eventually became Michigan Avenue, the most important shopping street in Chicago.

The keys to Chicago's greatness lie in its location. To the north and east are the Great Lakes and the St. Lawrence Seaway running out to the Atlantic Ocean. To the south is a network of rivers that join the Mississippi and flow down to the Gulf of Mexico. Chicago is the central point between the two waterways, and people have been using it as a trading post for thousands of years. When the Erie Canal opened in 1825, Chicago found itself with a direct water route to New York City. Products that were grown or manufactured in the Midwest were brought to Chicago and transported through the Erie Canal to the East Coast, or south along the Mississippi River system.

Because of its location, Chicago was able to make a major contribution to the success of the Union armies during the Civil War. When the war began, the South closed the Mississippi River to trade from the Midwest. Grain and stock had to be rerouted: Instead of being moved by boat down the Mississippi, they were brought to Chicago and then shipped by train or by canal to the East Coast. As a result, the Union armies, as well as the soliders' families at home, were well fed throughout the war. There was even a surplus of food that was sold to England and France—trade that discouraged those countries from recognizing the Confederacy. By the time the Civil War ended, Chicago was a major food center and one of the nation's most important commercial hubs.

WHERE'S THE BEEF? AND PORK?

Chicago's reputation as a cattle town was built during the Civil War. The Union Stockyards, which opened on Christmas Day 1865, could house 10,000 head of cattle and 100,000 hogs. In those days, pork was more popular than beef in the United States. Driven overland from the West, cattle would lose quite a bit of weight, so the animals were held in Chicago feedlots and fattened before being shipped to markets in the East. The stockyards made Chicago the beef capital of the world. Today that standing is reflected in its love of steaks, hot dogs, and Italian beef sandwiches.

WHERE'S THE BEEF?
"Italian beef" appeared on the Chicago streets after World War I. It consisted of thin (shaved) slices of beef roasted in broth with garlic, oregano, and spices. Italian beef, along with mozzarella and roasted green peppers, was stuffed into Italian bread, which was then drenched with beef broth. This was called an Italian beef sandwich, and it was an immediate hit in Chicago. It remains a hit, but today there are many different ways of making them. They can be bought on the streets through vendors or in many Italian restaurants.

In 1868, Philip Danforth Armour came to Chicago and set up a food processing company; by the 1890s, Armour and Company was the largest meatpacker in the nation.

★ WHAT TO TASTE AND WHERE TO TASTE IT ★

Italian Beef Sandwich

MR. BEEF
666 North Orleans Street ★ Chicago ★ (312) 337-8500
Well-done roast beef, thinly sliced, dipped in its juices, and served on Italian bread.
Optional topping: sweet peppers.

HOTDOGGING IN CHICAGO

The foundation is an all-beef sausage in a natural casing that snaps when you bite it, and it is served on a steamed poppyseed bun. Things get interesting with the addition of mustard, relish, chopped raw onion, pickle slices, pickled hot peppers, celery salt, and diced or wedged tomatoes. The required side is an order of French fries smothered with cheddar cheese. The Maxwell Street–style hot dog is served on a plain bun with fried or grilled onions and mustard. A good place to sample Chicago-style hot dogs is at Fluky's or at Superdawg Drive-ins.

In the 1870s, Gustavus Swift built refrigerated railroad cars and forever changed the way the beef industry operated. Instead of shipping live animals, he started slaughtering, processing, and packing beef for shipment throughout the country—an innovation made possible by Swift's refrigerated cars. At first, the railroads tried to stop him—they got paid more to ship a live steer than to move a dressed beef carcass—but eventually Swift won out. He created a nationwide distribution and marketing organization, and Swift & Co. became one of most important meatpackers and distributors in America.

Another familiar name from Chicago's golden age of meatpacking is Oscar Mayer. Mayer was a German immigrant who started out working in the stockyards, then joined his brother, a sausage maker and ham curer, in opening a small retail butcher shop in a German neighborhood on Chicago's Near North Side. In 1929, the Mayers took the bold step of putting their own name on their products and began selling America's first brand-name meats.

★ WHAT TO TASTE AND WHERE TO TASTE IT ★

Chicago Hot Dogs

SUPERDAWG DRIVE-IN
6363 North Milwaukee Avenue ★ Chicago ★ (773) 763-0660

This 1950s-style drive-in, complete with carhops, serves what many Chicagoans consider the best dog in town. If you miss the Superdawg experience while in the city, you can get another shot at it by visiting the branch at Midway Airport.

FLUKY'S
520 North Michigan Avenue ★ Chicago ★ (312) 245-0702

Serving Chicago-style hot dogs and Polish sausages, this small chain's locations are convenient and the prices are rock bottom. Naming a hot-dog stand appears to require more creativity than the actual skill in the kitchen. Some of the more unusual are Relish the Thought, Red Hot Mammas, Dog Day Afternoon, Weiner's Circle, and Mustards Last Stand.

Confectioners settled in Chicago in the early nineteenth century. By 1859, forty-six confectioners in the city were making candy, like hard candies, licorice, chicken feed (candy corn), and candy eggs. German immigrants brought the art of spun sugar, which was used to create cotton candy or floss. They also made lollipops by dipping slate pencils into spun sugar to create a handy confection.

One of the most significant events in the city's history was the Great Chicago Fire, which ravaged the city in 1871. Within days after the fire, the city passed a law requiring all new buildings to be constructed of fireproof stone and brick. As Chicago rebuilt after the fire, the city took on a greater importance than ever before.

Frederick W. Rueckheim, an immigrant from Germany, was among the many who came to Chicago to assist in rebuilding the city. He felt that he could do the most good (while succeeding in business) by helping to feed the workers who were rebuilding the fire-damaged city, so he opened a popcorn stand. Hoping to come up with an original twist on the old-fashioned popcorn ball, Rueckheim experimented with sugar coatings and combinations of marshmallows, nuts, and other ingredients before finally settling on a combination of popcorn and peanuts with a molasses glaze. At Chicago's Columbian Exposition, in 1893, Rueckheim's new confection attracted crowds to his popcorn stand. It wasn't until two years later that he worked out the details of mass production for the new confection, and at that point finally gave it a name: Cracker Jack. This was America's first snack food, which by 1896 was the best-selling confection in

CALL ME TOOTSIE

In 1896, Leo Hirschfield emigrated from Austria to New York and opened a little shop where he made candy from a secret family recipe. He named the candy after his daughter Clara, whose nickname was Tootsie. Sweet as it was, Leo decided to sell the business, and in 1922 it went public and was listed on the New York Stock Exchange. Starting in its earliest years, the Rubin family supplied the Tootsie Roll Company with its paper boxes, and during the 1930s the Rubins bought control of Tootsie and moved the headquarters to Chicago. Today, Ellen Gordon, the daughter of William Rubin, is president of the company. In addition to the traditional Tootsie Rolls, the company makes Tootsie Pops, which were the original Tootsie Roll–centered lollipops, Caramel Apple Pops, Child's Play, Charms, Blow Pop, Blue Razz, Cella's Chocolate Covered Cherries, Mason Dots, Mason Crows, Junior Mints, Charleston Chew, Sugar Daddy, Sugar Babies, Andes, Fluffy Stuff Cotton Candy, Dubble Bubble, Razzles, Cry Baby, Nik-L-Nip, and El Bubble.

the country. During the early twentieth century, Rueckheim began exporting Cracker Jack to Europe, and by 1913 it was the best-selling commercial confection in the world.

Cracker Jack's success may have inspired other Chicagoans to try their hand at commercial candy production. Emil J. Brach, with his sons Edwin and Frank, opened E. J. Brach & Sons in 1904. It sold caramels, butterscotch disks, and mints, and it became nation's largest seller of bagged sweets. In 1908, the Ferrare Pan Candy Company was started. It manufactured Atomic Fire Balls, Jaw Breakers, Boston Baked Beans, Lemonheads, and Red Hots.

In 1916, Otto Y. Schnering opened a bakery with a small candy department. By 1920, he had perfected a chocolate-coated candy bar filled with peanuts and caramel, and he named it Baby Ruth. Once Schnering began manufacturing this specialty, he stopped at nothing to promote it. His most famous stunt was chartering an airplane and having Baby Ruth bars dropped by parachute over major cities. No one-hit wonder, in 1926 Schnering invented the Butterfinger candy bar.

★ WHAT TO TASTE AND WHERE TO TASTE IT ★

Baked Goods

THE SWEDISH BAKERY IN ANDERSONVILLE
5348 North Clark Street ★ Chicago ★ (773) 561-8919

The Swedish Bakery in Andersonville opened in 1928 and continues to bake breads, cakes, and pastries. A neighborhood favorite is the Andersonville Coffee Cake.

George H. Williamson, a salesman for a candy broker in Chicago, knew little of candy making, but in 1914 he opened a shop and began to make his own candy. One chocolate-coated peanut bar proved especially popular, and he decided to manufacture it on a large scale. All he needed was a memorable name. Williamson was a fan of short-story writer William Sydney Porter, whose pen name was O. Henry, and Oh Henry! became the candy bar's name. First appearing on the market in 1920, within three years Oh Henry! was the best-selling candy bar in America.

In 1920, Archibald Candy Company opened the first Fannie May store in Chicago. By 1935, Fannie May candies were being sold in forty-seven stores across the Midwest; the company merged

LETTUCE ENTERTAIN YOU

Chicago is the home of one of the most interesting restaurant groups in the United States. It's called Lettuce Entertain You, and was started in the early 1970s by Richard Melman and his partners. Today it has over thirty-one restaurants. But unlike most restaurant groups, which have one strong idea that is taken across the country, Melman has opened almost all of his dining spots in Chicago, and each one is different. Curious to find out what commercial insight lay behind this unusual decision, I once asked him why he did almost all of his work in one town. His response: "I hate to travel. I don't like the aggravation you go through at airports. I have a horrible sense of direction. In a new town I never know where I am. I want to be with my family."

★ **WHAT TO TASTE AND WHERE TO TASTE IT** ★

Candy

MARGIE'S CANDIES
1960 North Western Avenue ★ Chicago ★ (773) 384-1035

Margie's Candies is a classic America ice-cream parlor. It opened in 1921 and very little has changed since then. Go for broke with the house special, a giant bowl filled with ice cream, whipped cream, caramel sauce, and sugar wafers.

MARSHALL FIELDS
111 North State Street ★ Chicago ★ (312) 781-1000

In 1918, the Frederick and Nelson Company of Seattle created Frango Mints, a confection composed of chocolate and mint. Eleven years later, Marshall Field's acquired Frederick and Nelson Co. and began selling Frango Mints in their State Street store in Chicago. Frango Mints became a Chicago icon. Additional flavors were added, like dark mint, double chocolate, toffee crunch, caramel, raspberry, coffee, cherry, and Frango chocolate.

with Fanny Farmer to form the largest retail candy chain in the country. Later, big corporations such as Mars set up factories in Chicago. In 1945, there were more than six thousand candy firms in America, but their days were numbered. Since then, some candy manufacturers have gone out of business, many have merged, and now a few candy companies now dominate the field. By 2010, there are projected to be only 150 candy companies in America.

A CITY OF NEIGHBORHOODS

Chicago has always been a haven for African-Americans coming up from the South. The two biggest migrations took place after the World Wars I and II. The newcomers settled on Chicago's South Side, which was close to the train station where they had arrived, and where there were plenty of jobs. Today, this area, called the Bronzeville district, is being restored and has become an important destination for African-American heritage tours.

Between 1840 and 1925, more than 40 million people immigrated to the United States, the majority passing through Ellis Island. Many of those who didn't stay in the New York area moved on to Chicago, among them Italian, Irish, German, Polish, eastern European, Scandinavian, and Greek immigrants. Their descendents still live in the neighborhoods chosen by their great-grandparents, and they keep their ancestral cuisines alive. In recent years, they have been joined by new groups, notably Asians and Mexicans.

★ WHAT TO TASTE AND WHERE TO TASTE IT ★

Mexican

FRONTERA GRILL AND TOPOLOBAMPO
445 North Clark Street ★ Chicago ★ (312) 661-1434

Chicago has a large Mexican community, which was established during the second half of the twentieth century. Topolobampo and the Frontera Grill, two of the best Mexican restaurants in North America, were created by Rick Bayless, who grew up in his family's barbecue restaurant in Oklahoma City. As an undergraduate, Bayless majored in Spanish and Latin American culture. Asked for his three favorite dishes on the menu, he came up with tortilla soup with pasilla chile, fresh cheese, and avocado; fish braised with tomatoes, capers, olives, and herbs; and fried shrimp with sweet toasted garlic. Each restaurant features outstanding margaritas and a great wine list.

WHEN CHICAGO WENT SOFT

Ice cream is generally served at five degrees Farenheit, but F. J. "Grandpa" McCullough and his son, H. A. "Alex" McCullough, believed that it would be more flavorful if it were served at a higher temperature, because cold temperatures numbed the taste buds. The McCulloughs owned the Homemade Ice Cream Company in Green River, Illinois, and they began experimenting with what would later be called soft-serve ice cream. They found that it was best when it contained about 6 percent butter fat and when it was served at eighteen degrees. In 1938, they thought they had found a winning flavorful combination, so they asked a friend to test-market it with his customers. It was a big hit.

After the war, Dairy Queen expanded quickly, from 17 outlets in 1946 to 2,600 in 1955. In 1950, Leo Maranz invented a small freezer to make soft-serve ice cream. With a partner he formed a new Chicago-based chain, which they named Tastee-Freez.

TWINKLE TOES?

Continental Baking Company made sponge cakes that were used for strawberry shortcake. Unfortunately, shortcakes were only sold when strawberries were in season, and the company needed products that could be sold year-round. Jimmy Dewar, a Chicago bakery manager, came up with an idea for filling shortcake with a banana cream, and selling it in small packages at the price of two for a nickle. Dewar claimed that he named the new product Twinkies after he saw an advertisement for the Twinkle Toe Shoe Company on a trip to St. Louis. During World War II, it was difficult to import bananas, so they shifted to a vanilla cream filling. After the war, the snack became an American icon. Twinkies have been deep-fried and served with ice cream. They have even been placed in the nation's Millennium Time Capsule. Twinkies have appeared in many movies and in a trial where the "Twinkie Defense" didn't cut the . . . cake?

★ WHAT TO TASTE AND WHERE TO TASTE IT ★

Greek

PAPAGUS
620 North State Street ★ Chicago ★ (312) 642-8450

Papagus means "Grandpa Gus." The restaurant is divided into areas that represent different parts of Greece. The Paros room represents northern Greece—the walls are whitewashed, handmade fabric lines the ceiling, and sea-blue bottles symbolize the Mediterranean. Examples of this region's cuisine are roasted jumbo shrimp in phyllo, served on a bed of saffron rice, and whole fish grilled over a wood fire. The grill is 150 years old and is fired only with cherry wood. Other corners of the restaurant correspond to other geographic regions of Greece and present their traditional dishes.

French Onion Soup

MAKES 6 TO 8 SERVINGS

Commissioned by the French government in 1673, Louis Joliet and Father Jacques Marquette became the first explorers of Chicago.

For hundreds of years, the cooks of Europe were organized into very specialized craft unions and each group controlled the production and distribution of their product. Then one day in the 1760s, a Parisian named Boulanger noticed a loophole in the law which would allow him to sell food to the public without belonging to a guild. What he found he could legally sell was soup. The major claim that he made for his recipes was that they were healthful and would restore one's strength. The word *restaurant* comes from the sign on Boulanger's shop, describing his "restorative" soups.

3 tablespoons unsalted butter

2 tablespoons olive oil

5 medium yellow onions, thinly sliced

Salt

½ teaspoon sugar

1 teaspoon chopped garlic

½ teaspoon chopped fresh thyme

3 tablespoons all-purpose flour

½ cup white wine

8 cups chicken stock

Freshly ground black pepper

Dash of Worcestershire sauce

12 to 16 baguette slices, each 1-inch thick, toasted

4 cups grated Jarlsberg or Swiss cheese (about 1 pound)

1. In a large heavy-bottomed pot, melt the butter and heat the oil over medium heat. Add the onions and cook, stirring frequently, for about 15 minutes, until they are soft. Season to taste with the salt, add the sugar, and continue to cook for 30 minutes more, until the onions turn dark brown and caramelize. Be sure to stir the onions frequently to prevent them from scorching. Add the garlic and thyme and cook 3 minutes more.

2. Add the flour and stir constantly for 2 minutes. Add the wine and 1 cup of the chicken stock and whisk vigorously until thick. Stir in the rest of the chicken stock, increase the heat to high, and bring to a boil. Reduce the heat to medium-low and simmer for 30 to 40 minutes more. Season to taste with the salt and pepper and a dash of Worcestershire sauce.

3. Preheat the oven to 375 degrees F. Ladle the soup into ovenproof soup bowls and place 2 slices of the toasted baguette in the soup. Cover each bowl with about ½ cup of the cheese and bake 20 to 30 minutes, until the cheese has melted and turns golden.

★ WHAT TO TASTE AND WHERE TO TASTE IT ★

French

CHARLIE TROTTER'S
816 West Armitage Avenue ★ Chicago ★ (773) 248-6228

Chef Trotter insists on the finest seasonal ingredients, preparing them with classic French techniques enlivened by American creativity. This is his flagship restaurant and is well worth visiting.

AMBRIA
2300 North Lincoln Park West ★ Chicago ★ (773) 472-5959

Ambria offers a luxurious combination of creative but easy-to-understand food, impeccably paced, unobtrusive service, and an elegantly romantic atmosphere. You can see it as old and clubby, or modern and polished, depending on your mood. The Art Nouveau setting and the view of Lincoln Park make the dining room a perfect backdrop for the seasonally changing menu. Don't miss the sublime dessert soufflé.

EVEREST
440 South La Salle Boulevard, 40th Floor ★ Chicago ★ (312) 663-8920

If the elevator ascent to Everest's fortieth-floor dining room doesn't make you giddy, the creations of chef-owner Jean Joho will. Inspired by his native Alsace, Jean creates sumptuous and elegant dishes out of simple and earthy ingredients. The menu changes seasonally, and the wine list embraces a huge selection of Alsatian wines. Ask for a window table so you can enjoy unobstructed views of the city along with your meal.

Horseradish-Crusted Filet Mignon

MAKES 4 SERVINGS

The origin of Chicago's importance lies in its location: For thousands of years, people have been using this spot as a central trading post. As the United States moved west, Chicago became a commercial center. Everybody who grew or manufactured something in the Midwest brought it to Chicago for sale, especially the guys who were raising cows and pigs. Each year, millions of steaks pass through Chicago, and some of the best of those steaks end up in the kitchens of Chicago.

FOR THE HORSERADISH CRUST

6 tablespoons (¾ stick) salted butter, at room temperature
3 to 4 tablespoons grated fresh horseradish or prepared white horseradish
Salt and freshly ground black pepper
½ cup panko (Japanese bread crumbs)

FOR THE HORSERADISH SOUR CREAM

3 to 4 tablespoons prepared white horseradish
1 cup sour cream
Salt and freshly ground black pepper

FOR THE MEAT

Four ½-pound, center cut filet mignons
4 slices good-quality bacon (optional)
Salt and freshly ground black pepper

1. **TO MAKE THE HORSERADISH CRUST:** In a medium bowl, with a wooden spoon, cream the butter. Once the butter is light and fluffy, stir in the horseradish and season to taste with salt and pepper. Add the breadcrumbs and mix until they have been incorporated. Use your hands to shape the mixture into 4 flat disks the diameter of the filets. Place on a plate, cover with plastic wrap, and refrigerate for at least 1 hour.

2. **TO MAKE THE HORSERADISH SOUR CREAM:** In a medium nonreactive bowl, mix together the horseradish and sour cream until smooth. Season to taste with salt and pepper. Cover with plastic wrap and refrigerate until ready to use.

3. **TO PREPARE THE FILETS:** If using the bacon, wrap each filet around circumference with one slice and secure the ends with a wooden toothpick. Repeat this with the three other filets and three slices of bacon.

4. Preheat the broiler to high. Place the oven rack on the top third of the oven. Heat a large, heavy, ovenproof skillet over medium-high heat. Season the filets with salt and pepper. Sear the sides of the meat by standing the filets on their sides until the filet or bacon just begins to brown and become crispy, about 30 seconds per side. Then sear the first flat side until dark golden, 2 to 3 minutes. Turn the filets over and sear the other side, cooking another 3 to 4 minutes for medium-rare.

5. Place a horseradish-bread crumb topping over each filet and place under the broiler until the crust becomes golden. Allow the filets to rest for 5 minutes before serving. Serve the filets with the horseradish sour cream on the side.

> Horseradish is native to southeastern Europe and western Asia, and most of the horseradish grown in the United States comes from Illinois farm country, just across the Mississippi River from St. Louis. Horseradish is the pungent root of a member of the cabbage family. It's called horseradish because it looks like a giant beige-colored radish.

★ WHAT TO TASTE AND WHERE TO TASTE IT ★

Steak

GIBSON STEAK HOUSE
1028 North Rush Street ★ Chicago ★ (312) 266-8999

The spot where the elite meet to eat. A powerhouse bar with an intense social scene, this is the place where aged beef joins cold beer for a hot date.

GENE & GEORGETTI
500 North Franklin Street ★ Chicago ★ (312) 527-3718

This is the old-style Chicago steakhouse at its best: Packed with old-time regulars there for its excellent grilled steaks and salads.

TRU
676 North St. Clair Street ★ Chicago ★ (312) 202-0001

Tru exudes an atmosphere of passion for the fine dining experience—passion for food, presentation, drama, and perfection. Rick Tramonto and Gale Gand work their magic to create complex and flavorful "progressive French" dishes, which are presented in original, nontraditional ways. You can choose from two prix-fixe menus: a well-designed three-course tasting menu, or the sumptuous eight-course Tramonto's Collection. Tables are generously spaced, and the service is impeccable.

Chicken with Mustard Cream Sauce

MAKES 4 SERVINGS

Mustard is one of the most widely used spices in the world. Mustard seeds were imported into America by European colonists, and mustard has been one of America's most important condiments ever since. Mustard cream sauce was popularized in the late nineteenth century and remains popular today.

1 1/2 tablespoons vegetable oil
One (3 1/2 pound) chicken, cut into 8 pieces
2 teaspoons kosher salt
1/2 teaspoon freshly ground black pepper
1 small onion, diced
1 shallot, diced
1 carrot, diced
2 sprigs fresh thyme, or 2 teaspoons dried thyme, crushed
1 cup white wine
1 cup heavy cream or crème fraîche
3 tablespoons Dijon-style mustard

1. Preheat the oven to 375 degrees F. Heat the oil in a Dutch oven or ovenproof skillet. Season the chicken pieces with half the salt and all the pepper, and brown the chicken in batches over high heat on all sides. Transfer the chicken to a plate, and add the onion, shallot, carrot, and thyme to the pan. Cook the vegetables over medium heat, until the onions are lightly browned. Return the chicken to the pan, cover with a round piece of parchment, or the lid slightly ajar, place the pan in the oven, and bake for 15 minutes.

2. Remove the chicken from the pan to a warm spot while you make the sauce. Pour the wine into the pan and, with a wooden spoon, scrape up any browned bits clinging to the pan. Simmer the wine and reduce to about 1/3 cup. Add the cream and simmer gently until thickened and the satiny sauce coats the back of a spoon. Whisk in the mustard, and season with the remaining salt. Return the chicken to the sauce to heat through, and serve immediately.

Steak with Garlic Butter

MAKES 4 SERVINGS

Garlic was introduced into America by European colonists, who mainly used it for medicinal purposes. Cooks in New Orleans and in the American southwest used it extensively, and by the late nineteenth century garlic became a common ingredient in American cookery. Yet the first written record of garlic butter does not appear until the 1940s. Garlic butter was popularized first as a spread to make garlic bread, but it found a variety of other uses, such as in this recipe.

1 tablespoon kosher salt, plus more to taste
2 cloves garlic, chopped
½ cup (1 stick) unsalted butter, softened
½ shallot, minced
½ cup chopped fresh parsley
½ teaspoon fresh lemon juice
½ teaspoon chopped fresh tarragon leaves
Freshly ground black pepper
Four 9-ounce top sirloin steaks, each ½-inch thick
2 tablespoons canola oil
French fries
Watercress

1. Sprinkle the salt over the garlic and continue to chop, smearing the garlic with the flat side of the knife, until the garlic becomes pastelike. Into a medium mixing bowl, place the softened butter. Add the shallot, garlic, parsley, lemon juice, tarragon, and season to taste with the salt and pepper. Stir the ingredients together until all are thoroughly combined. Spoon the mixture out onto a small sheet of parchment or wax paper and roll the butter up in the paper to form a log that is 1½ inches in diameter. Refrigerate the herb butter for at least 1 hour to set.

2. Heat a large heavy skillet, preferably cast iron, over high. Preheat the skillet for 3 to 5 minutes to ensure a good sear on the steaks. Rub each steak with the canola oil and season with the salt and pepper. Lay the steaks in the hot skillet and sear for 2 minutes on the first side. Turn the steaks over and continue to sear for 2 minutes on the second side for medium-rare. Allow the steaks to rest for 5 minutes before serving.

3. Remove the parchment paper from the herb butter and slice into 4 equal disks. Top each steak with the herb butter and serve with French fries on the side. Garnish each plate with a few sprigs of watercress.

Parmesan-Crusted Creamed Spinach

MAKES 4 SERVINGS

Parmesan Creamed Spinach is the perfect side dish for a steak.

3 (10-ounce) boxes frozen chopped spinach
5 tablespoons salted butter
1 small onion, minced
2 cloves garlic, minced
Pinch of ground nutmeg
1 cup heavy cream
3/4 cup freshly grated Parmesan cheese
Salt and freshly ground black pepper
1 cup fresh breadcrumbs

1. Thaw the spinach and squeeze out the excess liquid. Set the spinach aside. Preheat the oven to 450 degrees F.

2. In a large skillet, melt 3 tablespoons butter over medium heat. Add the onion and sauté for 5 minutes. Add the garlic and nutmeg and cook for 1 minute. Pour in the heavy cream, reduce the heat to medium-low, and simmer the mixture until it is reduced by half. Keep an eye on the cream as it reduces, in case it starts to boil over. The reduced cream will be very thick and turn a buttery yellow color when ready. Add 1/4 cup cheese and stir constantly until it has completely melted. Remove the skillet from the heat and add the spinach. Season to taste with the salt and pepper. Pour the spinach mixture into a 5-cup baking dish.

3. In a small skillet, melt the remaining 2 tablespoons butter. Pour the melted butter over the breadcrumbs in a small bowl and toss until the crumbs are thoroughly coated. Sprinkle the buttered crumbs over the spinach, then sprinkle on the remaining 1/2 cup cheese. Bake the creamed spinach for about 10 minutes, until the cheese has melted and becomes golden brown. Serve hot.

Lemon Bars

MAKES SIXTEEN 2-INCH SQUARES

There is an interesting historical reason why most people like sweets. In the wild, most things that taste sweet are safe to eat; most things that taste bitter are dangerous. So those of our early ancestors who loved sweets, in moderation of course, had a better chance of survival, and we have descended from them. Lemon bars are a common in Chicago—try them for breakfast with fresh brewed coffee.

½ cup (1 stick) unsalted butter, at room temperature, plus more for the pan
1 cup plus 2 tablespoons all-purpose flour
¼ cup confectioners' sugar, plus more for dusting
½ cup granulated sugar
½ teaspoon baking powder
2 eggs, beaten
4 tablespoons fresh lemon juice

1. Preheat the oven to 350 degrees F. Butter an 8-inch square pan.

2. In a bowl, blend together 8 tablespoons butter, 1 cup of the flour, and ¼ cup confectioners' sugar. Press this dough into the prepared pan. Bake for 15 minutes. Remove the pan from the oven, but leave the oven on.

3. While the dough base is baking, mix together the granulated sugar, the remaining 2 tablespoons flour, the baking powder, eggs, and lemon juice. When the base is removed from the oven, pour this lemon mixture over it and return the pan to the oven. Bake for another 20 to 25 minutes.

4. Cool in the pan. Cut into squares and sift confectioners' sugar over all.

Place lemons in a plastic bag and keep the bag in the refrigerator. That should keep them moist for about 2 weeks. A sliced lemon can hold for about 10 days if the exposed side is covered with plastic wrap and kept in a small tightly closed container.

Chocolate Deep-Dish Pizza

MAKES 10 SERVINGS

Italians started coming to Chicago during the 1850s; by the 1940s there was a significant population of Italian immigrants and their descendants. Many were successful in the restaurant and bar business. Deep-dish pizza became popular with more and more people, and soon Chicago became known for creating it. Everyone—not just Italians—adopted it as a "Chicago" food. Chocolate Pizza is a blending of Chicagoan's love of deep-dish pizza and their devotion to sweets.

FOR THE PIZZA CRUST

½ cup (1 stick) unsalted butter, plus more for the pan
½ cup brown sugar
½ cup granulated sugar
½ teaspoon baking powder
½ teaspoon vanilla extract
2 large eggs
1 cup all-purpose flour
½ cup of your favorite kind of chocolate chips

TOPPINGS (All or any combination of the following)

½ cup peanut butter
½ cup mini marshmallows
½ cup butterscotch chips
¼ cup semisweet chocolate chips
¼ cup dark chocolate shavings, loosely packed
¼ cup milk chocolate shavings, loosely packed
¼ cup white chocolate shavings, loosely packed
¼ cup chopped pistachio nuts
¼ cup chopped almonds
¼ cup coconut flakes

1. Preheat the oven to 375 degrees F. Lightly grease a 9-inch springform pan.

2. TO PREPARE THE CRUST: In a mixing bowl, cream together the butter and the sugars until smooth. Beat in the baking powder and vanilla. Beat in the eggs, one at a time. Beat in the flour. When the mixture is evenly blended, stir in the chocolate chips.

3. Spread the batter into the prepared pan and bake for 15 to 20 minutes. The dough will still be quite soft and lightly browned. Remove the pan and turn off the oven.

4. TO ASSEMBLE: Using a tablespoon, evenly distribute the peanut butter on top of the pizza crust. Scatter the mini marshmallows and the butterscotch chops on top. Return the pan to the oven for 10 minutes. (The heat should be off.)

5. Scatter the remaining toppings on top of the pizza. Return the pan to the oven for 10 minutes longer.

6. Cool in the pan on a rack for 30 minutes. Remove the springform sides. Cut pizza into wedges to serve.

TWO CRUSTS ARE BETTER THAN ONE

Chicago-style deep-dish pizza begins with a thick crust, lined with meats, like pepperoni or sausage, vegetables, or just about anything else. Mozzarella is added on top. A layer of dough is placed over the cheese and a thick tomato sauce is poured on top. In some cases there are additional toppers, like Parmesan cheese. Then it's baked in a traditional pizza oven. Ike Sole of Pizzeria Uno is credited with creating Chicago-style deep-dish pizza. In addition to the deep-dish pizza, Chicagoans are also known for a thin-crust style of pizza with a light spicy tomato sauce, sausage, green peppers, and mozzarella. It is usually cut into squares and is eaten folded in half.

★ WHAT TO TASTE AND WHERE TO TASTE IT ★

Deep-Dish Pizza

THE ORIGINAL PIZZERIA UNO

29 East Ohio Street ★ Chicago ★ (312) 321-1000

Ike Sole is credited with creating Chicago-style deep-dish pizza, because he wanted to serve something more substantial than regular pizza.

Swedish Cardamom Cake

MAKES 12 SERVINGS

Much of the food in Chicago is based on the cooking found in the ethnic neighborhoods. A perfect example is The Swedish bakery in Andersonville. It opened in 1928 and continues to bake the breads, cakes, and pastries that were dear to its founder. The Cardamom Cake is a neighborhood favorite. It's a light, cardamom-scented yeast cake with a topping of almonds.

FOR THE CARDAMOM DOUGH

2 packages (½ ounce each) dry yeast
½ cup warm water (between 100 and 115 degrees F)
2 cups all-purpose flour, plus more for kneading
¼ cup sugar
½ teaspoon ground cardamom
Pinch of salt
4 tablespoons (½ stick) unsalted butter, at room temperature
2 eggs
Vegetable oil, for the bowl and the baking pan
¼ cup slivered almonds

FOR THE ALMOND FILLING

8 ounces (1 cup) almond paste
2 tablespoons sugar
4 tablespoons (½ stick) margarine, at room temperature
2 tablespoons (¼ stick) unsalted butter, at room temperature

1. TO MAKE THE DOUGH: In the bowl of a stand mixer, dissolve the yeast in the warm water. Allow the yeast to stand for 10 minutes, until foamy.

2. In a medium bowl, with a whisk or fork, combine the flour, sugar, cardamom, and salt.

3. In the stand mixer, with the dough hook attachment, stir the flour mixture and the butter into the yeast on low speed. Add 1 egg and continue to beat the dough until it is smooth and sticky. Turn the soft dough onto a floured surface and gently knead a few times. Place the dough into a large oiled bowl, turning the dough once to coat the top. Cover with plastic wrap and allow it to rise for 1 hour, until it doubles in size.

4. TO MAKE THE FILLING: In a clean bowl of a stand mixer with the paddle attachment, beat the almond paste, sugar, margarine, and butter until smooth. Set aside at room temperature.

5. Preheat the oven to 375 degrees F. Generously grease a 12-inch round cake pan.

6. TO FORM THE CAKE: Gently deflate the dough. Turn the dough out onto a generously floured surface and roll out to a large rectangle, about 9 x 16 inches. Spread the almond-paste mixture over the surface of the dough. Starting from the long side, roll the dough, jelly-roll style, towards you to form a long loaf. Then turn the ends towards each other to form a ring and tuck one end into the other, pinching to seal the seam.

7. Transfer the ring to the greased cake pan, leaving a 1-inch border from the side of the pan to allow the cake to expand. With kitchen shears, make diagonal cuts, three-quarters of the way into the dough, every 2 inches, all the way around the ring. Be careful not to cut all the way through the dough. Lift up a snipped piece and move it towards the center of the ring, move the next snipped piece and turn it towards the outside of the ring. Continue until you have gone completely around the ring.

8. In a small bowl, lightly beat the remaining egg. Generously brush the surface of the dough with the egg and sprinkle the top with the slivered almonds.

9. Bake for 45 to 60 minutes, until the top of the dough is shiny and a deep golden brown. Allow the cake to cool on a rack. Serve warm or at room temperature.

> The aromatic spice cardamom is the dried seeds of a fruit that is a member of the ginger family. Cardamom is native to India and Sri Lanka, and is widely used in Arab countries and by northern Germans and Scandinavians, especially in cookies and cakes.

FROM BAKE SHOPS TO SARA LEE

Over the years, Chicago has been home to many bakeries whose products became famous throughout the United States. Charles Lubin, for instance, bought a small chain of neighborhood bakeries called Community Bake Shops in 1935. Fourteen years later, he named a cheesecake after his daughter, and he changed the name of the company to the Kitchens of Sara Lee, which was later shortened to just Sara Lee.

Chicago-Style Chocolate Cheesecake

MAKES 10 SERVINGS

Cheesecake is one of our earliest baked goods. Culinary lore claims that the ancient Greeks took goat cheese and sheep cheese, sweetened it with honey, and made a cheesecake that was fed to the athletes at the first Olympics which took place in 776 B.C. Whatever its origins, cheesecake reached its height of perfection in the United States.

Like many cities in the United States, Chicago has a love of sweets that includes a group of of specialty bakers. One of the most famous is Eli's, which has been baking cheesecake since 1977. Chicago is the largest cheesecake market in the country. And Eli's is the largest specialty cheesecake bakery, turning out 16,000 cakes each day.

FOR THE CRUST

Butter, for the cake pan
1 cup crushed graham crackers
4 tablespoons (½ stick) unsalted butter, melted
2 tablespoons sugar

FOR THE FILLING

2 (8-ounce) packages cream cheese, at room temperature
¾ cup sugar
3 eggs
2 tablespoons whole milk
2 tablespoons heavy cream
½ cup sour cream
2 teaspoons vanilla extract
5 ounces bittersweet chocolate, melted and cooled

FOR THE DECORATIONS

1 cup chocolate sprinkles
Heavy cream, sweetened and whipped
Chocolate shavings

1. Butter a 9-inch round cake pan.

2. TO MAKE THE CRUST: In a bowl, blend together the ingredients and. Press the mixture into the bottom of the cake pan. Refrigerate for 1 hour.

3. Preheat the oven to 350 degrees F.

4. TO MAKE THE FILLING: In a bowl, cream together the cream cheese and sugar. Add the eggs, one at a time, blending well after each addition. Blend in the milk, heavy cream, and sour cream. Fold in the vanilla and melted chocolate.

ABOUT GRAHAM CRACKERS

Graham crackers are sweet whole-wheat crackers made from graham flour. Graham flour is whole-grain wheat flour with the husk or bran and center or germ left in. The Reverend Sylvester Graham (1794–1851) gave his name to the flour because of his rigid views on temperance and the virtue of eating whole grain and unadulterated foods. The Reverend Graham believed that a healthy diet would produce better citizens of superior moral fiber. Nabisco, the world's largest cookie and cracker factory, is located in Chicago.

5. Pour the filling into the prepared pan and bake for 45 minutes. Turn off the heat and let the cheesecake sit in the oven for 1 hour. Do not open the oven door. (The cool air may cause the cheesecake to crack.)

6. Let the cake cool completely. Invert the cake to unmold it. Press the chocolate sprinkles into the sides and decorate the top with swirls of whipped cream and chocolate shavings.

CHEESECAKES, ANYONE?

Chicago is the largest cheesecake market in the United States, and Eli's is the country's largest specialty cheesecake bakery—the company turns out sixteen thousand cakes each day in seventy-five different flavors. Mark Schulman, an attorney who gave up suing for sifting, is president of the company. As he led me on a tour of the plant, Schulman reeled off his daily "shopping list": 15,000 pounds of cream cheese, 4,000 pounds of sugar, 265,000 fresh eggs, 5,000 pounds of sour cream, and 200 pounds of Madagascar vanilla. Adjacent to the plant is a dessert café where you can sample some cheesecake-based creations. The Dipper is frozen cheesecake on a stick, dipped in chocolate and coated with a topping of your choice. A Smush is cheesecake and ice cream smashed together. There's also a wide selection of shakes made from cheesecake and ice cream.

INDEX